DECADE DIAMONDS &
MONTH, DAY, HOUR AND MINUTE DIAMONDS

Your Destiny in Action
HOW TO FIGURE IT OUT

by LOUISE STOREY

Copyright ©2010 by Louise Storey

All rights reserved. No part of this publication may be reproduced or transmitted in any form, or by any means - electronic, mechanical, photocopy, recording or otherwise - without prior written permission of the copyright owner or publisher, except as provided by international copyright law. For further information please contact:

Louise Storey
Email: info@numbersalive.com.au
Web Site: www.numbersalive.com.au
Mail: Numbers Alive, P.O.BOX 584, Mt MARTHA, Victoria, Australia, 3934

National Library of Australia Cataloguing-in-Publication entry
Author: Storey, Louise.

Title: Decade diamonds & month, day, hour and minute diamonds : your destiny in action - how to figure it out /by Louise Storey.

Edition: 1st ed.

ISBN: 9780980392920 (pbk.).

Subjects: Numerology.
         Tarot.
         Astrology.
         Cabala.

         133.335

Designed and produced by Powerhouse Design

Disclaimer
No responsibility for loss or harm occasioned to any person or entity acting on any of the material in this publication can be accepted by the author/composer or publisher. The subject matter is for the information of readers only. Any extreme practices resulting from any of the information contained herein are absolutely negated.

Illustrations from the Rider-Waite Tarot Deck ® reproduced by permission of U.S. Games Systems Inc., CT 06902 USA. Copyright © 1971 by U.S. Games Systems, Inc. Further reproduction prohibited. The Rider-Waite Tarot Deck is a registered trademark of U.S. Games Systems, Inc.

DEDICATION

I dedicate this work to Pythagoras and all Masters of Wisdom

SPECIAL THANKS

Special thanks honour the abiding support that Donna McKinnon and Judith Dunne gave so selflessly throughout this endeavour. I am indebted to their mutual sense of humanity, friendship, support and, above all, to their belief in this work.

Special thanks also go to the team at Powerhouse Design for the extraordinary effort they put into this work. Nicky Chanter, you are an "NChanter"; you weaved your magic to help produce a truly beautiful book.

WILLIAM BRYAN:

"Destiny is not a matter of chance,
It is a matter of choice.
It is not a thing to be waited for
It is a thing to be achieved."

TABLE OF CONTENTS

PREFACE	11

PART 1: MONTH, DAY, HOUR AND MINUTE DIAMONDS

Chapter 1: INTRODUCTION — 14
- Long and Short Cycle's Natures — 16
- Life, Decade and Short-Term Diamond Differences — 16
- New Terminology — 16
- ◇ Major Cautionary Advice — 17
- ◇ Further Cautionary Advice — 19

Chapter 2: A DIAMOND'S BASIC STRUCTURE — 20
- ◇ Each Diamond's Basic Structure — 20
- ◇ Each Diamond's Basic Components — 21
- ◇ Each Diamond's Magickal Facets — 22
  - Points Regarding Magickal Facets — 23
  - Points Regarding this Book's Subject Matter — 23

Chapter 3: PERSONAL MONTH DIAMONDS — 25
- ◇ About Personal Month Diamonds (PMDs) — 25
- ◇ How to Calculate Personal Month Diamonds (PMDs) — 26
  - How to Calculate a PYN Family (PYNF) — 26
  - How to Calculate a PMN Family (PMNF) — 28
  - Steps and Diagram for Calculating SD and WN PMDs — 28
- ◇ Case Study: September 2007's SD PMD for Phoebe — 29
  - Interpretations — 30
  - A Lesson on Themes: Keys 1, 11 and 19 — 31
- ◇ Case Studies: THE IRWIN FAMILY — 34
  - STEVE IRWIN — 34
  - TERRI IRWIN — 35
  - BINDI and BOB IRWIN — 37
  - "TIGER" WOODS — 39
  - Mother and Son Reunion — 42
- ◇ PMD Interpretation Tips — 43
- ◇ General Tips and Comments — 45
- ◇ Points to Remember — 47
- ◇ Checklist of Significant Features — 48

Chapter 4 : PERSONAL DAY DIAMONDS   49
- About Personal Day Diamonds (PDDs)   49
- How to Calculate a Personal Day Number Family (PDNF)   50
- Steps and Diagram for Calculating SD and WN PDDs   51
  - Case Studies: AZARIA CHAMBERLAIN—Believed Killed by Wild Dingo   51
  - STEVE IRWIN—Death by Poisonous Stingray Barb to Heart   54
  - LADY DIANA—Fatal Car Crash   57
  - DODI FAYED—Fatal Car Crash   58
  - PRINCE WILLIAM—News of Mother's Death   60
  - PRINCE "HARRY" (Henry)—News of Mother's Death   61
  - PRINCE CHARLES—News of Ex-wife's Death   62
  - St JOAN of ARC—Execution Day   63
  - Words of Caution   66
- Universal Day Diamonds (UDDs)   66
  - PRINCE HARRY—PYD and UDD for day of his Mother's Death   67
  - STEVE IRWIN FAMILY—UDD for day of Steve's Death   67
  - SUSAN BOYLE— PYD and UYD Meteoric Rise to Fame   68
  - Interpretation Tips   68

Chapter 5 : PERSONAL HOUR DIAMONDS   70
- About Personal Hour Diamonds (PHDs)   70
- How to Calculate a Personal Hour Number (PHN)   70
- Steps and Diagram for Calculating SD and WN PHDs   71
- Case Study: LEON and DANA's End of their Relationship   72
- PDDs in Action   73
  - Leon   73
  - Dana   74
- PHDs in Action   74
  - Leon Announces Relationship's End   75
  - 15:00 Hrs: Leon—The End Begins   75
  - 15:00 Hrs: Dana   76
  - 16:00 Hrs: Dana—Quarrel Continues   76
  - 16:00 Hrs: Leon   77
  - 17:00 Hrs: Dana—Dana Leaves   77
  - 17:00 Hrs: Leon   78
- Case Study: "TIGER" WOODS—Dramatic Fall From Grace   79
  - Interpreting Woods' Magickal Facets and Constellations   81

Chapter 6 : PERSONAL MINUTE DIAMONDS   83
- About Personal Minute Diamonds (PMinDs)   83
  - Steps and Diagram for Calculating SD and WN PMinDs   84
  - Case Study: JESSICA WATSON—Sails Into The Record Books   85
  - Points of Interest   87

PART 2: WINDOWS TO THE FUTURE

Chapter 7 : PERSONAL YEAR TAROT SPREAD — 90
- A Personal Year's Windows of Opportunity — 90
- How to Calculate a PYN Family's Tarot Spread — 92
- How to Interpret a Personal Year's Tarot Spread — 92
  - 2007: S.O.S. — 93
  - 2009: "TIGER" WOODS — 95
  - 2010: "TIGER" WOODS — 96
  - 2009: SUSAN BOYLE — 97
  - 2010: SUSAN BOYLE — 98
  - 2010: KEVIN RUDD — 99

Chapter 8 : PERSONAL MONTH TAROT SPREAD — 100
- A Personal Month's Windows of Opportunity — 100
- How to Calculate a PMN Family's Tarot Spread — 100
- How to Interpret a Personal Month's Tarot Spread — 101
  - JULY 2004: Family Rift — 101
  - NOVEMBER 2009: "TIGER" WOODS—Family Crisis — 103
  - PRACTICE: MAY '10, JESSICA WATSON, JUNE '10, KEVIN RUDD — 104

Chapter 9 : PERSONAL DAY TAROT SPREAD — 105
- A Personal Day's Windows of Opportunity — 105
- How to Calculate a PDN Family's Tarot Spread — 106
- How to Interpret a Personal Day's Tarot Spread — 106
  - 30th MAY 1431: St JOAN of ARC—Burned at Stake — 106
  - 27th NOVEMBER 2009: "TIGER" WOODS—Day of Reckoning — 108
  - 24th JUNE 2010: KEVIN RUDD—Political Assassination — 108
  - 15th May 2010: JESSICA WATSON—Day of Victory — 109

Chapter 10 : THE PERSONAL MONTH GRID — 110
- How to Set Out a PMG — 110
- Personal Month Idiosyncrasies — 111
  - September and October — 111
  - The New Year — 112
  - Repeat Patterns — 112
  - Merging Years — 112
  - A Cycle within a Cycle — 113
- Using the PMG as a Forecasting Tool — 113
  - Parallel—Accidents — 114
  - Parallel—Events — 115
- WORKSHEET: Tarot Spreads & PMG — 116

PART 3: PERSONAL DECADES

Chapter 11 : INTRODUCTION TO DECADES — 118
Introduction to Decades — 118
- Emergence of a Fixed Agenda — 119
- Emergence of a Timetable — 119
- Emergence of a Preset Destiny — 120
- Predictive Basis to Our Numbers — 120
- Cosmic Origins to Our Cycles — 120
- Awareness of an Earthly Assignment — 120
- Special Turning-Points — 120
- Cyclic Rotation of Numbers — 121
- Developing Informed, Self-help Skills — 121

Chapter 12 : DECADE IDIOSYNCRASIES — 123
Decade Idiosyncrasies and Patterns — 123
- The Year of Birth's Exceptional PYD—Age 0 — 123
- Indelible Imprinting—Single Digit Years from 1 to 9 — 124
- Indelible Imprinting —Tens' Digit Years — 125
- ♥0 PYDs — 126
- Indelible Imprinting—Unit 9 Years — 127
- ♥0 and ♥9 Patterns for a LPN2 — 128
- Inner □s in 10s and 9 Years — 129
- Our most Personal Decade's Rare Features — 129
- The PYD's ♥ Number and the Wheel of Life — 130
- A PYD and UYDS' CA Cycles are Generic — 131
- The PYD's Second Cycle Repeats Every Tenth Year — 132
- Introducing the Decade Diamond (DD) — 132
- A DD's Goal (DG) and Challenge (DC) — 133
- A DD's Ruler — 133
- 10 and 9-Age Years' Vertical Axes — 133
- Zero Challenges — 134
- The ♥6 Year — 134
- Ideas for Further Investigation — 135
- Practice Tips — 135

Chapter 13 : DECADE DIAMONDS		**137**
◆	Advent of Decade Diamonds (DDs)	137
	• How to Calculate SD DDs	139
◆	Case Study: JAMIE OLIVER'S ("The Naked Chef") Twenties' DDs	140
◆	Jamie's SD DD's Numbers	140
◆	Interpreting Jamie's SD DD	141
	• Background Information	141
	• SD Interpretations	141
	• Number-pairing Interpretations	142
	• Decade Ruler Interpretations	143
	• Decade Determinants	146
	• DDs Bring to Light	146
	• DDs' Special Considerations	146
Chapter 14 : WHOLE NUMBER DECADE DIAMONDS		**147**
◆	Whole Number Decade Diamonds (WN DDs)	147
◆	Case Study: JAMIE OLIVER	148
	• Steps for Calculating a Set of SD and WN DDs	149
	• Insights from Jamie's Twenties' WN DGs	149
	• Insights from Jamie's Twenties' WN DCs	150
	• Insights from Jamie's Twenties' WN DRs	151
◆	Famous People's Prominent Decades	152
	• Cameo: Sir WINSTON CHURCHILL	152
	• Cameo: ADOLF HITLER	153
	• Cameo: OSAMA BIN LADEN	154
	• For Study: SADDAM HUSSEIN	155
	• Case Study: ALAN BOND	156
	• Cameo: SUSAN BOYLE'S Special Decade	159
Chapter 15 : MAKE YOUR DECADES WORK FOR YOU		**160**
◆	Getting the Most from Decades	160
◆	A Decade's Pattern and Order	162
	• First Decade: DG6 with DC6	163
	• Second Decade: DG7 with DC5	163
	• Third Decade: DG8 with DC4	164
	• Interpretation Tips: Decade Goals and Rulers	165
	• Interpretation Tips: Decade Challenges	166

PART 4: TREASURE HUNT

Chapter 16 : UNCOVERING PERSONAL GEMS — 168

- Your Lifetime Tarot Card and its Spread — 168
- Diagram: Minor Arcana's Decans, Planetary Rulers and Decan Dates — 170
- How to Create a Lifetime Tarot Spread — 172
- Case Study: LADY DIANA'S Lifetime Tarot Spread — 173
  - General Interpretations — 173
  - Specific Interpretations — 176
  - Cameo: 14th DALAI LAMA — 177
  - Cameo: JESSICA WATSON — 178
  - Cameo: STEVE IRWIN — 178
  - Cameo: OPRAH WINFREY — 179
  - Cameo: AZARIA CHAMBERLAIN — 179
  - Cameo: "TIGER" WOODS — 180
  - Cameo: ELVIS PRESLEY — 180
  - Additional Points — 180
- Table 1: Suits, Symbols and Meanings — 181
- Table 2: Decan's Dates, Minor Keys, Names, Planets and Signs — 182
- Table 3: Planets and their Meanings — 184
- Table 4: Zodiac Signs and their Meanings — 186
- Table 5: Hebrew Letter Placements and Meanings ⇔ Major Arcana Keys — 190
- Four TREES of LIFE Displaying Various Attributes — 192
- General Tips — 193
- Conclusion — 194

- **APPENDIX 1:** Meanings for Acronyms & Symbols — 196

- **APPENDIX 2:** Conversion Table from Numbers to Tarot Keys — 197

- **APPENDIX 3:** All Number Family Calculations — 198

- **APPENDIX 4:** All Diamond Calculations — 200

- **APPENDIX 5:** All Tarot Spread Calculations — 204

RECOMMENDED READING LIST — 206

PREFACE

This esoteric, numerology journeybook carries on from where the *Yearly Diamonds* journeybook left off. It presents the advent of Personal Months, Days, Hours, Minutes and Decade Diamonds. They took many years to evolve to their present level and complete the Mini Maps to Life series.

Decade Diamonds are new to numerology. They are basic in construction yet profound in their 10-yearly directions. By comparison, Personal Month, Day, Hour and Minute Diamonds have very short cycles. Even so, they are as comprehensive as Life and Yearly Diamonds. They are particularly useful self-help tools for keeping up-to-date with current trends. Their abundant directions are extremely insightful for all aspirants searching for ways and means to stay in sync with their Soul's requirements. The depth and detail that can be retrieved from them is unsurpassed, which makes their present and future indications indispensable to all those on the Path.

Simple, numeric formulas are applied to all diamonds. Interpretation techniques continue to use numerology and Tarot in their capacity as tools for self-determination and self-direction. This premise is maintained in all fields for study in this journeybook. A brief account of each is outlined below.

- **Decades and Decade Diamonds**, a totally new branch of numerology, emerged due to intense Personal Yearly Diamond research. When Decade Diamonds are put with their Personal Yearly Diamonds, everyone's unique, pattern and order from birth until death is revealed in a numeric sequence. This pattern and order conceals a major portion of the matrix upon which the many, varied stages and phases of life are mapped out. Once revealed, a large part of the Soul's hidden agenda for this incarnation may be accessed by those who earnestly desire to realise their Destiny.

- **Personalised Year, Month and Day** *Tarot spreads* evolved many years later. They spawned the concept of a whole number, **Personal Month Grid**. Much later again, the Personal Month Grid's predictive elements emerged.

- **Personal Month, Day, Hour and Minute Diamonds** are recent developments. Their more current maps to life fine-tune and update long-term diamonds' life directions.

◆ **Your Tarot card at birth** reveals a major part of this lifetime's Personality/Soul requirements. *It is equal in importance to your Life Path and Destiny Numbers.* To my knowledge, this Tarot card's extremely personal aspects are not utilised, therefore, not recognised for their enormous significance. **Lifetime Tarot Spreads** are created from the birth Tarot Key. Their amazing insights reveal many important clues to other aspects of this life's journey that cannot be found otherwise.

This journeybook's Diamonds unfolded over many years. Taken altogether they reveal that our lives are patterned upon *a predetermined matrix fixed in numbers*. Each map identifies the specialised fields that the Soul has chosen for its Personality to come to know and experience during each map's period of operation. Each map also identifies the hidden agendas, timetables, cycles, goals and challenges that, when collated, reveal much of the Souls' overall Plan. Given that, anticipate a personal revelation when you calculate all Personal Yearly Diamonds from age 0 to age 99; it will affect your thinking forever …it has mine …. and it leaves no doubt that our numbers are the product of a purposeful, Intelligent Design! These enthralling prospects lie in store when you learn how to create your own set of Personal Year and Decade Diamonds.

Advanced esoteric methods that include Numerology, Tarot, Astrology, the Qabalah and the Tree of Life show how to get much more from our numbers. Chapter 16 epitomises that where they are applied to individual, Lifetime Tarot Spreads. Their integration reveals the spread's deeper meanings as well as increasing the amount of hidden clues therein. By obtaining greater knowledge, we learn to gain a keener awareness of ourselves and our Destinies.

Decade Diamonds is the third "How to" or "D.I.Y." esoteric, numerology journeybook in what has now grown from one to a series of six! As increasingly advanced numerology and Tarot methods are introduced in each book, a background in metaphysics and occult sciences is helpful. However, every attempt is made to make the subject matter suit beginners.

My hope is that your Personality awareness and Spiritual resolve grow from this study. Another, is that the product of these studies will expand the parameters of this Sacred Science further by transplanting and propagating new ideas and methods in other's minds.

In Light and Love,
Louise

PART 1

PERSONAL MONTH, DAY HOUR AND MINUTE DIAMONDS

Chapter 1:
INTRODUCTION

All diamond cycles in this journeybook, except for Decade Diamonds, scale down the element of time. As their cycles sequentially reduce, their numbers and Keys become more and more "alive". This is due to their numbers and Keys being *transient* which means that their possibilities have less time in which to manifest. **Force** (from shortening) and **less time** are the two fundamentals that alter their mode of operation. Hence, transiting numbers' indications are *specific* and *dynamic*; long term numbers' indications, *general* and *steady*. These basic differences between short and long term numbers and Keys, means that all transiting numbers and Keys are interpreted with more emphasis and urgency.

To understand this better, visualise what occurs when adding more spice to a recipe or increasing the amount of coffee in your cup or pressing harder on the accelerator pedal. Then you can imagine how the potency and velocity of the energies and forces of transiting numbers and Keys work. Their outcomes become more defined as their time constraints become more and more condensed. Therefore, their fortunate aspects seem more beneficial and their less fortunate, more upsetting. As short-term numbers and Keys are temporary and more transparent, forecasts have the potential to be more accurate due to less time that their directions have to manifest.

Transiting numbers make up Parts 1 and 2 of this journeybook. They greatly expand on what was introduced in preceding books by revealing additional methods that disclose increasingly more advanced tools with which to plan your destiny. Thus, this book introduces many new Maps to Life that teach how to fathom your present and future. These Maps to Life, as with the Life, Yearly and Universal Maps to Life from books 1 and 2, are partly derived from the birthdate and the current age and partly from current, calendar points in time.

There are countless personal guidelines, options and possibilities hidden in all numeric maps and all occult sciences that depict macro/micro existence. Each map is programmed to meet the exclusive requirements of each level and stage of our unfoldment throughout our lifetime. When accurately interpreted, the right guidance at the right time is revealed. This is when the true nature of numbers and Tarot are recognised as "*wayshowers*".

Learning how to apply *Year, Month, Day, Hour and Decade Diamond* directions to our lives lays the foundation for this. It is achieved via the esoteric study of numerology to gain a holistic view of what our numbers truly represent. This study requires knowledge of the meanings of numerology and Tarot's ancient symbols and a smattering of astrology and the Tree of Life. It also requires knowledge of how the numbers' and the Tarot Keys' infinite representations can be manipulated to reflect all aspects of our human nature and worldly experiences. Knowledge of their exoteric (everyday/worldly) and esoteric (spiritual) prospects can then be used to unveil the Divine Guidance concealed therein. Thus the Soul's requirements for each lifetime are revealed; hence, our powers and the powers within our numbers and Keys' wayshower side.

Used for these purposes, numerology is one means among many to understand and know *you*, your potential, scope and options so that you may figure out your Soul's requirements for this lifetime. Studying how your numbers operated in past cycles furnishes you with a solid premise from which to forecast present and future prospects. Foreknowledge such as this enables you to plan, initiate and then manifest the highest qualities in your numbers and Tarot Keys. Foreknowledge of their negative indications alerts you to where your faults and flaws lie. These are your *self-corrector* signs. Knowing them enables you to plan, initiate and then manifest means to transform them.

To assist you in this endeavour, graded steps and many case studies are presented throughout this journeybook as each new branch of numerology is systematically introduced. They provide you with ways to access each period within a lifetime. Most importantly, they illustrate how to get personal updates at any time so that you have a means among many to remain in touch with your "Soul's Agenda".

This journeybook is organised into four parts; a brief outline follows.

- **PART 1:** As their names indicate, **Personal Month, Day, Hour and Minute Diamonds** break down Personal and Universal Yearly Diamonds into shorter, then shorter self-guidance cycles.
- **PART 2: Year, Month and Day Personalised, Tarot Spreads** are introduced in this section. These unique Tarot spreads expand on Personal Year, Month and Day Diamonds and are each other's companions. Then the **Personal Month Grid's** self-guidance and predictive nature concludes this section.

- **PART 3: Personal Decades and their Diamonds** are introduced here. They bring a new branch to numerology.
- **PART 4:** This section introduces your *special* **Tarot Key at birth**. It is then expanded to create your unique **LIFETIME TAROT SPREAD**.

Except for the *Lifetime* Tarot Key, its Tarot spread and decades, each numerological field studied, starting with Yearly Diamonds, condenses life cycles into shorter and shorter timeframes. The shorter the life cycle, the more dynamic, refined and detailed its hidden, personally tailored agendas within specialised fields of life become. A summary of each follows.

- Personal Yearly Diamonds contain 3x4 monthly cycles
- Universal Yearly Diamonds contain 4x3 monthly cycles
- Personal Month Diamonds contain 4x1 weekly cycles
- Personal Day Diamonds contain 4x6 hourly cycles
- Personal Hour Diamonds contain 4x15 minute cycles
- Personal Minute Diamonds contain 4x15 second cycles
- The Personal Month Grid contains 12x1 monthly cycles.
- Decade Diamonds represent 10-yearly cycles

LONG AND SHORT CYCLE'S NATURES

Long cycles such as those in Life Diamonds and Decades project long-range, future possibilities and options. Their themes are *unfolding* in nature and their forecasts, being long term, are *generalised*. This makes it difficult to pinpoint exact times for events. However, when the timeframe is narrowed, all diamonds with shorter cycles hone guidelines accordingly. They provide the missing steps that fill in all longer cycles' gaps.

LIFE, DECADE AND SHORT-TERM DIAMOND DIFFERENCES

Life Diamonds (LDs) provide an "eagle" view of an entire lifetime. Decade Diamonds are similar in that they also provide an "eagle" view for their 10-yearly cycles. Long term cycles such as those in LDs and Decades are only capable of producing *general, overall* forecasts. Diamonds with shorter cycles provide the "mouse" view as their depth and detail is *specific*. As all diamonds are spawned from one birthdate, they are connected therefore, share an integral relationship. Ideally, they are worked together. Only in this way can the many steps needed to reach the Life Path's long-range goals be kept in mind and sight.

NEW TERMINOLOGY

As many new fields of numerology are presented in the following pages, their names and terms are reduced to acronyms after their initial introductions. To make it easy to remember and to apply them, they are listed at the head of each chapter: eg Personal Month Diamond (PMD). Although loath to rely on the use of acronyms and certain symbols throughout the text, they not only save much repetitive writing but also dramatically speed up working this system once committed to memory. A Table for all acronyms and symbols is located in Appendix 1.

The following points summarise the basic requirements for all Diamonds introduced in this book.

- Learn to modify the principles and methods introduced in the *Life and Yearly Diamonds' journeybooks* and then apply them to suit all Diamonds and Tarot Spreads introduced in this journeybook
- Learn how to calculate and utilise Life, Year, Month and Day Number Families
- Explore the application of associations drawn from astrology, the Qabalah and the Tree of Life to enrich and expand this comprehensive, numerology system further

MAJOR CAUTIONARY ADVICE

Cautionary advice pertaining to "death" numbers and Keys was addressed at this point in *Yearly Diamonds—Your Soul's Yearly Maps to Life*. You may wish to refresh what was written there. It is being stated again at the outset in this book because "death" types of numbers and Keys (really transitions or endings) appear even more frequently in shorter cycles but happily death *rarely* occurs. As several of the case studies in this book depict accounts of death, it would be wrong to get the impression that the numbers and Keys highlighted for those occasions mean that a death will occur whenever they appear. Hence, the caution here is to refrain from forecasting a death from them. An anecdote from my own personal experiences highlights this.

Years ago, when I was deeply into astrology and not so much numerology, I found myself facing a potential "threat to life pattern" regarding one of my sons.

I had set up his current astrology charts only to see a sinister pattern in them; "a classic life-threatening signature". It was very marked which made me worried and anxious. So I set up his array of numerology configurations in a bid to confirm what I saw. I knew if I did that, they would either validate or dispel my fears; they validated them. That created a dilemma. He was a sceptic and anti astrology and numerology and …. <u>*I might be wrong*</u>! (He knew that I updated his charts. However, the irony was that when he found it too hard to resist, he would inquire of them!) Nevertheless, I had to decide what to do with this information, as the warning was stark. It was a disturbing position to be in and a difficult decision to make; I felt I was damned if I told him and damned if I did not. A long time was spent wringing hands and considering what to do and the best way to go about it when the right time arrived.

The day that I knew I could not live with myself if something serious did happen to my son, and had said nothing to warn him, made up my mind. Then I waited for the right moment to arrive. When it did, I toned things down by passing a warning onto him. I did this by informing my son that I had noticed signs of accident-proneness in his charts. I then went on to suggest that he try to be more focussed when driving (he was a speedster and prone to taking risks) and more careful when in potentially "dangerous" situations or places or around potentially dangerous people or equipment. I also asked him if he could think of times or situations when he might be vulnerable and needed to be vigilant. I approached the matter along these lines, *without mentioning death*, although that was my main concern because of so many ominous signs.

Months later, my son set out to buy a Christmas tree not far from his home. Just as he drove over the crest of a hill that hid the right-hand turn a little farther on to the Christmas tree farm's driveway, a 4-wheel-drive vehicle had stopped there unable to complete its turn. This was owing to the driveway's entrance being blocked by a stationary car.

Needless to say, he crashed headlong into its rear. His airbag inflated but was asphyxiating him. As luck would have it, a police car with two policemen in it was coming over the crest of the hill on the opposite side to my son's. My son told me that one police officer actually said to the other when he saw the stationary vehicle that this was "an accident waiting to happen". They quickly came to my son's aid when they heard the crash and saved his life by prising the airbag from him. My son escaped with shock and a cracked sternum.

So what does that tell us? ……. Sons don't listen to their mothers? That warnings do or don't work? That my son had a bad memory? That airbags can be potential killers? or lifesavers? Or, that matters close to his chest were not being dealt with and this was the way that his Inner Guidance showed him that? Was it because he was not dealing with matters that were squeezing the life from him? Or, that in his subconscious he was wanting to push something obstructing his Path out of the way? Or, that he needed to stop and take a good look at his life, right *now*?

OR, does it tell us to be super circumspect when confronted with many daunting numbers?

When I heard of my son's accident and that he might have died if not for the policemen, I was very relieved to say the least. Even though his planets and numbers were foreboding, it is much more common for a life-threatening situation to occur than actual death as was so in his case. On the next page, some Keys that were present in my son's Personal and Universal Yearly Diamonds are shown on the right, his Personal Month Diamond, on the left.

The Keys on the right are from my son's Personal and Universal Yearly Diamonds. Other warning Keys were there as well but these are the ones that usually intimidate people.

The numbers from left to right are:
20, 13, 7, 0, 16, 64 and 34. Accident-proneness often results when 7, 16 and 34 appear together.

The Keys on the left are from my son's Personal Month Diamond. However, many of the Keys shown for both examples were in all three diamonds.

The numbers from left to right are:
21, 27, 24, 1, 10, 78 and 48.

FURTHER CAUTIONARY ADVICE

When potential "death" or harmful numbers and Keys appear in short term diamonds, they tend to evoke feelings of fear and trepidation. This is a natural reaction as we are all human. But there is an inherent danger in this type of reaction to create self-fulfilling prophesies, hence the need to caution against this kind of likelihood. As the potential in all numbers and their Keys is infinite, see other possibilities in them instead of emphasising their threatening or dark side.

To lessen any apprehension, acknowledge that you have experienced these numbers and Keys many, many times in past cycles. *Recall that you have journeyed through them unscathed*. Ending signs usually forecast that a *transition* is immanent; transitions *precede growth*. Welcome these times knowing that you might be entering a metamorphic period that tells you that it is timely to become the "butterfly" and grow; that is something to relish, *not* the reverse! Try the "Hanged Man approach". Use the Hanged Man concept to see things in a different light and from a different angle. Doing this allows new waves of Light, Love, inspiration and aspiration to flow into your mind. They dispel negative thinking, conditioning, attitudes and behaviours that keep multiplying if not curbed.

It is also good to bear in mind that our numbers and Keys are guides and describe "a" future: a future out of many possible futures. The futures that we seed are generated by our levels of intent, integrity, awareness, knowledge, understanding, wisdom and maturity and the subsequent choices made from them. We need to take responsibility for and learn from the seeds we sow and, more importantly the crops they grow.

Chapter 2:
A Diamond's Basic Structure

LD = Life Diamond	**G** = Goal	**TCR** = Top Cycle Ruler
CA = Current Age	**GR** = Goal Ruler	**SD** = Single Digit
PYN = Personal Year Number	**C** = Challenge	**WN** = Whole Number
PYD = Personal Yearly Diamond	**CR** = Challenge Ruler	
UYD = Universal Yearly Diamond	**DR** = Diamond Ruler	

All Diamonds in this Part 1 are based upon a diamond-shaped construction of personal numbers that address specific points in time, namely: months, days, hours and minutes. Their construction follows the same principles as those used for Life Diamonds (LDs) and Universal Yearly Diamonds (UYDs); their interpretation, essentially the same as Life and Yearly Diamonds.

EACH DIAMOND'S BASIC STRUCTURE

The diagram below illustrates a Month, Day, Hour and Minute Diamonds' basic structure.

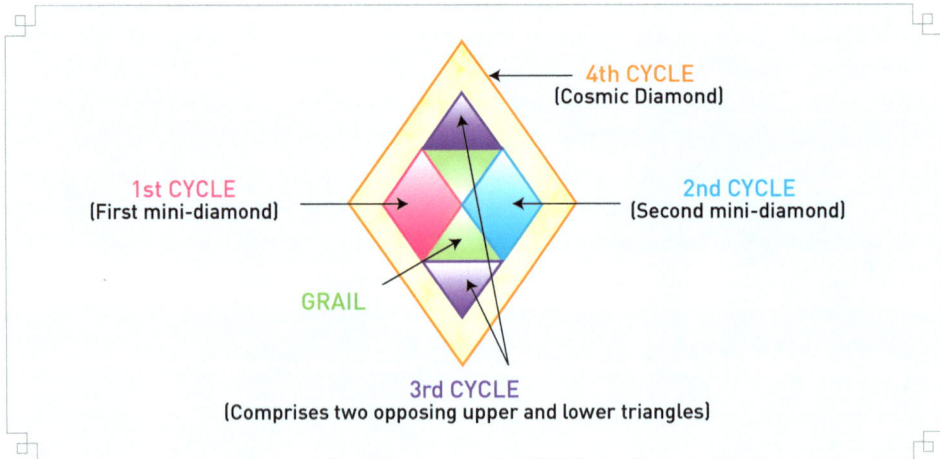

When separated from its structure, a ◇'s basic components are as follows:

- **Two side-by-side mini-diamonds** (first and second cycles)
- **Two opposing triangles**—one upper (▲), one lower ▼(third cycle)
- **One large "auric" Diamond**— the **COSMIC DIAMOND**
- **A Grail**—the "empty spaces" at the centre of the ◇'s structure
- **4 Cycles** of varying periods that are determined by a ◇'s individual time spans

EACH DIAMOND'S BASIC COMPONENTS

The following is a comprehensive list of components that make up all diamonds found in Part 1.

1. HORIZONTAL AXIS (Baseline) ⇨ 3 numbers that represent a **specific point in time**
2. VERTICAL AXIS ⇨ perpendicular number-line in a ◇
3. 3 GOALS (**Gs**) ⇨ 3 numbers above baseline
4. **GRs** ⇨ Goal Rulers: 3 Goals' totals
5. 3 CHALLENGES (**Cs**) ⇨ 3 numbers below baseline
6. **CRs** ⇨ Challenge Rulers: 3 Challenges' totals
7. **DRs** ⇨ Diamond Rulers: CR totals + BASELINE totals + GR totals
8. Two side-by-side MINI-DIAMONDS ⇨ *first and second* cycles
9. Two opposing TRIANGLES (Goals' ▲ + Challenges' ▼) ⇨ *third* cycle. (Each ▲▼ has its own Ruler. When added, their Rulers equal the ✿'s Rulers.)
10. COSMIC DIAMOND ⇨ *fourth* cycle; the large "auric" diamond
11. TOP CYCLE RULERS (↻**TCRs**) ⇨ totals of all four Cycle Rulers
12. CONSTELLATIONS ⇨ Baseline's Totals, **YGRs, YCRs, YDRs and TCRs**
13. HEART NUMBER (♥) ⇨ is the *Personal* Number for each time period

14. **INNER SQUARE** (□) ⇨ first two Goals and first two Challenges
15. **GRAIL** (⧖) ⇨ ♥ Number + first two Goals + first two Challenges
16. **STAR of DAVID** (✡) ⇨ revealed by all three Goals and all three Challenges
17. **✳'s 4 NUMBER-LINE CONSTELLATIONS** ⇨ 2 in VERTICAL ✚ and 2 in DIAGONAL ✖
18. **WHEEL** (✳) ⇨ VERTICAL (✚) + DIAGONAL (✖) CROSS totals = the ✳'s Rulers
19. **MAGICKAL FACETS** ⇨ Numbers 13 to 17 constitute a ◇'s Magickal Facets

The following diagrams reveal the elements that comprise all 3-numbered Diamond's sacred geometry. Although Personal Yearly Diamonds featured in Book 2 have 3-numbered baselines, they are the only diamonds without a Cosmic Diamond.

EACH DIAMOND'S MAGICKAL FACETS

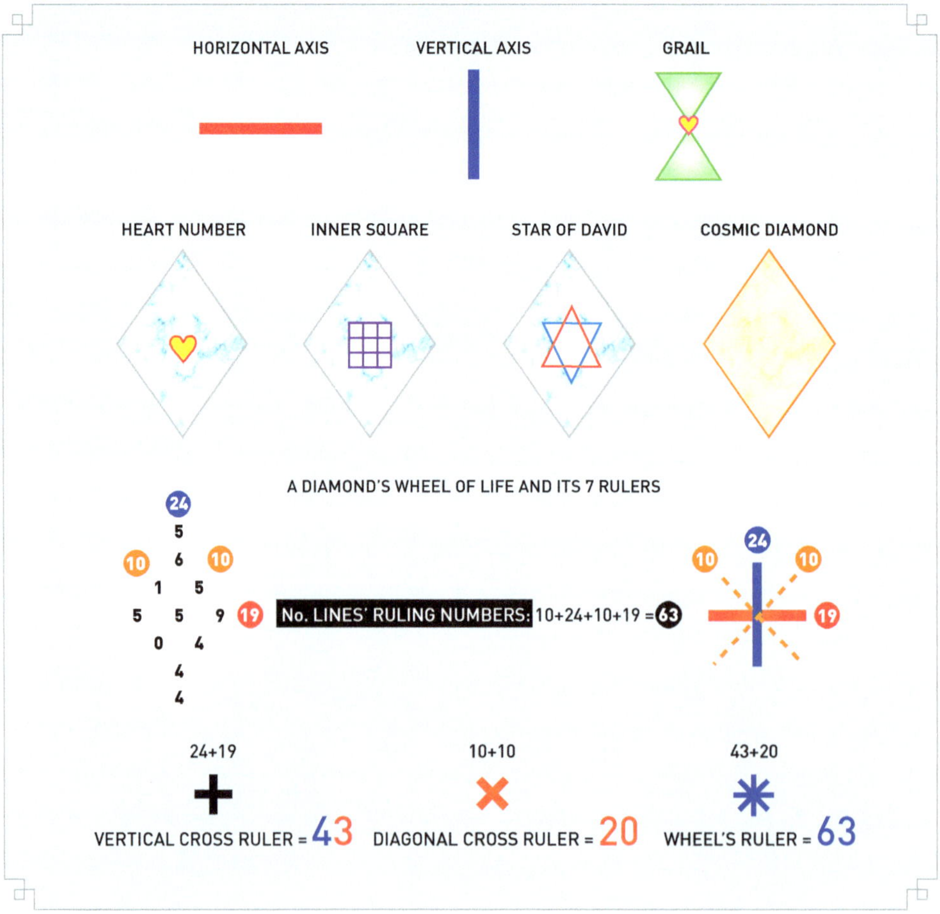

POINTS REGARDING MAGICKAL FACETS

- Magickal Facets are concealed in all ◇s except for Decade Diamonds (Part 3). This is because Decade Diamonds do not have 3-numbers on their baselines.

- Comprehensive Magickal Facet meanings for interpretation purposes are provided in the *Life and Yearly Diamonds'* books; <u>they are not repeated in this book</u>.

- When interpreting a diamond's directions, it is unwise to assume that Magickal Facets monopolise spiritual indications; they do not. If we can agree that all life aspires to unify the duality at the foundation of our existence, we may also agree that each number and Tarot Key, being part of this dual existence mirrors that duality; they have their yin and their yang, their positives and their negatives as well as their mundane and their spiritual aspects. Hence, neither needs to be part of a Magickal Facet in order to be interpreted esoterically.

- Magickal Facets interpreted esoterically are of particular use to those seeking Soul direction.

POINTS REGARDING THIS BOOK'S SUBJECT MATTER

- Assuming that you are familiar with number-pairing and how to decode ◇s by now, <u>full instructions for either are not repeated in this book</u>. The reason being that all new case studies' calculations and interpretations are essentially the same as those for Life and Yearly Diamonds.

- Each chapter provides a detailed diagram of the ◇ for the opening case study. It illustrates how they are set up. Its Constellations and Cycle Rulers are displayed on either side of the ◇. Its Magickal Facets and their Rulers are listed below it to demonstrate a quick, easy way to show them.

- Calculations for the case studies are kept basic to encourage you to hone your skills as you complete them. To complete them is important as Constellations and Magickal Facets are referred to often in their analyses; and this is the case in all chapters to follow.

- It may assist you to copy each case study's name, birthdate and ◇'s construction onto a note-pad as you go. This makes it easier to follow the instructions and references to teaching points. Also take out the Tarot cards when referred to. Moreover, take particular note of any number or Key that is the same as your own and draw comparisons. Once you have finished working a case study, do not throw your work away. Keep it in the book in case you need to return to it at a later time or to use it to compare with other ◇s in this book or the other "Diamond" books or your research. Once these ◇s are mastered, you have self-revelatory, divinatory tools as guides that keep you abreast of current trends and the stages and phases that you pass through at different times during your life.

- One tip is to copy out each chapter's abbreviations onto a separate piece of paper and keep it by you as you work through each chapter. See **Appendix 1** for a list of all acronyms.

- The table for converting numbers to Tarot Keys and vice versa is found in **Appendix 2**.

- Knowing how to calculate **number families for each point in time** that a particular Diamond represents, is essential to this work. Full instructions are provided as each arises. These instructions are repeated in **Appendix 3**. The same applies to all ◇ constructions and their formulas. They are repeated in **Appendix 4**. **TAROT Spread** instructions are repeated in **Appendix 5**.

- THE PARADOX: Although each Month, Day, Hour and Minute Diamond cycles' directions become activated by turn, paradoxically, any or *all* of their numbers may be activated *at any given time*—they are no different in this respect to any other diamond.

- Interpretations for all numbers from 0 to 99 and all 78 Tarot Keys are found in the *Life Diamond's* Appendices. Refer to their interpretations and take out the Keys as they appear in each case study's analysis. It is recommended that you have other numerology and Tarot resources to enrich and expand your findings. A recommended reading list concludes this book.

Chapter 3: Personal Month Diamonds

PYN = Personal Year Number	**G** = Goal	**PYNF** = Personal Year Number Family
PMN = Personal Month Number	**GR** = Goal Ruler	**PMNF** = Personal Month Number Family
PMD = Personal Month Diamond	**C** = Challenge	**P** = Personal **F** = Family
S = Single	**CR** = Challenge Ruler	**UYN** = Universal Year Number
W = Whole	**DR** = Diamond Ruler	**UDN** = Universal Day Number

ABOUT PERSONAL MONTH DIAMONDS (PMDs)

Personal Month Diamonds continue from where Personal and Universal Yearly Diamonds left off. They begin by taking our self-directional journey into much shorter periods of time so that we can access more immediate guidelines and trends.

Personal Month Diamonds (PMDs) commence this study; Personal Minute Diamonds (PMinDs) conclude it.

Diamonds that represent shorter periods condense the element of time. This sequential, concentrated process intensifies their energy fields making them more dynamic. It effectively hones guidelines as they have less time in which to manifest the promise of opportunities and options hidden in their numbers and Keys. This *fine-tuning* process is their forté. It greatly improves prospects of knowing how and when to plan everyday and spiritual objectives for the present and future. Most importantly, it provides other means to keep our fingers on the pulse of our Destinies.

The formulas used to create all ◇s in Part 1 are essentially the same as those for LDs, PYDs and UYDs. However, their baselines use the *current, Universal Number* (calendar number) or the *current point in clock time* (hour or minute) as part of their equations. Being *generic* numbers, they take **first position** on the baseline. This is the same as the generic number taking first place on the LD's baseline. The enduring or longest-lasting number takes third place. These numbers sit either side of the most personal number, the Personal Month, Day, Hour or Minute Number—**the ♥ number**.

All diamonds in this section are like LDs and UYDs in that they contain **four cycles**. They are calculated from the point in time when their diamonds begin.

Hence, each PMD begins and ends on the first and last days of each calendar month. Their four cycles represent one week each and each week starts on the **1st, 8th, 15th, and 22nd days**.

HOW TO CALCULATE PERSONAL MONTH DIAMONDS (PMDs)

All formulas in this section are based on *number families* that represent specific points in time. They are calculated prior to setting up their diamonds. Hence, the Personal Year Number Family (PYN**F**) is calculated first to obtain the Personal Month Number Family (PMN**F**); the Personal Month Number Family (PMN**F**) to obtain the Personal Day Number Family (PDN**F**), and so on. (See Appendix 3 for Life Path Number Family calculations.) We begin this adventure with PYN**F** calculations with **F** being the acronym for Family.

HOW TO CALCULATE A PERSONAL YEAR NUMBER FAMILY (PYNF)

The purpose of this exercise is to create a **range** of *personalised* yearly numbers—the **PYNF**—so that a **range** of SD and WN Personal Month Diamonds may be calculated for each month. The calculations are based on a series of reduction steps until all numbers are finally reduced to SDs. Once this step is reached, the root digit is then included to complete the PYNF.

The number of steps required depends on how many compound numbers are present in the birth date's day and month numbers and the current year's number. Those that produce the greatest range of PYNs have compound numbers in all sectors. Those that contain a combination of low birth day, month and current year numbers such as 5–1–2001, take only three, short steps to calculate.

The formula used to calculate the Personal Year Number Family is the same as the traditional formula:

> **PYNF FORMULA:** BIRTH **DAY** + BIRTH **MONTH** + CURRENT CALENDAR **YEAR**

To calculate a year's Personal Year Number Family (PYNF), use the current Calendar or Universal Year Number (UYN) for the chosen year. Then add it to the birth *day* and birth *month* numbers. For the following example, the year selected is **2010**; the birthday **27**; the month **6**.

NB: as this formula is based on a calendar year, the PYNF is in force from January 1 to December 31 for that year only.

PYNF FORMULA: BIRTH DAY + BIRTH MONTH + CURRENT CALENDAR YEAR

The number of steps is governed by compound numbers appearing anywhere in the equation.

STEP 1: No Reductions
a. To begin, 2010 is split into 20 and 10.
b. Next, retain the whole birthday (27) and month (6) numbers.
c. Add: 20+10+27+6= **PYN**⇨**63**
d. **63** is the highest, *personalised*

STEP 2: Century Number Reduction
a. Reduce 20 to **2** and retain **10.**
b. Do not reduce other numbers.
c. Add: 2+10+27+6= **PYN**⇨**45**
d. **45** is the second highest, *personalised* PYN.

STEP 3: Year Number Reduction
a. Retain **2** and reduce **10** to **1**.
b. Do not reduce other numbers.
c. Add: 2+1+27+6= **PYN**⇨**36**
d. **36** is the third highest, *personalised* PYN.

STEP 4: Birth Day Number Reduction
a. Retain **2** and **1**.
b. Reduce 27 to **9**.
c. Add: 2+1+9+6= **PYN**⇨**18**
d. **18** is the second lowest, *personalised* PYN.

Note: When all SDs appear as totals, no further steps are required except to reduce **18** to **9** to complete the number family. If the birth day number is high like 29, use it first, then 11 and finally, 2. Then go to step 5.

STEP 5: Birth Month Number Reduction
If the month number is 10, 11 or 12, reduce until the final SD step is reached.

STEP 6: Additional Step
Set out the numbers this way:

    2010 (use full **year** number)
    27 (use full birth **day** number)
    6 (use full birth **month** number)

Then ADD: **2043** ⇨ **Root 9**

STEP 7: Compile the PYNF
Set out **2010's PYNF** including its root digit: **63, 45, 36, 18 and 9**. (also **90** as 9's reverse)

Note: Each number in the PYNF's group must reduce to the same root digit.

Note: Step 6 is well worth doing. It brings to light other numbers that have significant influences during the year when the total is spilt and paired. The numbers you obtain from **2043** are **20** and **43**. **20** is generic having little effect. However, **43** is the hidden "gem". It can be regarded as a "personal year number" and its indications can be counted on; its reverse number and root digit, as well. From **43** you get **43/34** and **7/70** besides **4, 3, 7** and **0**. They enrich and expand the yearly directions. These numbers stand out if they bring other numbers to the year or match personal numbers or numbers in major configurations. The main point of this exercise is to use **43** and its offshoots as **"surrogate PYNs"**.

Decade Diamonds & Month, Day, Hour and Minute Diamonds

HOW TO CALCULATE A PERSONAL MONTH NUMBER FAMILY (PMNF)

PMNF FORMULA: CURRENT MONTH NUMBER + PYNs from PYNF

Steps to find the Personal Month Number Family

1. Calculate the **PYNF**
2. ADD the **current month's number** to all PYNs in the PYNF
3. Their totals yield the **Personal Month Number Family (PMNF)**

Note: All PMNs become the ♥number in each PMD baseline.

STEPS AND DIAGRAM FOR CALCULATING SD AND WN PMDs

PMD FORMULA: CURRENT CALENDAR MONTH + PMN + PYN

STEPS FOR CALCULATING SD and WN PMDs

1. **SD Baseline:**
   - (a) Select **current month's number**; reduce to a SD
   - (b) Select **current SD PYN** from its PYNF
   - (c) Add a) and b) to get **PMN**. Reduce to a SD.
   - (d) **Baseline:** Place SD Cal. Mth No. first, **SD ♥ PMN second**, SD PYN third

2. Calculate all Goals, Challenges, Cycle Rulers, Constellations and Magickal Facets
3. Calculate Interim and WN PMDs to broaden and confirm findings

Each CALENDAR MONTH divides into 4 x 1 WEEK CYCLES

WEEKLY CYCLE CALCULATIONS

Each PMD cycle is active for **1 week**

- ✧ **1st week** (first mini ◇): Day 1 → Day 7
- ✧ **2nd week** (second mini ◇): Day 8 → Day 14
- ✧ **3rd week** (two opposing ▲▼s): Day 15 → Day 21
- ✧ **4th week** (cosmic ◇): Day 22 → Last Day of the month

When creating a baseline for a SD or a WN ◇, begin with SDs. Then select the lowest WN in the PYNF series for the next WN PMD and work up from there. Numbers in WN ◇s tend to grow large and unwieldy very quickly. Regardless, the enthusiast will find much to learn from higher numbered WN ◇s as they often reveal vital data that confirms findings. Ideally, work with two or three, WNs from each number family unless a more in-depth study is required.

CASE STUDY: SEPTEMBER 2007'S SD PMD for PHOEBE

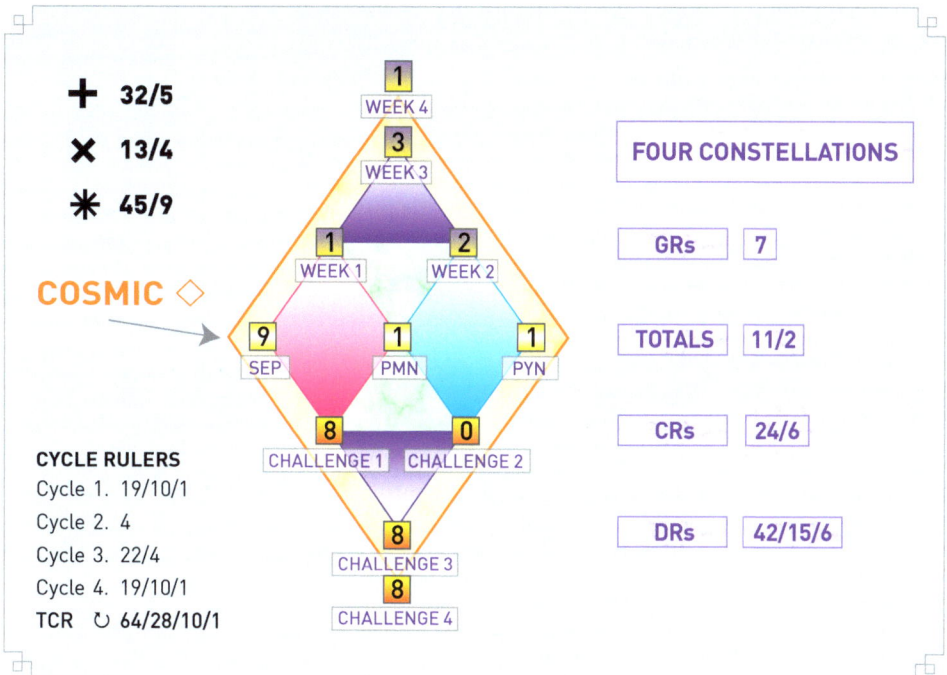

CYCLE RULERS
Cycle 1. 19/10/1
Cycle 2. 4
Cycle 3. 22/4
Cycle 4. 19/10/1
TCR ↻ 64/28/10/1

FOUR CONSTELLATIONS

GRs 7
TOTALS 11/2
CRs 24/6
DRs 42/15/6

SEP. MAGICKAL FACETS: □ 11/2; ✕ 12/3; G▲6; C▼16/7; ✲'s △11/2, ▽11/2; ✤22/4; ◇19/10/1

PHOEBE, A SENIOR NURSE: ALL SEPTEMBER'S CYCLES

- DOB: 2–8–1969 = LPNF ⇨ 98, 89, 80, 26, 17, 8
- 2007 PYNF ⇨ 37, 19, 10, 1 (20+7+2+8)
- SEP. PMNF ⇨ 46, 28, 19, 10, 1 (Add 9 to each PYN)

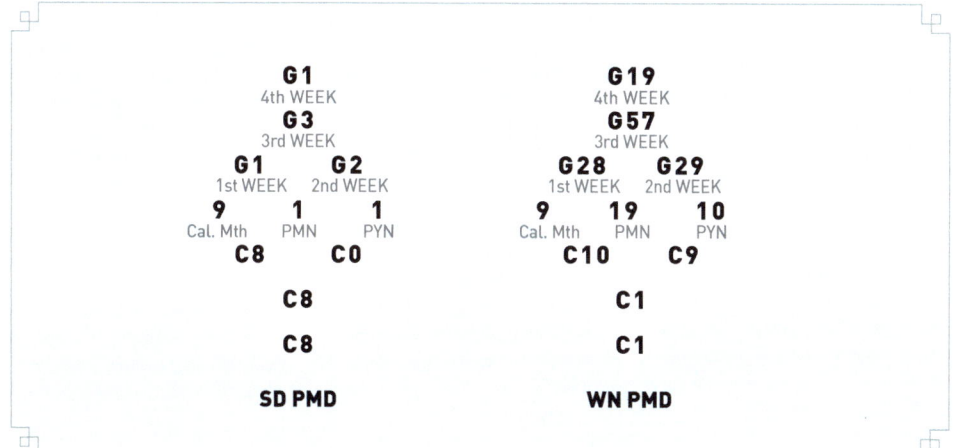

Decade Diamonds & Month, Day, Hour and Minute Diamonds

Interpretations

As was highlighted in the *Life and Yearly Diamonds'* books, always begin your interpretations by scanning both ◇s to take in their salient features. Then scan the ♥, □, ✡, ✸ Rulers, Cycle Rulers, ☋ and other Constellation Rulers to pick up quick impressions. Apply these preliminary steps before any ◇ is interpreted. Use the Checklist at the end of this chapter to help you.

When these initial steps are taken, relate what you intuit to Phoebe's current objectives and situation. ♥ numbers are always a good place to start. When the month began, Phoebe was ensconced in politics surrounding her position at work. So ♥1 did not reflect new beginnings as such as she was not planning anything new. On the contrary, it indicated *personal issues* and the <u>start of problems at work</u>. This is a subtle example of when we see the start of problems as the beginnings of something instead of applying **1**'s typical interpretations.

Although SD PMDs have unique directions, WN PMDs' directions are more authentic in my opinion. This is because they are not reduced, thus, kept true to what they represent. Being authentic makes their trends more specific, therefore, more apt for the current circumstances and times. In addition, whole numbers' details are more accurate. They provide more scope besides improving timing prospects. This case study exemplifies these points as the month began in earnest. Hence, **WN☐28** and **WN♥19** picked up the **paired 19s** in the **SD PMD's first cycle**. In doing so, they provided timing clues that power struggles (**28**) would be likely issues to face (**19**) and that they would begin during the first week's cycle, which they did.

Other reliable clues as to what might eventuate for that month nestle in the ◇'s □. It is ruled by **11/2/20**. **11** suggests matters to do with work, work contracts, administrative duties and negotiations; **2** relationships, politics and diplomacy; **20** decisions, likely difficulties and stress. As the □ mostly points to Personality issues, we take from it that the □ provides the clue that Phoebe's ego or character is likely to be tested according to what its numbers and Keys imply. This being so, consider appropriate negative aspects from the □'s **SD 1, 2, 8** and **0**; its number pairs: **12/21, 80/8, 28/82, 88, 20/2** and **10/1** and its Rulers: **11/2/20** that are likely to reflect Phoebe's Personality's tests, trials and triumphs in the current environment. As things were brewing at work and Phoebe was anxious about her senior position and duties, we would consider possibilities related to ego bruising, work, work politics, negotiations, contracts, criticisms and decisions.

Hence, the month's theme essentially reflected ego, self-awareness and Karma surrounding these issues rather than starting new things (**1s** and **19s** signify beginnings). The ways in which Phoebe conducted herself then <u>*and in the past*</u>, determined the positive and negative extent of the experiences and encounters she was likely to face that month.

8, 10, 18, 19, 20, 21, 28, 45, 57 and **64** implied that the issues to be faced at work would not be easy. They indicated that September was a time when circumstances would force Phoebe (**10s**) to defend herself in her executive role; both **SD C8s** and **11** indicate executive duties. Situations arose that tested those aspects within her. This is due to our numbers and Keys reflecting back to us what we share in common. As **11** is primarily about *self*-learning (two **1s** in **11**⇨**self** and **11**⇨**learning**), the "trials" and stress she was experiencing (paired **20**), would enable her to see where some of her strengths and weaknesses lay *so long as she had the awareness to observe (1s) what was unfolding at the time*. What she was facing (**19**) matched these specific traits in her numbers and Keys as they in turn matched the situation she was in. Hence, self-learning from **11** resulted from the month's experiences. Many **10s** hinted that matters would be forced into the open; paired **18, 80, 88s and 20** warned that they were likely to be harsh, err on the judgemental side and have long-term ramifications depending which way things unfolded.

Taking the view that our numbers are our instruments and that we are to learn how to use them and not allow them to use us, implies that we should look for ways and means to figure out how to get them to work *for* and not against us.

For example, paired **11s;** and the SD Grail's Ruling **12** gave clues as to how Phoebe could solve her problems. **11's** aspects of being just and fair, seeking amicable resolutions that serve everyone's best interests and learning from what we think, say and do fit well with **SD PMRs 6's** discriminative aspects and **12's** aspects of viewing things from a different angle to seek the best options. They gave **11's root 2's** negotiation traits a better chance of attaining a win-win situation. Knowing what might happen and how to use these numbers provides the ways and means. For example, **11s** always provide an opportunity to judge when and where things might go wrong or are wrong and then apply corrective measures to right them.

A LESSON ON THEMES: KEYS 1, 11 AND 19

This is an esoteric lesson. It looks at Numbers and Keys' allotted attributes that include their Hebrew letters to uncover more clues and insights. The purpose of doing so is to enrich findings and to find common themes among them. This approach is important because common themes verify forecasts.

The best way to go about this is to pretend that this is your PMD and then ask yourself what you would do if this were your **SD♥1, WN♥19** and □ **Ruler 11**? Begin by thinking of and/or looking up their interpretations. Then decide how best you can apply them to yourself and your circumstances. Ask yourself which aspects about you and your life they might be reflecting. Do this for any ♥number in any ◇.

For example, ♥**1**s signal that you have entered a time to provide yourself with an opportunity to focus on how well you really know yourself and your capabilities. Your "**1** work" is to observe yourself in action as well as to evaluate what you accomplish. The aim of a **1** is to develop that awareness each time it appears as self-awareness via self-observation and self-appraisal are majorly **1's** "work". These are wonderful aspects for an aware aspirant to utilise knowingly. A significant part of what a **Personal Month 1** is depicting is that this is a good time to get to know yourself and to essentially, "put your house in order" by being watchful.

1 **How to use 1:** If we turn to the Qabalah for deeper meanings, we find that **1** links to *house* and *order*. This is where the aspects of *house* and *order* originate. They come from the translation of the Hebrew letter *Beth* which is assigned to **The Magician Key**. *Beth* means *house* and **The Magician** attention, observation and concentration as well as *organisation*. This is evident by the way His "tools" are deliberately laid out on His table (His environment). If this were your ♥**1**, are you able to get from it clues to aspire to be *in charge of yourself (house) and your life (environment) by paying attention to how watchful, efficient and orderly you are throughout this month?*

11 **How to use 11:** With **11** being the SD PMD ◻'s Ruler, and **11** reflects results of past works, would you anticipate that "times of reckoning" that lead to learning via *self-correction* will underpin the month's experiences? If so, then certain mistakes and wrongdoings from past deeds are likely to require attention this month. *Attention, observation and concentration* are **1's** main characteristics and there are two **1**s in **11**. Therefore, **11** also contains many "**1**" elements. The word "self" is added to the following keywords to exemplify **1's** elements in **11**. Hence, **11's** *self-education, self-knowing, self-corrective, self-balancing* aspects provide major clues to the work required when **11** appears as a transiting number.

Lamed is the Hebrew letter assigned to **Key11 (Justice)**. Knowing some of what Lamed means enables us to apply other **11** aspects to ourselves and our lives. Lamed means *"ox goad"* which translates into provoke, drive, urge, push, stimulate, spur and incite. These keywords uncover **11's** little known "prodding", "*get going*" side. To make it personal, it is when we use the ox-goad to *self*-goad ("self" from the **1**s in **11**) to self-motivate. Or, the goading can come from others or outside forces.

The **Sword, Judge and Scales** in the Key's picture imply austere aspects. But, austerity needs love's temperance to be merciful. There is a lovely *balanced* **combination** of head and heart in this Key and so in **11**. (**MARS rules the mind** and **VENUS, the** ♥. Note the use of their colours in the Key.) Love, mercy and temperance stem from **LIBRA'S rulership of Key11** as **LIBRA** brings **VENUS' merciful and loving aspects** to the fore. So, we have **11's higher aspect of loving, discriminative understanding**. Without balance, too much intellect or emotion impairs our ability to be just and fair.

19 How to use 19: *Resh* is the Hebrew letter assigned to **Key 19**; it means *face*. I often use the noun *face* as the verb *to face* and find that it works well in that context. When you see **1, 11** and **19** appear in your numbers, consider that their theme might be one that *prods* you to *face* something; something for you to *observe*, analyse and *learn* from *in order to improve* aspects of yourself and the way you live your life.

Applying the above to Phoebe, how could she take advantage of this month's possibilities in her numbers, Keys and Hebrew Letters? Firstly, she needed to see her **1s** as signs that she was entering a period that would test her authenticity, self-image, her leadership skills and how well she managed herself and her affairs. Her numbers held a warning against maintaining poor relationships (paired **11s and their 2s** and **SD PMDRs42/15/6**) if she denied herself the chance to grow (self-change aspects of paired **18s**) in self-awareness (**1s**) by refusing to face (paired **WN19s**) the consequences of her actions or, more importantly in this case, *non*-actions i.e., Karma (paired **11s**). Considering the *collective* tone of her numbers, **11** and **20** would be interpreted as harbingers of reckoning that require balancing her scales where appropriate. This Karmic theme is one to consider.

What other themes can you find?

What else can you add to these interpretations?

CASE STUDIES: THE IRWIN FAMILY

STEVE IRWIN: FIRST SEPTEMBER CYCLE

The PMD of Steve Irwin's unusual death is below. His wife and children's case studies appear in the following pages to reveal their numbers and Keys for that tragic day.

DOB: 22–2–1962 = LPNs ⇨ 105, 96, 87, 33, 15, 6
DIED: 4–9–2006 = UDNs ⇨ 39, 21, 3
2006 PYNF ⇨ 50, 32, 14, 5 (20+6+22+2)
SEP. PMNF ⇨ 59, 41, 23, 14, 5 (Add **9** to each PYN)

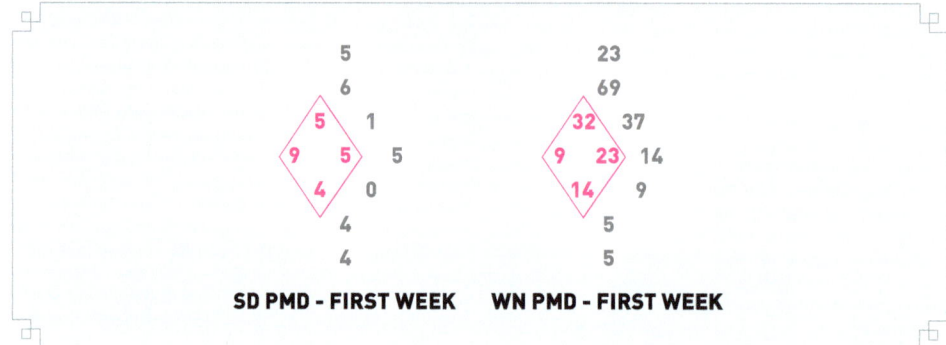

SD PMD - FIRST WEEK   **WN PMD - FIRST WEEK**

Steve Irwin's tragic death occurred during the first week of **September 2006**. Several numbers in his PMD's first cycle have a potential, life-threatening signature. They are **SD9**, paired **55**, two **45s** and Cycle Ruler, **23** (**23** often appears when something significant or unexpected occurs). Further warnings of an ending become clearer when these numbers are viewed in combination with the WN PMD's first cycle's ♥number **23** and then **9, 41** (**C14's** reverse) and its Ruling **78**.

We have already seen in Tom, Kevin Rudd, Jan and Brian Naylor's case studies in the *Yearly Diamonds'* book how harsh paired **45, 50, 55 and 59** can be if they appear in a ◇. Now we see similar effects arising from their presence in Steve's SD PMD and the effect his sudden, unexpected demise had on his family (**50s**).

The presence of master or **10s** numbers intensifies a ◇'s effects. They add forcefulness, intensity and sometimes greater levels of risk to its trends. Steve's ◇ had many **10s** in powerful positions and he was notorious for taking risks. They ruled his □, the ✿'s △ and ▽ triangles and both arms of his SD ✕.

Note the menacing composition of his SD ✿'s △. Both the SD ✕ and ✿ rulers added to **20**⇨**Judgement** from their separate **10s' Rulers**. This is an awesome build up of powerful energies and forces. The **10s** warned of forced change and the **20s** warned that great care is best exercised when making decisions under its influence. We learnt from the media of Steve's decision to change his diving location. This turned out to be a fatal decision and cost him his life! It was based on his judgement (**20**) of unfavourable weather conditions at an earlier, filming location.

Each **10** reduces to **1**. In the Qabalah, the aspects of **Life and Death** are assigned to it. Many **1s** in this ◇ placed a heavy emphasis on one or the other—for Steve it was the latter.

Although many warning signs were evident in Steve's PMDs for the week he died, his Personal Day Diamonds (PDDs) need to be compared with them to better gauge this event. (See next chapter.)

TERRI IRWIN: FIRST SEPTEMBER CYCLE

DOB: 20–7–1964 = **LPNF**⇨**110, 101, 92, 47, 38, 29, 11, 2**
Event: 4–9–2006 = **UDNF**⇨ **39, 21, 3**
2006 PYNF ⇨**53, 35, 17, 8** (20+6+20+7)
SEP. PMNF⇨ **62, 44, 26, 17, 8** (Add **9** to each PYN)

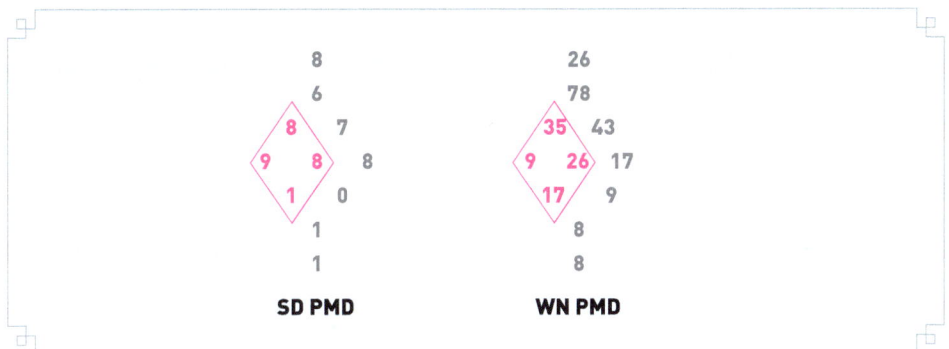

The overall nature of Terri Irwin's SD and WN ◇s are now considered.

TERRI IRWIN'S SD PMD appears daunting with its **8s**, three paired **80s** and three **88s** (with another on the **WN PMD's Vertical Axis**). Just one of these can be harsh or cruel if negative. But when no fewer than *five* paired **18s** plus **81** as the ✶'s ruler in the ◇ are added to them the potential for tragedy in **18/81** is intensified. When **PMDR57** is included, it increases this ◇'s warnings. Then each **88** reduces to **16/7** making these signs even more formidable especially when their **root 7s** are taken into account. These **7s** stem from potentially threatening numbers. Because of this, they warn of the possibility of something unforeseen, strange or bizarre unfolding.

Such a high concentration of **8s** in Terri's ◇ requires attention. Although they brought great hardship, they also meant that Terri had much greater than normal courage and inner strength to draw on if needs be. She used these traits positively when she pulled on her inner reserves to cope with the enormity (**88s**) of her personal tragedy and its effects. She also used them to be strong for her children and for when she was forced to deal with a full-on media hype. Terri also demonstrated remarkable maturity and love in the face (paired **19**) of so many challenges.

The SD baseline rulers are **25/7**. They indicated travel (**25**) over water (**7**). When linked to **39**, one of Terri's SD PMDR totals, they signified the holiday (**39**) she and her children were enjoying in Tasmania at the time of Steve's death. **57**⇨**3 of Swords** was the highest SD PMDR. It signified her heartache and its reverse, **75**⇨**7 of Pentacles**, all she no doubt felt she had lost at the time. **12**⇨**Hanged Man**, also belonging to the PMDR's number family, signified her life being turned upside down by the news of her husband's bizarre death. **21**⇨**The World**, likely signified the end of her world at that time and **12**'s its reverse, there being little to do but be tied to the situation and make the best of it (note that the Hanged Man is bound).

The lowest SD PMDR and Challenge Ruler are both **3s**. **3**'s positive and negative sides shown here are stark. The month began with **3** being symbolic of a mother and her children indulging in fun and excitement (the pleasure and light-hearted aspects of **3** and indulgence aspects of **39**) until sudden disaster (**16** and **57**) struck (**3** now as heartache and distress).

WN PMD: As the **Page of Wands, WNs26** highlight the Page's aspect of receiving news—news that brought Terri grief (**62**). Being her WN ♥number, WN 4th goal and SD Cosmic ◇ Ruler, **26/62** indicated the huge impact this news had, not only on her and her family, but also worldwide (**root 9** from ✱ **ruler, 81**). This ordeal brought her to a temporary impasse and her pain and suffering were unmistakable (**62**). This is readily seen in the **8 of Swords Key** when **26** is reversed. **Key62** clearly depicts grief, shock and trauma. **60** is the WN Cosmic ◇'s Ruler. Being a tens' number, it emphasised the serious nature of this tragedy and the effect it had on the family unit. As the **6 of Swords**, it signified Terri in troubled times trying to protect (**7s**) her children. The good thing to bear in mind re **Keys62 and 60** is that they describe *temporary* states of affairs; they inevitably *pass*.

SD/WN PMD: Intensified **1s**, paired **10s** and **19/91** in Terri's SD PMD challenge area indicate her "test" which was to face (**19**) losing her mate and then being forced (paired **10s**) to take control (**1 and 7**) of the family's corporate affairs (paired **88s**). She also had to orchestrate Steve's very public funeral (executive traits in *three* paired **88s**). Her **WNC17** linked to her

PYN17. We saw her thrust even more than usual, into the spotlight. But these **17s** also indicated the vast support she received both at home and abroad.

Terri's SD **+**, adds to **49**. This is highly significant because **49** can depict the loss of a male; in this instance, Steve. To confirm this, **WN78** implies a phase in the life is about to end: for Terri it did; but it can also be a warning of potential loss. Both **78** and **49** also relate to matters of estate that must be attended to when death occurs. When you link ♥**26, 49 and WNG78** together, you get news (**26**) of her husband's (**49**) death (**78**).

BINDI SUE IRWIN: FIRST SEPTEMBER CYCLE

DOB: 24–7–1998 = LPNF ⇨ 148, 139, 130, 58, 49, 40, 22, 4
Event: 4–9–2006 = UDNF ⇨ 39, 21, 3
2006 PYNF ⇨ 57, 39, 21, 3 (20+6+24+7)
SEP. PMNF ⇨ 66, 48, 30, 12, 3 (Add **9** to each PYN)

ROBERT CLARENCE IRWIN (BOB): FIRST SEPTEMBER CYCLE

DOB: 1–12–2003 = LPNF ⇨ 36, 18, 9
Event: 4–9–2006 = UDNF ⇨ 39, 21, 3
2006 PYNF ⇨ 39, 21, 12, 3 (20+6+1+12)
SEP. PMNF ⇨ 48, 30, 21, 12, 3 (Add **9** to each PYN)

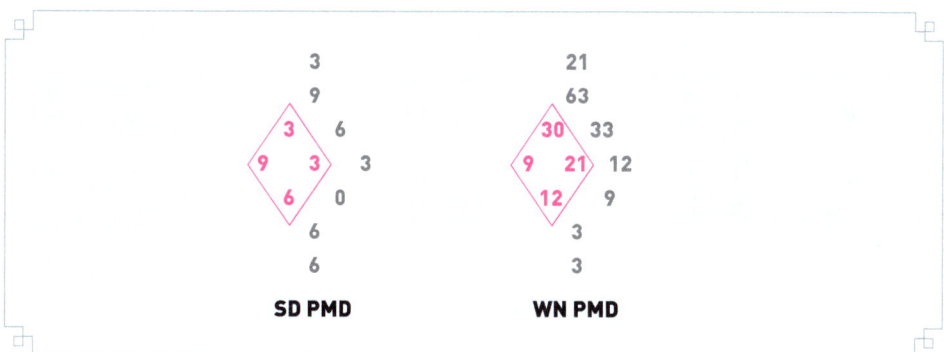

Both Bindi and Bob's PY and PM numbers are almost identical for this tragic event. This is due to both their birth day plus month numbers reducing to **4**. Therefore, the same SD and *first* WN PMD serve both children for this event *but their experience of it will not be exactly alike because some of the numbers are different in their number families*. Eg, Bob had a **21** and Bindi a **57** and a **66**. If these WN PMDs were set up for each child, they would show up any differences. If their Tarot spreads were calculated for the month, they would more easily show where the differences lie. Monthly Tarot spreads are introduced in Chapter 8.

Excellent clues to this event lie in the children's number families. They contain indications not found in the children's ◇s such as **PYN57** for Bindi. It was highly relevant for her as it depicted her heartache and sorrow. **PMN48s** are others; both children had one. They provided a sure sign that something about the children's lives would significantly change. **48s**, being Cup Keys, have an emotional component. They indicated that this change in the children's lives contained elements of sadness and that the sadness might even be death related. **57, 48, 30, 21** and **12** can imply death. Why **30**? …read on.

The appearance of **30** in both PMNFs showed its relationship to happy times as well as death. **30's** relationship to death stems from it being the number of the **Sun's Path on the Tree of Life**. The Sun rules the **19th Key** and **19** reduces to **10** and **10** to **1**. Then, **1's** Qabalistic, dual attribution is "Life and Death"; hence, 30s' associations to death via **19**. **30's** picture depicts a celebration. Is this why we celebrate someone's life when they pass on? Making these associations from **30** to the "Tree's" Paths of Wisdom helps us to understand why such a "happy" Key can have dire connotations; something that mystified me until I made these connections. The numbers, Keys and the Sun's Path on the "Tree" are shown below. **Keys 1, 10 and 19s'** attributes are written below them. The **esoteric name for Key 30** is written below it.

1	10	19		30
Life/Death	Wealth/Poverty	Fertility/Sterility	Sun's Path: 30	Perfected Work

The children's SD and WN PMDs interpretations are not confined to the active cycle; they are read over all. This approach avoids missing other important signs that contributed to the event.

The trauma of this close knit family's loss is seen in the emotional nature of the ◇'s **3s**, **6s** and **9s** but more so in their pairings eg, multiple **63s** with **60s** were foreboding (**63** also rules the SD ✳). Yet, they also indicated the children's happy times and indulgences (**3s and 39s**) travelling (**60s**) and holidaying (**39**) with their mother (**60s and 66**) before they received the devastating news of their beloved father's death (**54**⇨ **Page of Swords**). **54/18/9** are the SD PMD rulers. The news (**54**) was of a tragic (**18**) loss (**9**). **18/9** also ruled the children's SD Grail! Several **69s** can depict a family gathering or reunion. In the children's case it was at their father's funeral.

21 was the SD ◇ first week's Ruler and the WN ◇'s ♥number. It marked an end to a phase in the children's lives and when reversed as **12**, a cruel twist of fate. It depicted their lives being "suspended" and turned upside down (**Hanged Man**) while they adjusted to their loss. Then ☋**84** depicted a possible death in the family; three **C6s** provided the "family" clue. However, several **3s** and **6s** epitomised the enormous outpouring of love from a shocked public.

Paired **36s** and reversed ✱ ruler and **WN G63** indicated the childrens' heavy burden (**36**⇨**10 of Wands**) and distress (**63**⇨**9 of Swords**). Family stress is highlighted in the repetitive **6s, 60s, 63s and 66s** in the challenge area of their SD PMD. They dampened the joy that many **3s** and paired **WNG33** are more noted for. Was such a clue in **WNC33?** ….. that it was a Challenge?

"TIGER" WOODS: LAST NOVEMBER CYCLE

DOB: 30–12–1975= **LPNF** ⇨**139, 127, 118, 55, 46, 19, 10, 1**
Event: 27–11–2009 = **UDNF**⇨ **67, 49, 40, 22, 4**
2009 PYNF⇨**71, 53, 26, 17, 8** (20+9+30+12)
NOV. PMNF⇨ **82, 64, 37, 28, 19, 10, 1** (Add **11** to each PYN)

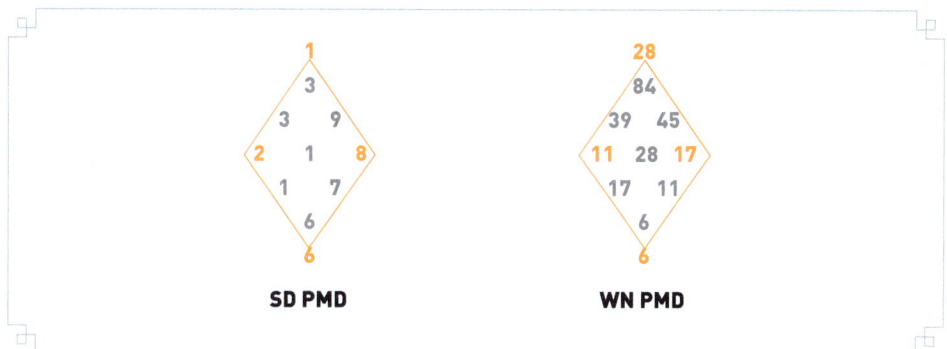

SD PMD's Magickal Facets and Constellation Rulers:
- ◇ □ **20/2**; Grail **21/3**; ✿'s △**11**; ▽**18/9**; ✵**29/11/2**; +**28/10/1**; ×**22/4**; ✱**50/5**; ◇**17/8**; ☋**78/15/6**
- ◇ PM CR **20/2**; PMD Baseline Rulers**11/2**; PM GR **16/7**; PMDR **47/11/2**; Current Cycle Ruler: **17/8**

Decade Diamonds & Month, Day, Hour and Minute Diamonds

Here we have Tiger Woods' PMDs for late November **2009** when he crashed his car close to his home; look for **16**. It was caused by an overdose; look for **7** and **15**. Having just found evidence of his infidelities; look for **3, 15, 16** and **39**, his wife reportedly assaulted him; look for **2, 8** and **28** and family matters were uppermost; look for **6, 46, 64** and **66**. If these numbers are present, intensified and appear in both ◇s or are powerful Rulers and Woods has set up the right conditions for such an event, anticipate that things will very likely turn out according to the numbers and Keys' indications.

This event transpired during the PMD's last cycle. It is an excellent example of a month's major indications not occurring until close to its end. The same thing happened in Woods' 2008-2009 PYD and 2009 UYD when his "Fall from Grace" occured near the end of November. Woods' PYD was featured in Part 4 of *Yearly Diamonds*. Most importantly, the PMD's numbers matched his LPNs. They pointed to a significant month.

Apparently the dispute between Woods and his wife stemmed from her discovery of his lover's message on his mobile phone. Considering what transpired, we would be looking for numbers and Keys that correspond to: messages, wife, family and lovers, relationships, romance, sex, lies, drugs, an accident, suddenness, conflict and anger and hospitals. They were well represented by relevant numbers and Keys in his ◇s.

3s and **Pages** can indicate messages. Paired **26**⇨**Page of Wands** was active in the challenge area of the last cycle; it was made stronger because the SD Grail Ruler was also **26**. Once the infamous messages were discovered, they instantly brought Woods grief. This is graphically portrayed in the **Page's** reverse Key: **8 of Swords** (**62**). (Note the same news/grief outcomes for Terri Irwin's **26** and **62**.)

The first case study in this chapter had a **SD♥1** like Woods'. True to a **♥1**, Woods' transparency or authenticity was tested that month. It was time to face his actions from the past and present (note his Karmic **11**). His Personal Day Ruler was **10** and the **Wheel of Fortune** represents the past, present and future. Hence it also has strong Karmic implications relating to how well or not Woods had conducted himself up to that point in time. **19** is found in his **PMGR19**; nowhere else. Even taken from there, it depicted that he had something to face. The dreaded fame/shame numbers (paired **16s** with **17s**) were in the SD PMD's Challenge area. **16**⇨**The Tower** and **17**⇨**The Star**, the active cycle's Ruler and Ruler of the Vertical Axis were in the last cycle with a hidden **10** from paired **28** at its base. **10, 16, 17** and **19** all have Karmic implications. The media went berserk broadcasting (**26**) the scandal (**17**) via every media outlet around the world (paired **21s**⇨**The World**). What a cosmic smack that was (**16**)!

Woods' WN Rulers were well worth calculating. His WN✱Ruler: **378** had **78**⇨**10 of Pentacles** in it and matched his SD☋Ruler. **78** signified an end to a phase in his life, as did the *hidden* Ruling Day Number which was **13**⇨**Death**. Hidden **73**⇨**5 of Pentacles** from **37** (**378**) signified his wife and sponsors abandoning him soon after his double life was exposed and **37** itself, loss of riches. **WN♥28**⇨**2 of Wands** and **WNG28** in the last cycle pointed to power struggles and a role reversal between husband and wife.

When analysing a ◇, remember to factor in that all numbers on the face (front) of their Keys also contribute to an interpretation; eg, **2** on the face of the **2 of Wands**. Hence, this **2** provides a strong indication that relationship issues are likely. Why strong? Because it is the Key for the WN ◇'s ♥number and all ♥numbers are strong. Key **28**'s esoteric name *"Dominion"* provides more clues as it has such connotations as power, authority, control and dominance. If a relationship is tense, then *Dominion* hints that relationship matters could be an issue. **2** in **28** and **42** implies power struggles (**28**) in relationships (**42**). Two of **WN CR42**'s aspects are "Wisdom and Folly". Not much imagination is required to fit its folly aspect to Woods' indiscretions.

Did his WN ♥**28** signify an actual physical attack due to being a ♥number and intensified by **WN G28** atop the Vertical Axis? Phoebe's "**28** situation" was more of an inquisition; it was a different type of a power struggle.

Can you find the elusive **43** that warns of a third party interfering with the marriage (**CR42**)? Which SD Ruler warned of the family's peril? Which one of poor decisions? Did you find the number of treachery? Where was **14**, the number of wrath hidden? It depicted his wife's fury. Which numbers indicated the children?

Did you notice some similarities between Woods' experiences and Phoebe's?

Decade Diamonds & Month, Day, Hour and Minute Diamonds

MOTHER AND SON REUNION: LAST DAY OF THIRD CYCLE

Event: 21–4–2010 = **UDNF** ⇨ **55, 28, 10, 1** (21+4+20+10=**55**; 21+4+3=**28**; 3+4+3=**10/1**)
2010 PYNS⇨ Mother **SD PYN9**; Son **SD PYN3**
APR. PMNS⇨ Mother **SD PMN4**; Son **SD PMN7** (Add **4** to each PYN)

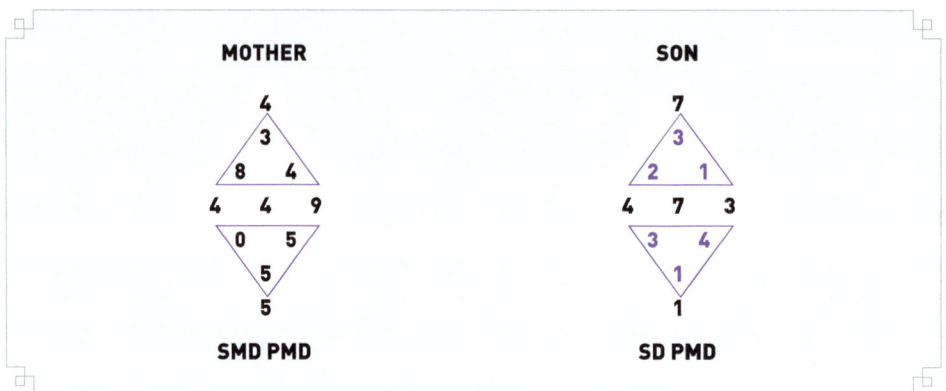

Mother's Magickal Facets and Constellation Rulers:

- ◇ □ **17/8**; Grail **21/3**; ✿'s △**8**; ▽**17/8**; ✿**25/7**; **+38/11/2**; ×**25/7**; ✳**63/9**; ◇**22/4**; ☊**85/22/4**
- ◇ PM CR **15/6**; PMD Baseline Rulers**17/8**; PM GR **19/10/1**; PMDR **51/15/6**; Current Cycle Ruler: **25/7**

Son's Magickal Facets and Constellation Rulers:

- ◇ □ **10/1**; Grail **17/8**; ✿'s △**10/1**; ▽**4**; ✿**14/5**; **+33/6**; ×**24/6**; ✳**57/12/3**; ◇**15/6**; ☊**60/24/6**
- ◇ PM CR **9**; PMD Baseline Rulers**14/5**; PM GR **13/4**; PMDR **36/18/9**; Current Cycle Ruler: **14/5**

This cameo demonstrates how some numbers that were prominent in other case studies brought forth different aspects to consider; **49, 55 and 50** are such numbers. Another reason for including this cameo is to provide an example of "cuspal" timing of an event. It shows how indications can, on occasion, take up until the last day of their mini or overall cycle to manifest.

Mother and son had been parted for years. On the last day of the third weekly cycle, the mother set off to collect her son from the airport as he was returning home to live with her.

MOTHER: Only relevant points in the mother's ◇ are highlighted. Firstly, the strong presence of paired **49s** indicated a relative coming *into*, her life; *not* leaving it and *no one dying* as in other case studies. Paired **G84**, reversed to bring forth **48**, not only indicated the journey (**3rd Cycle Ruler 25** also indicates travel) to the airport (**34** has links to air travel) but also that she would voluntarily sacrifice her solitary way of life and suddenly leave it behind that day (**84/48**). This radical life-change was plainly evident in the current cycle. Paired **C55s** and **50s** in the **Challenge** ▼ and its **Ruling 10** especially hinted at that. So did **reduced 12 from 84** and the **Goal** ▲'s **Ruling 15**. These numbers besides **40s, 44s and 45s**, also in the ◇ have depicted tragic events in other case studies. Although this was essentially an upheaval of sorts for the mother, it marked a *happy* occasion. **Paired G43 and C50s** indicated mother and son's celebration at being reunited once again.

SON: Paired **42s** and **43s** in the son's ◇ more clearly signify the reunion and celebration. He had strong indications of completion and culmination in his **10s** and **21s**. He also had those that suggest re-establishing himself (**4s, C1s,** two **31s** in the current cycle and *four* **73s**). Then **3s** and **PMDR hidden "63"** hinted that he had certain reservations about his new life. However, two paired **32s** and **74s** with **+33** and **☋60** would likely counterbalance them. **32** meant that he had success on his side, **74** that he would receive assistance, **33** that he had the wherewithal to overcome obstacles and **60**, that he had his mother's support.

PMD INTERPRETATION TIPS

Do not reduce the calendar month if it happens to be October, November or December for WN PMDs.

To obtain the best results, work PMDs with other relative data. At the very least, calculate their LDs and YDs. Go further if needs be.

The Irwin family's ◇s are excellent examples of the highly improbable occurring. The best way to test an hypothesis that a warning might be present in a ◇, is to set up the entire family's charts. If the warning is consistent in all of them, then there is a strong possibility that something untoward might occur especially if they contain repetitive themes and numbers that criss-cross between ◇s. This reinforcement generally validates theories.

Unlike Terri's ◇, Bindi and Bob's ◇s provided a clear-cut example of when starkly contrasting events took place. Eg, their **3s, 6s and 39s** suddenly swung from happiness to horror. One minute they were enjoying a wonderful holiday with their mother and the next, suffering grief and turmoil on learning of their father's fate. Such stark contrasts make forecasting this event from their ◇s very tricky but Terri's was the exception.

If you sense daunting trends in a ◇, beware of seeding self-fulfilling prophesies. **If the ◇ is someone else's, be aware that your place is to inspire, inform, empower and guide, not instil fear.**

Universal Day Numbers (Calendar Day): When a major life event occurs, always check the day's date (Universal Day numbers) against the person's numbers. More often than not, they reflect the event in some way. Eg, this occurred for each member of the Irwin family on the day Steve's death occurred. That day's date had **day 4** and **month 9** in it. When paired to make **49**, they signified Steve's death and the loss (**9**) of a male (**4** father) as well as acting as a major trigger to Terri's PMD's SD **+49** Ruler.

As a comparison, "Tiger" Woods' day's date added to **49** when his double-life was exposed to all and sundry. In his case, it signalled an end to a way of being (ending aspect in **13** which is **49's** first reduced number). But, current day numbers cannot be gauged on their own merit even if a ◇ is set up for them. (Universal Day ◇s are introduced at the end of the next chapter.) The whole chart needs to be considered in conjunction with them. By the whole chart I mean all that you know to put up on a person numerologically, even astrologically if necessary, as verification is the key to accurate interpretation.

Why does **49** often signify difficulties, relatives (mostly males but *not always*), finances, endings and sometimes death? You need to **reduce 49** to find the answers. They are in the Keys displayed below. Note the blue-green curtain in **Key 49**. It corresponds to Key 13 as blue-green is this Key's Qabalistic colour. From this well hidden association we find the clues that hint at **49's** darker side.

The Keys below show **number 49 with its reductions, 13/31 and 4/40.**

Keys 49 and 31 display their esoteric names; **Keys 13, 4 and 40,** one of their aspects.

49's REDUCTIONS:

Material Happiness Transformation Strife Reason Immaturity

GENERAL TIPS AND COMMENTS

Several tips and comments re long and short cycles appear below.

- longer cycles *rule* shorter cycles
- shorter cycles break up longer cycles into intermediary steps thus provide vital, missing details
- shorter cycles refine, hence define their longer cycles' indications
- shorter cycles' refining process provides vital clues as to how a longer cycle's goals may be attained
- shorter cycles produce more current time-frames
- shorter cycles *trigger* longer cycles' possibilities
- all cycles' positive and negative signs whether long or short, reveal the options you have to gain greater control over your life
- shorter cycles' up-to-date directions indicate how best to modify and refine your Personality while strengthening spiritual resolve with the aim of growing in spiritual stature
- it is wise to work long and short cycles together

Realistically assess what you anticipate might occur from short-term cycles that is relevant to *you*. Learn to devise strategies that fortify strengths as well as those that overcome self-undoing. The sting can be erased from your lessons when they are perceived as revealing what needs to be learned in order to grow in loving understanding and appreciation of others, the world and yourself. As a wise teacher once said, "Instead of putting so much energy into self-flagellation put that energy into correcting what has gone wrong." If we all remembered to do that, how much better would our lives, worlds and the world be?

Take time to ponder *what you are thinking, therefore, creating*.

Are you succeeding to plan—therefore planning to succeed? Or, failing to plan—therefore, planning to fail?

Use your long and short-term cycles to figure out how numbers and Keys work. Aim to use them to achieve success, satisfaction and fulfilment. At all times, remember that their numbers and Keys are for you to use, not for them to use you! They are your *tools*, always responding according to the way that you *handle* them. See them as being neutral until you activate them. **You are the Magician.** Like The Magician in Key 1, use your "tools" to exercise control over your Destiny. Until they are mastered, mistakes are inevitable. So, liken yourself to a pencil that has a point at one end (focus) and an eraser at the other (for correcting life's mistakes). Keep your pencil point sharpened and wisely directed as you write your "recipes for success, satisfaction and fulfilment". As your skills and wisdom grow, revise and modify your "recipes" often.

If PMDs are new to you, a good tip on how to make best use of them is to calculate a full 12-month set at a year's start. It not only provides a handy overview of a current year's trends in detail but also makes it easier to plot when and where monthly cycles mesh with their ruling PYD and UYDs' cycles; especially the latter.

Another tip is to calculate the PMD at the beginning of each month in your journal and make projections for it. Try the same for each weekly cycle before or when they become active. With practice, these jottings teach you how to forecast future trends. Over time, they provide a trusty resource that deepens your awareness of how transiting numbers and Keys' operate. *The hoped for objective is to reach the stage when you know how to activate them to achieve intended results.*

When you isolate one week's numbers from the rest in your journal, what do you see in the week's Goal, Challenge and Ruler/s? How can these three numbers help you to understand specific aims, traits and capabilities about you that they reflect? Which fields of your life do they *currently* represent? What are they calling to your attention? What are in their positive aspects that you can cultivate; in their negative aspects that you can transform? Consider how your current circumstances and aims correspond to each week's directions. What do you see in their guidance? What are their options, opportunities and scope? What can be made the most of? What needs correction? Are any cautionary aspects there?

PMDs are wonderful *Wayshowers*; they could well become one of your favourite tools to learn how numbers and Keys operate. Apart from yourself, practice putting up PMDs for people close to you and events you know well. Then practice on famous people and people who experience the same event. The media, internet and libraries provide abundant sources for this type of research material.

See Part 2, Chapter 10 for more hints and clues re Personal Months.

POINTS TO REMEMBER

1. **Finding Emphasis:** Use the same methods to find emphasis for PMDs as for LDs and YDs. Eg, scan for significant features, such as intensification of numbers, and links to major personal numbers and other ruling configurations.

2. **Timing:** Use the same principles for decoding PMDs as for LDs and YDs. Eg, numbers in a PMD other than those in the current week can be activated at any time during the month. When major personal numbers and significant numbers or patterns from other configurations appear in the PMD, then that PMD's matching numbers act as timing triggers to them.

3. ♥ **Number:** The ♥ number has a significant influence on its month.

4. **Grail:** The Grail also has a significant influence on its month.

5. **Inner □, + Cross and Horizontal Axis:** As with LDs and YDs, an excellent impression of a month's Personality trends may be quickly ascertained from these facets and their Rulers.

6. ✡, × **Cross and Vertical Axis:** Their numbers and Keys contain spiritual or Soul guidelines.

7. ↻ **Rulers:** Provide excellent clues to a month's tone, themes or outcomes.

8. **PMDs' Number Line Rulers, Cross Rulers and ✴ Rulers** always contain significant directions.

CHECKLIST of significant features

1. Heart number
2. Current cycle
3. First two Goals' paired compound number
4. First two Challenges' paired compound number
5. All Goal, Challenge, Cycle and Constellation Rulers
6. Top Cycle Rulers (TCRs ↺)—total of all Cycle Rulers
7. The third cycle's Goal ▲ and Challenge ▼ Rulers
8. Inner □
9. Grail ⌛
10. Star of David and its separate △▽ Rulers
11. 4 Number lines, + and × and ✳ Rulers
12. Vertical Axis
13. Major personal numbers appearing in a ◇
14. Numbers from within the ◇ that link to its Rulers intensify each other
15. Numbers that are the same as any major personal numbers
16. Does the current date link to any personal or ◇'s numbers?
17. Master or tens numbers intensify positive and negative aspects
18. Intensification—repeating numbers
19. Intensification—repeating Major Arcana and Minor Arcana Keys
20. Intensification—repeating Royal Keys or Aces
21. Intensification—Tarot suit or element emphasis
22. Intensification—astrological influences if known
23. Isolated number or Key
24. Thematic numbers
25. Thematic number "strings" (when groups of numbers have similar aspects)
26. Decade Diamond's numbers—are shorter cyclic numbers triggering them?

Chapter 4:
PERSONAL DAY DIAMONDS

> **PMN** = Personal Month Number **P** = Personal **PYNF** = Personal Year Number Family
> **PMD** = Personal Month Diamond **U** = Universal **PMNF** = Personal Month Number Family
> **PDN** = Personal Day Number **G** = Goal **PDNF** = Personal Day Number Family
> **PDD** = Personal Day Diamond **GR** = Goal Ruler **YD** = Yearly Diamond
> **UDN** = Universal Day Number **C** = Challenge **S** = Single **W** = Whole
> **UDD** = Universal Day Diamond **CR** = Challenge Ruler **PYD** = Personal Yearly Diamond
> **UYN** = Universal Year Number **DR** = Diamond Ruler **UYD** = Universal Yearly Diamond

ABOUT PERSONAL DAY DIAMONDS (PDDs)

The Personal Day Diamond (PDD) represents a single day in the life and its numbers and Keys point to events that are likely to occur on that day. If Personal Day Diamonds are worked for general purposes, they make excellent self-directional tools for uncovering each day's possibilities. When worked for specific purposes, they delineate the best day to plan for a special occasion or to research noteworthy events; this is their forté.

PDDs are also invaluable for experiencing firsthand the infinite ways that numbers and Tarot Keys work in tandem with us. This is primarily due to their quick rotations and short life spans. Since their daily pointers lend themselves to journal-keeping, much can be learnt from this practice. It pays to maintain a habit of noting what occurs beside each diamond. This can be done prior to the day's events for forecasting practice and again at the end of the day to test your accuracy besides making additional jottings that reflect what actually transpired. These notes will prove to be an invaluable resource over time.

Two types of PDD are introduced in this chapter, one PERSONAL (PDD), the other UNIVERSAL (UDD).

The PDD's baseline is calculated using a combination of personal numbers together with current, universal numbers. The UDD is calculated solely from the day's date; its diamond contains no personal numbers. UDDs serve to provide cosmic influences as well as being a further indicator of a day's possibilities. This is similar to the way that a PYD works with its UYD. Perhaps the UDD's best use is to help confirm findings. Three basic UDDs conclude this chapter.

PDD IDIOSYNCRASIES

SD Personal Day and their SD Personal Day Diamond numbers repeat every *tenth* calendar day.

This phenomenon occurs because each successive, tenth day's number reduces to the *same root digit* as the calendar day, *ten days prior.* Quite often similar events occur on these days while not on others. The latter is attributed to the fact that once compound or WN, calendar day numbers become current, daily encounters and events reflect their specific energies and forces. This is no different to the way that a "parent" number (compound number) defines its reduced numbers. When applied to a day's number, **day 14's root 5** is very different to **day 23's root 5**.

Two examples of a ten-day (*inclusive*) monthly sequence are:

1st–10th–19th–28th Day	and	5th–14th–23rd Day
1 1 1 1		5 5 5

HOW TO CALCULATE A PERSONAL DAY NUMBER FAMILY (PDNF)

PDNF FORMULA: CURRENT CALENDAR DAY + CURRENT PMNs from PMNF

Steps to find the Personal Day Number Family

1. Calculate the current PYNF and then the PMNF
2. ADD the **current calendar day's number** to all PMNs in the PMNF
3. Their totals yield the **Personal Day Number Family (PDNF)**

Note: All PDNs become the ♥number in each PDD baseline.

STEPS AND DIAGRAM FOR CALCULATING SD AND WN PDDs

STEPS FOR CALCULATING SD and WN PDDs

1. **SD Baseline:**
   - (a) Select **current Day Number**; reduce if a WN.
   - (b) Select **current SD PMN** from its PMNF.
   - (c) Add a) and b) to get **Personal Day Number (PDN)**. Reduce to a SD.
   - (d) **Baseline:** Place SD Cal. Day No. first, **SD ♥ PDN second** and SD PMN third
2. Calculate all Goals, Challenges, Cycle Rulers, Constellations and Magickal Facets.
3. Calculate Interim and WN PDDs to broaden and confirm findings.
4. Apply "Points to Remember" and Checklist from Chapter 3.

Note: DAYLIGHT SAVINGS TIMES—Use real clock time.

Each 24–HOUR DAY divides into **4 x 6 HOURLY CYCLES.**

CALCULATIONS FOR EACH 6-HOURLY TIME SPAN

1st	6 hours begins at	**MIDNIGHT**	1st mini ◇: Midnight—6am (first cycle)
2nd	6 hours begins at	**6 a.m.**	2nd mini ◇: 6am—noon (second cycle)
3rd	6 hours begins at	**NOON**	2—opposing ▲▼: Noon—6pm (third cycle)
4th	6 hours begins at	**6 p.m.**	Cosmic ◇: 6pm—midnight (fourth cycle)

SD PDD FOR BABY AZARIA

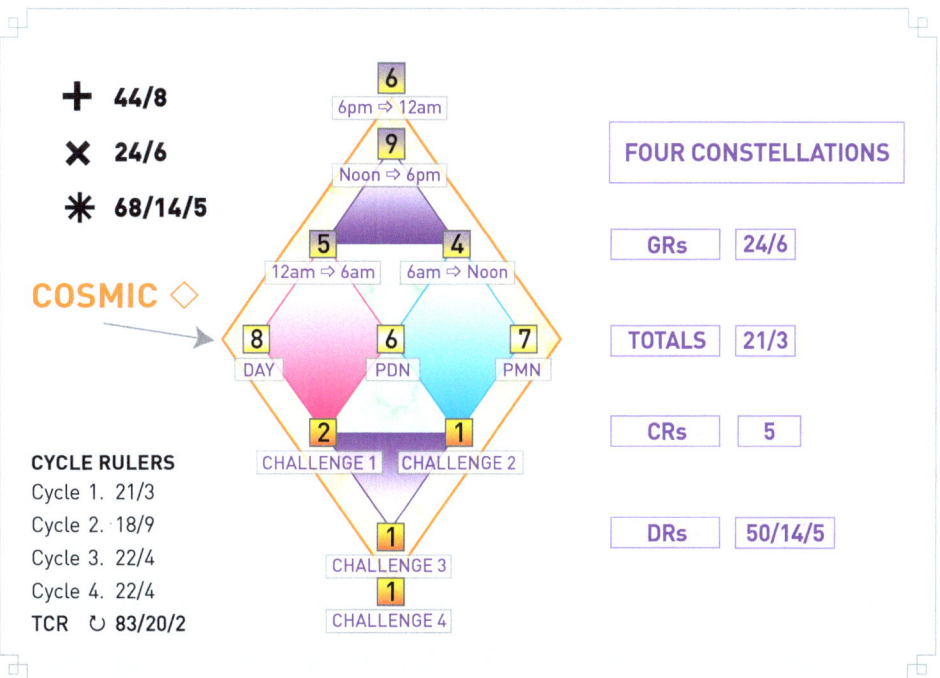

SD PDD'S MAGICKAL FACETS: ☐ 12/3; Grail 18/9; G▲18/9; C▼4; ✡'s △12/3, ▽10/1; ✤22/4; ◇22/4

AZARIA CHAMBERLAIN: 6PM TO MIDNIGHT CYCLE

Event: Baby Azaria presumed taken by a wild dingo in the Australian outback.
Died: 17-8-1980 ⇨ **UDNF 124, 115, 106, 43, 34, 25, 7**
Birth date: 11-6-1980 ⇨ **LPNF 116, 107, 98, 35, 26, 17, 8**

1980 PYNF: 116, 107, 98, 35, 26, 17, 8 (The PYNF is *always the same* as the LPNF for the first year of life)
AUG. PMNF⇨**124, 115, 106, 43, 34, 25, 16, 7** (Add **8** to all members of Azaria's PYNF.)
DAY17 PDNF⇨**141, 132, 123, 60, 51, 42, 33, 24, 6** (Add **17** to all members of Azaria's PMNF.)
PDD Baseline Calculations: DAY8 + **SD PDN6** + SD PMN7 or WN DAY17+ **WN PDN33** + WN PMN16

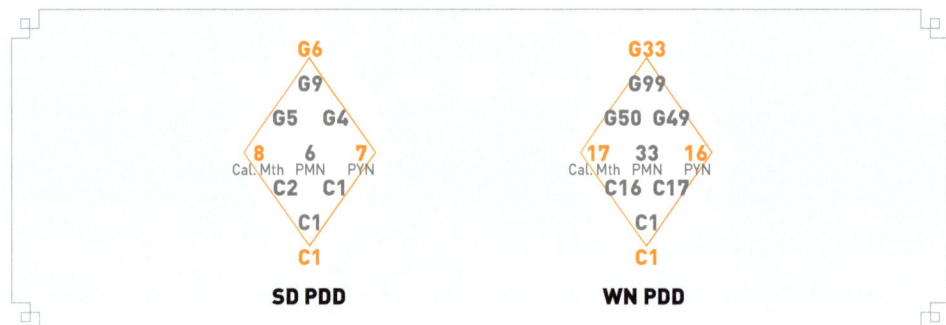

Azaria was only nine weeks old—a helpless, sleeping babe—when this freak event occurred. It provides an example of mystifying 7s at work when someone is at the mercy of unknown forces. The UDN's root digit 7 triggered Azaria's PMNF and is why **7** is significant in this instance. True to form, **PMN7**, in sync with the day's **UDN7**, accounted for the extraordinary events that unfolded that eerie night.

It was during the last cycle that Azaria disappeared never to be seen again. Azaria's ◇s and number families contain many potential death numbers. They are: **1, 10, 12/21, 16, 17, 18, 22, 24, 44, 49, 58, 64 and 78.** As many were treated in this vein in other case studies it is left to the reader to compare case studies and to look up their meanings. To add to this list, paired **86** warned of a potentially hazardous situation. Then, **22 and 17** are known for receiving public attention. A blaze of publicity followed Azaria's death for months, even years afterwards.

LINKS TO ANIMAL THEME

When Azaria's Keys are looked *into*, four in particular link to an animal theme via their associations or symbols. They are **Keys 17, 8, 18 and 24**: **The Star, Strength, The Moon and the Queen of Wands**. We can use them when interpreting their possibilities to take a different approach such as verifying an animal theme due to being major personal numbers, intensified and relevant to what occurred that night.

Firstly, **Key 17** is important for two reasons. One is that it was the day's number and two that it was one of Azaria's **LPNs**. Why single out **Key 17**? Because it has links to nature and the animal kingdom and *an animal was the catalyst for this event*. When **17** is reduced to **Key 8 ⇨ Strength** its links to animals via the lion on **Key 8** are clear. However, this is no ordinary lion—he is King of the Beasts, so he represents the entire animal kingdom as does **17** indirectly via its association to **8**. Two prominent **8**s from Azaria's birth date link to root **8** from **UD17**. Now we have established that **Key 8** is intensified. Hence, it is likely that the lion's negative side would manifest and suggest a *wild* beast—a *predator* —**a dingo** in Azaria's case.

This predator theme grows more likely as **18 ⇨ The Moon** resides in Azaria's birth year. **Key 18** has a *wolf* on it, not unlike a dingo—*a wild, undomesticated animal that scavenges at **dusk***. The links being unravelled are **Moon ⇨ dusk and nighttime; the wolf ⇨ dingo**! Hence, **The Moon Key** provides a plausible, association of ideas to consider for the events that took place, especially when **8**, paired **17** and **18** were all active in Azaria's last SD PDD's cycle!

Paired 24 in Azaria's ☐ introduces yet another animal to the mix. It has links to animals via the cat in its Key's picture. (I repeatedly find that **24** depicts people who love cats or dogs or loathe either.)

ALL KEYS LINK TO AN ANIMAL THEME

STEVE IRWIN: Bizzare Death During First or Second Cycle
Event: Death caused by a stingray barb penetrating Steve's heart.
Died: 4–9–2006 ➾ UDNF **39, 21, 3**
Age: 44 (Pronounced dead during morning.)
Birthdate: 22–2–1962 ➾ LPNF **105, 96, 87, 42, 33, 15, 6**

2006 PYNF: 50, 32, 14, 5
SEP. PMNF: 59, 41, 23, 14, 5 (Add **9** to each PYN)
DAY 4 PDNF: 63, 45, 27, 18, 9 (Add **4** to PMN's)
PDD Baseline Calculation: SD DAY4 + **SD PDN9** + SD PMN5 or WN DAY4 + **WN PDN18** + WN PMN14

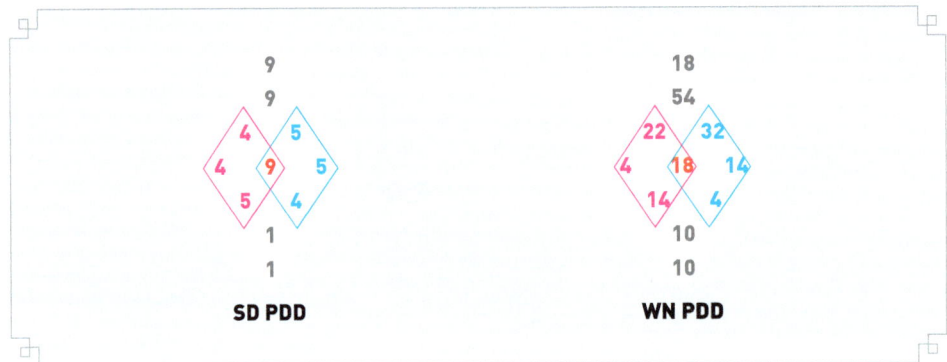

Important Points

With the intent to be pro-active rather than seem morbid, if what appears to be a remote death signature or a warning in a YD appears again in one of its PMDs, then it is wise to set up PDDs to find which day might be the one to guard against. Naturally, we would prefer if it were a special event. As Steve died on this day, his PDD naturally confirmed such a possibility. However, it is not that simple if you are trying to find when death might occur as it is like searching for a "needle in a haystack".

To predict a death is one of the hardest things to do and maybe that is a very good thing! *Many* factors need to be considered and a *lot* of figuring done. It is wise to consult the charts of family member's as well as others who may be involved. Their astrology charts should also be consulted for such a serious possibility but do not confine this practice to tragic events; the same approach applies to celebrations and noteworthy occasions. Those versed in astrology will find that this system works in tandem with it.

Timing

Steve Irwin's time of death was given in the morning so one of the first two cycles for that day is the one when his death occurred. As it happens, both cycles contain life-threatening numbers such as **9s and WN22** (**22** is also the **SD PDD's first Cycle Ruler**), paired **55** in the second cycle and hidden **13s** (from paired **49s** in his first and second SD cycles. There were *five 13s overall!*). These numbers' links to endings or death make it difficult to choose which cycle is "the" one. It leads to the assumption that death occurred near the end of cycle one or shortly into cycle two and was likely a "cusp event".

First or Second Cycle Active

Chance events and timing on that day synchronised with Steve's choices to help orchestrate his ultimate demise. Bad weather was the catalyst. It caused him to change his mind about work plans. This is seen in the four paired **45's** and two **1s**, as **5** relates to change, **4** to work and **1** to plans. This change of mind to proceed to another filming location can be seen in the four, paired **95's** (**5**, change and **9**, the mind).

Marine Animal Theme

Similar to Azaria, Steve's death was highly unusual. He died from a stingray's barb thrust deeply into his heart. Being a marine animal, ties the stingray to an animal theme.

18s in powerful positions relate this event to a marine theme. Steve's birth year adds to **18** and one of his Life Diamond Rulers (LDRs) is an **18**. Then Steve had three prominent **18s** in his current PYD. They were triggered by the high profile **18s** that ruled Steve's SD PDD's □, his ✱'s △ and PDN. **18** is his WN PDD's ♥ number and its final Goal. It is essential to seek out leading, multiple links like this to support hunches or theories.

If we use astrology and Qabalah associations allotted to the Keys, we find other connections that reinforce considering a marine theme.

Astrological Associations

This potent **18**⇨**Moon Key** emphasis is ruled by **Pisces, the *fish*,** and Pisces *rules the seas*. In addition, the **Moon Key** has a *crayfish* as one of its main symbols. Hence, this Key's associations to the sea and marine life support a marine animal theme. This theme was considered mostly because of **18** and **13s**' strong presence in that day's numbers. It was also considered to tie the events of the day to the prevailing, environmental conditions that contributed significantly to this outcome.

Qabalistic Associations

Why single out **13**? Steve had **LGR13** in his Life Diamond, which was triggered by the many hidden **13s** in his SD PDD. They relate to *fish* via the **Hebrew letter** *NUN* for **Key13,** which literally translates as *"fish"*, hence we get excellent backup from this multiple association to consider a marine theme.

Life Diamond Associations

Uncannily, Steve's Life Diamond's ✱Wheel Ruler was **57⇨3 of Swords**. As shown below, it depicts three swords piercing a red heart! Making the connection between this Key's image, the stingray's barb and that it actually struck Steve in the heart, gives cause to wonder just how remote the chance of being pierced in the heart by a stingray's poisonous barb was, when such a high profile Diamond Ruler Key portrays a heart pierced by swords? How astonishing and remarkable is that?

KEYS 13 & 18 LINK TO MARINE LIFE

NUN⇨FISH   PISCES⇨SEA   STEVE'S LD✱ RULER
⇨CRAYFISH

The following PDDs are of LADY DIANA and DODI FAYED, PRINCES WILLIAM and HARRY and CROWN PRINCE CHARLES. They depict Lady Diana and Dodi Fayed's tragic accident that caused their deaths. This set of PDDs proves how a common event is reflected in all members' numbers.

Try setting up PDDs for important occasions that affect a group. Wedding days, baby's births or team events make good practice.

ST JOAN of ARC'S PDD for her day of execution follows the royal family's. Her SD and WN LDs, SD UYD, PYD, PMD and PDD show the basics for such an occasion.

CASE STUDIES: LADY DIANA, HER FAMILY AND DODI

LADY DIANA: *First Cycle*
Event: Fatal Car Crash
Died: 31-8-1997 ⇨**UDNF: 74, 65, 56, 47, 20, 11, 2** (Pronounced dead at 4a.m.)
Birth date: 1-7-1961 ⇨**LPNF: 88, 79, 70, 25, 16, 7**

1997 **PYNF: 124, 115, 106, 43, 34, 25, 16, 7**
AUG. **PMN: 132, 123, 114, 51, 42, 33, 24, 15, 6** (Add **8** to each PYN.)
DAY31 **PDNF: 163, 154, 145, 82, 73, 64, 55, 46, 37, 10, 1** (Add **31** to each PMN.)
PDD Baseline Calculation: SD DAY4 + **SD PDN1**+ SD PMN6 or WN DAY31 + **WN PDN46** + WN PMN15

You may like to calculate each person's Life Diamonds through to their PDDs to appreciate how their numbers reveal the impact that this day had on their lives.

The first cycle in each PDD depicts when Lady Diana met with her fatal accident. Many potential death numbers show up more in Lady Diana's SD than her WN PDD (except for WN ♥**46** ⇨**4 of Cups** and its reverse, **64**⇨**10 of Swords**; they are in her SD Cosmic ◇ and part of the PDNF). They were: paired **13s, 21 and 22** in the Vertical Axis and **55, 73 and 57s** in her SD □. *All were in powerful positions.* Paired **34**⇨**8 of Wands** and **16s**⇨**The Tower** in each PDD (more intense in her WN PDD) warned of a possible accident. Besides being potential death numbers, **57** and **64** are passionate numbers and might account for Lady Diana being so upset with the paparazzi that day. Paired **35s**⇨**9 of Wands** stood for her weariness of their intolerable pestering and never being rid of them. Did **WN61's** running away aspect indicate her wanting to flee the paparazzi? The paired **53s**⇨**Knight of Swords and 37s**⇨**King of Cups** possibly saw Dodi as her "knight" valiantly trying to protect her from them (**33** in ✡'s △'s name is *Valiant*).

Decade Diamonds & Month, Day, Hour and Minute Diamonds

As death occurred, could we perceive the SD □'s **20**⇨**Judgement**, the **Grail's 21**⇨**The World** and paired **22**⇨**The Fool** with two **13 Death Keys** on the **Vertical Axis** collectively, as a transition to the next phase in life? Does **Key 64** as ♥**46**'s reverse depict the same thing? For high profile people, **22** often depicts public life or attention and sometimes state funerals; both were so in this case.

DODI FAYED (Lady Diana's Lover): First Cycle
Event: Fatal Car Crash
Died: 31–8–1997 ⇨**UDNF:** 74, 65, 56, 47, 20, 11, 2 (Died at approx. 1:20a.m.)
Birthdate: 15–4–1955 ⇨**LPNF:** 93, 84, 75, 39, 30, 21, 12, 3

1997 PYNF: 135, 126, 117, 54, 45, 36, 27, 18, 9
AUG. PMNF: 143, 134, 125, 62, 53, 44, 35, 26, 17, 8 (Add **8** to each PYN.)
DAY31 PDNF: 174, 165, 156, 93, 84, 75, 66, 57, 48, 39, 12, 3 (Add **31** to each PMN.)
PDD Baseline Calculation: SD DAY4 + **SD PDN3** + SD PMN8 or WN DAY31+ **WN PDN48** + WN PMN17

Taking a different approach, Dodi's SD PDD makes very strong connections to his **birth date** and the **UD's date**. They provide an excellent example of the synchronicity occurring between a ◇, major personal numbers and the current date.

Firstly, several high profile **15s** in Dodi's SD PDD connect to his birth **day** number **15**⇨**The Devil**. One is the baseline Ruler, one the first cycle Ruler; one the □ Ruler—with another at its base—and yet another, the ✿'s △ Ruler.

These **15s** were greatly intensified because they held major positions and were multiple. Dodi's high profile, romantic attachment to Lady Diana exemplified their intensification. We saw **Key15's** LOVERS' aspect in full operation as their romance attracted worldwide headlines (**21s** in PDD and one in LPNF).

Secondly, an even more powerful connection can be made from Dodi's PDDs to his **LPNs**. Note how SD ♥3⇨**Empress** (which is really a **12**⇨**The Hanged Man**) and paired **39s**⇨**Knight of Cups** (they reduce to **12/3**) perfectly match his **LPNF: 39/12/3**. **39** links to his playboy image, unabashed self-indulgence and love of beautiful women and expensive things. ♥**3** indicates that love, romance and having fun were high priorities for that day. Yet **12** strongly hinted at reversals and its reverse as **21**, possible transitioning to afterlife. ♥**48**⇨**8 of Cups** can also depict that; it reduces to **12** and then we get **reversed 21** again which can depict an end to life.

Thirdly, **SD 4**⇨**Emperor** from the calendar day's **31**⇨**5 of Wands** links to Dodi's **birth month 4**. Paired **31** appears in his fateful first cycle. As the **5 of Wands, Key31** graphically depicts the struggle Dodi was having dealing with trying to please Lady Diana on the one hand (♥**3**) and cope with the power struggle that was developing between them and the invasive paparazzi on the other (✡'s **ruling 28**⇨**2 of Wands**).

To act (paired **34**⇨**8 of Wands**) on his decision (**47**⇨**7 of Cups** number of choice) to escape the paparazzi is seen in the many Key**15s'** *releasing* rather than attaching aspect. But that decision may have been too impulsive and too forceful (**34**'s aspects) and ultimately led to his death: **Key 13**⇨**Death** (**WN31**'s reverse and WN ♥**48**⇨**8 of Cups** in the first cycle).

Did the *wrath* aspect from the **Temperance Keys** (**14s**) in both ◇s play its part in that melodrama when we saw Dodi trying to rid himself of an annoyance (**WN14s**), that was making his life a living hell (**15s**)?

To conclude, Dodi's SD Grail Ruler was **18**⇨**The Moon** which can be the number of tragedy. It picked up the wide public attention his death received through its reverse as **81**'s aspects. Their root **9s**⇨**The Hermit** that linked to his **PYNF** of **9s**, hinted at endings as well as the global portrayal of his death.

PRINCE WILLIAM: First Cycle —15 years old
Event: Father (Prince Charles) bringing news of his mother's (Lady Diana's) death.
Date of Event: 31–8–1997 ⇨ UDNF: 155, 146, 137, 56, 47, 20, 11, 2
Birth date: 21–6–1982 ⇨ LPNF: 128, 119, 110, 47, 38, 11, 2

1997 PYNF: 143, 134, 125, 53, 44, 35, 17, 8
AUG. PMNF: 151, 142, 133, 61, 52, 43, 25, 16, 7 (Add **8** to each PYN)
DAY31 PDNF: 182, 173, 164, 92, 83, 74, 56, 47, 38, 11, 2 (Add **31** to each PMN.)
PDD Baseline Calculation: SD DAY4 + **SD PDN2** + SD PMN7 or WN DAY31 + **WN PDN47** + WN PMN16

Prince William's SD, first cycle contains foreboding numbers. Eg, paired **64**⇨**10 of Swords** and **22**⇨**The Fool** aptly fit this tragic event. Two paired **26s**⇨**Page of Wands** in the Vertical Axis and two in this cycle indicate the tragic news he received from his father re his mother's fatal accident (**WN PMN16**⇨**The Tower**). But there is a real poignancy in the several **62s**⇨**8 of Swords** that convey his pain and suffering. They depicted the temporary, paralysing nature of this grief-laden news. His Magickal Facets and Constellations contain a prevalence of **13s**⇨**Death** and a harsh **55**⇨**Ace of Swords**. With **57, 64 and 62s**, they warn of a life-changing day. The **SD Grail Ruler** was **24**⇨**Queen of Wands**; it links to death on this occasion. It intensified the paired **24s** in the SD PPD's first cycle. **24** not only signified his mother (Queen of Wands) but as **42**⇨**2 of Cups,** in negative mode, their parting instead of union. Intensified **24/42s** also signified the close mother-son relationship so the wounding would likely be deeper. **WN C15s**⇨**The Devil** with ♥**11**⇨**Justice** also indicated a parting. **WN63**⇨**9 of Swords** represented the nightmarish news; **WN48**⇨**8 of Cups** a death and a new way of life. ☾**84** signified a death in the family as it did for Bindi and Bob Irwin.

PRINCE "HARRY": First Cycle —12 years old
Event: Woken from sleep by father bringing news of his mother's death.
Date of Event: 31–8–1997 ⇨ **UDNF:** 155, 146, 137, 56, 47, 20, 11, 2
Birth date: 15–9–1984 ⇨**LPNF:** 127, 118, 109, 46, 37, 28, 19, 10, 1

1997 PYNF: 140, 131, 122, 50, 41, 32, 23, 5
AUG. PMNF: 148, 139, 130, 58, 49, 40, 31, 13, 4 (Add **8** to each PYN)
DAY31 PDNF: 179, 170, 161, 89, 80, 71, 62, 44, 35, 8 (Add **31** to each PMN.)
PDD Baseline Calculation: SD DAY4 + **SD PDN8** + SD PMN4 or WN DAY31 + **WN PDN44** + WN PMN13

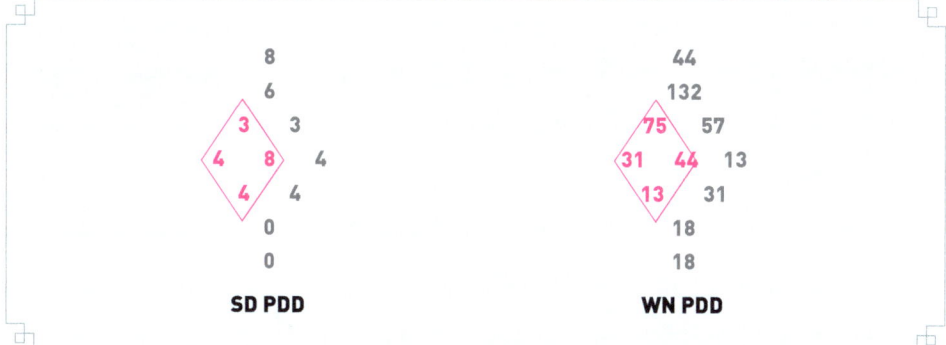

SD PDD   **WN PDD**

The make up of both Prince "Harry's" ◻s and **Grail's numbers** was extremely daunting. **WNC18s and SDC80s and 40s** only added to their threat. Both ◇s showed very clearly not only the possibility of a loss but also the enormous suffering that would be endured if it occurred. Indeed, Prince Harry's SD PDD first Cycle Ruler, **19/10/1**⇨**Sun, Wheel of Fortune and The Magician** with paired **34s**, depicted the sudden, untimely death of a senior family member, none other than his mother.

Paired **40s**⇨**Page of Cups** and **44s**⇨**4 of Cups** with **48s**⇨**8 of Cups**, **80s** and **86s** indicated the unimaginable stress of the day's events. His young life would be changed forever (paired **48s**—especially when intensified by the SD Grail's portentous **22**⇨**The Fool**). The ✶'s △ and ▽s contained double **64s**⇨**10 of Swords** and **30s**⇨**4 of Cups**. As the trends were negative, they were formidable. They signalled the collapse (**64**) of his family structure (**30**) which was confirmed by the ✶ Ruler, a fateful **20**⇨**Judgement**. It warned that something drastic might occur that could have long term effects. This was clearly a day of an "out-of-the-blue", life-shattering event (*six* **34s**⇨**8 of Wands**). Did ☋**79** signify the loss of his hero?

PRINCE CHARLES: First Cycle
Event: News of Lady Diana's death (ex wife).
Date of Event: 31-8-1997 ⇨ UDNF: 155, 146, 137, 56, 47, 20, 11, 2
Birth date: 14-11-1948 ⇨ LPNF: 92, 83, 74, 47, 38, 20, 11, 2

1997 PYNF: 141, 132, 123, 51, 42, 33, 24, 15, 6
AUG. PMNF: 149, 140, 131, 59, 50, 41, 32, 23, 14, 5 (Add **8** to each PYN)
DAY31 PDNF: 180, 171, 162, 90, 81, 72, 63, 54, 45, 36, 9 (Add **31** to each PMN.)
PDD Baseline Calculation: SD DAY4 + **SD PDN9** + SD PMN5 or WN DAY31+ **WN PDN45** + WN PMN14

The **SD Vertical Axis** reflected the enormous inner strength, compassion and wisdom Prince Charles needed to deal with that day's extraordinary events. Other Keys that served in this way included several paired **54s** in the SD PDD which identified Prince Charles with the **Page of Swords** and the **5s** with the **Hierophant**. They would have helped him to draw on the practical wisdom contained in each when conveying the tragic news of his former wife's death (**22**⇨**The Fool** as first SD Cycle Ruler plus two hidden **13s**⇨**Death** from paired **49s**⇨**9 of Cups**) to his young sons. The **SD Grail Ruler's 27** signified an ending, as did **SD ♥9**. The two **WN C17s**⇨**The Star**, thrust him into what was likely an uncomfortable spotlight given the nature of his and Lady Diana's strained relationship. **WN ♥45**⇨**5 of Cups** depicted his grief and heavy emotional state. Prince Charles' **SD □** ruler, **18**⇨**The Moon**, could signify Lady Diana and his mother (feminine aspect of the Moon). It could also signify his being put under public scrutiny as the public judged both his reaction and handling of such a delicate, very public, family matter. Can you find judgemental **11** and **20** that were influencing the day's events?

St JOAN of ARC (1412–1431)—19 years old
Event: Execution Day—burned at stake
Died: 30-5-1431 ⇨UDN: 80, 44, 17, 8
Current Age at Death: **19.4+mths**
Birth date: 6-1-1412 ⇨LPN: 33, 24, 15, 6

1431 PYNF: 52, 43, 16, 7
MAY PMNF: 57, 48, 21, 12, 3 (Add **5** to each PYN)
DAY30 PDNF: 87, 78, 51, 42, 33, 6 (Add **30** to each PMN)
SD PDD Baseline Calculation: SD DAY3 + **SD PDN6** + SD PMN3

Joan of Arc's LDs and YDs for the current year of her death are displayed along with their SD PMD and SD PDD for that historic day. The layout for this event exemplifies the very basic amount of preparation required for research of this nature. Interpretations for this event are confined to signs of death.

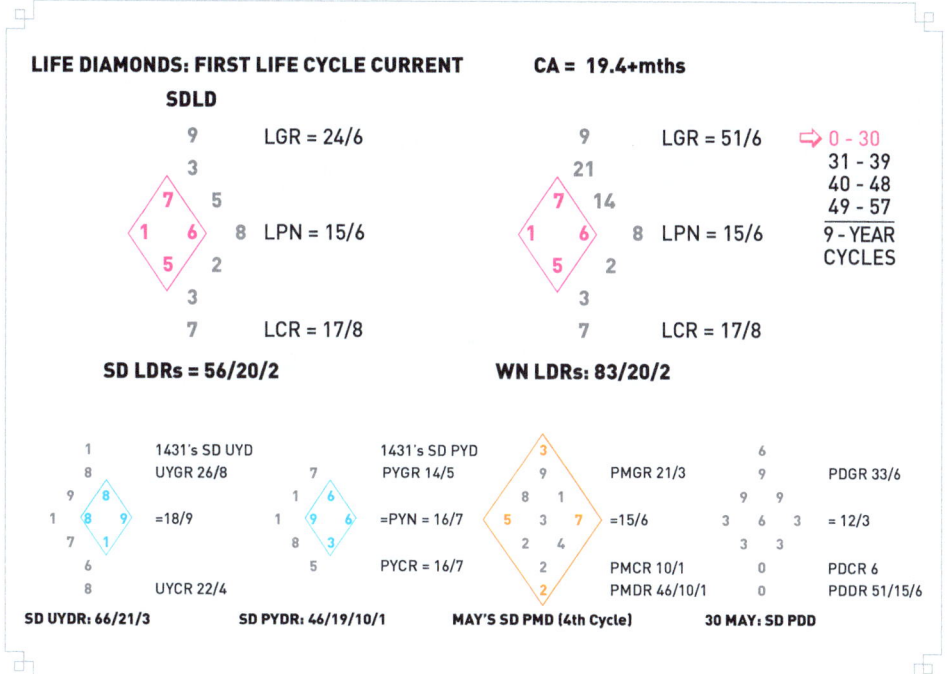

Activated Cycles
LD's 1st cycle: Rulers— **19/91; 10/1**
UYD's 2nd cycle: Rulers—**26/62; 8/80**
PYD's 2nd cycle: Rulers—**24/42; 6/60** (Contains one of St Joan's LPNs)
PMD's 4th cycle: Rulers—**17/71; 8/80** (Links to LD's 1st cycle)
PDD's cycle: Time of death not known

Examining all Diamonds

The point of this exercise is to demonstrate how to find significant links between ◇s to verify an event. Firstly, scan each ◇ for relevant signs and repetitive themes as this preparation strengthens and supports findings.

General Overview

As this was **execution day**, imminent signs of death should be mirrored and reinforced throughout these ◇s. As it happens, the ◇s do have strong links to each other that point to a likely death. They occur between the PMD and PDD to St Joan's major personal numbers, YDs and LDs. To find such links is essential. Note that the current UYD and PYD appear particularly menacing supporting the theme of an execution with a predominance of **8s** in her UYD. When paired to make **88**, they reduce to **16s** and link to the **PYD's 16s**. This build-up of energies and forces concentrates the trends' ominous potential. Then **UYCR22** provides further confirmation. Several **18s** as **81s** do the same as we know **18** can sometimes be the number of tragedy. Then, the PYD contained **19/10/1, 16, 15, 14, 48 and 12** in strong positions. These numbers along with the UYD's **8s, 88s and 98s, 22 and 18s** combine to either: herald unprecedented accomplishment; immense gain or loss; extreme cruelty; a harrowing experience; or death.

Findings

As there are many excellent links between ◇s and St Joan's major personal numbers, only the most relevant are dealt with here.

First are the major links to her **LPNF: 33/24/15/6** from the PDD's several **33s**⇨**7 of Wands** (**33** also ruled its ✱) and from her PYD's current Cycle Ruler, **24**⇨**Queen of Wands**. **15/6**⇨**Devil and Lovers** rule May's PMD SD baseline and are one of the SD PDDRs. Its ✱ adds to **69**⇨**Ace of Pentacles**—producing **15/6** when reduced—and several **69s** are present in the SD PDD as well. Then, the UYD's Grail Ruler was **33** and its □ Ruler, **25**! **25**⇨**Knight of Wands** ruled her LD's Grail, ✱ and cosmic ◇. To find **33, 24, 15 and 6 and 25** so prominent and frequent is extremely important because they not only confirm findings but also spring her major numbers into action. This synchronistic criss-crossing between ◇s certainly implies that aspects of her destiny were being activated that day.

Next, St Joan's birth *day*, **6**, happens to be the ♥ number of the PDD; that is significant. It is surrounded by **33s** (her top LPN) and **96/69s**. These strong **3, 6, 9s** and **15/6 pattern** in the SD PDD reproduce the **3, 6, 9s** in her LD's Vertical Axis. They form striking links to the active cycles in her SD PYD and her PDD and, of course, her full set of LPNs.

73⇨**5 of Pentacles** is the next number to consider. It appears in the SDLD's Goal▲ and both LD's Vertical Axes. It is the PYD's ☍ and appears in its ✡'s △. It also forms part of her current PMD's baseline. **Key 73** signifies St Joan not only being shunned by the King *and* the Church, but also being *forced* (**UYDR10**) to *face* something (**UYDR19**) entirely *alone* (**73's root 1**).

Due to its reliable links to fires, **16⇨The Tower,** in this case, is an extremely important number to verify findings as St Joan would be burned to death. High profile **16**s are seen in the SD PYD and one rules the UYD ✡'s △. *They trigger the 16 in the active LD cycle.* This gives its presence greater power.

Not to be surprised, the actual ruler of the UYD's ✡'s Ruler was **39⇨the Knight of Cups**, with two more within the SD LD's Vertical Axis, one in the PYD and *six* in the PDD. **FAITH** is a keyword, which can be attributed to **39⇨Knight of Cups** and its **root 3⇨The Empress** for this event. Such an abundance of **39**s and **3**s fortified her unwavering faith in God which most likely helped her to get through that terrifying day. It is comforting to know that the number of God (**26**) was in her UYD, too. It ruled its current cycle and was its Goal Ruler. I believe that **9**s also make a connection to God via the Hebrew letter, *YOD*, which is assigned to the **9th Tarot Key⇨The Hermit**— UYD ✶ Ruler was **90**. Other connections to God are found in the **17**s in each ◇ except for the PDD.

This case study provides an excellent example of when a most promising looking PDD has a dire outcome. Pretending that this event is not known, the first clue that it might warn of a bad day is that St Joan's LPNs appear in the PDD many times. This could have heralded something momentous in a *good* way. But I think the major clues that this turned out to be just the opposite were the **UYD's 8s, 88s and 89/98s**, its **18s**, its **UYC22** and the fact that its current cycle contained **88, 89/98, 18 and 19**. (Note the similarities to Terri's PMD's numbers.) Then the day's date added to **44/17/8**. **44** can be a cause for concern. It was strong in Prince Harry's PDDs. (Remember how Osama Bin Laden used his paired PYD's **44** catastrophically on September 11, 2001; Book 2! Could **44** have ominous traits due to being **double 22 or four times 11**?) Besides, **44's root 8** intensifies the **8**s in the UYD and **8**s are also numbers of God (from 26 and 17 reductions)!

Take out the **4 of Cups Key**. Discounting the four Aces in the Tarot deck, the **4 of Cups** is the *only* Key in the minor arcana that has a hand from Spirit making an offering to a person. It is most poignant to imagine this Key alluding to the cross offered to St Joan as a final act of kindness by one of the soldiers. She drew courage, strength and comfort from it in her dying moments.

You may wish to refer to St Joan's case study in *Life Diamonds'* Chapter 9.

WORDS OF CAUTION

Many things need scrupulous attention before assuming that a death is immanent in someone's charts. For example, St Joan was at the forefront of battle and could have been killed *at any time*. <u>Her numbers depicted this likelihood *from 1429, onwards*</u>.

The point is that signs of "death" *frequently appear* among progressed charts' numbers but *death seldom occurs*. This is due to all earth life being cyclic, ever changing and temporal. Hence, the numbers show ideas, feelings, habits and things coming to their natural end and these are what they mostly reflect. So you are urged once more to be thorough in your work before reaching such conclusions and to be *extremely cautious* if charts seem to threaten a death. Go by the adage: "If in doubt, don't!"

The cluster of PDDs for the day Lady Diana and Steve Irwin died provided an example of setting out a family's ◇s to verify an outstanding occasion. Their Magickal Facets and Constellations provide more validation for those who wish to calculate them.

UNIVERSAL DAY DIAMONDS (UDDS)

Personal Day Diamonds have Universal Day Diamonds (UDDs) like Personal Yearly Diamonds have Universal Yearly Diamonds. UDDs are simply calculated from the day's date. Their calculations follow the same methods as Life Diamonds in that the month number goes first, the day's number second and the year number third on their baselines.

Why bother with UDDs?—because days' dates are potent and this point has already been brought to your attention several times. UDDs can be used to designate the beginnings of a new life, a life-changing event or an enterprise or to verify findings. This being so, then each day's date can have a bearing on everyday events, especially those that are outstanding. The only way to verify that hypothesis is to set up many Universal Day Diamonds (UDDs) beside their PDDs for exceptional days.

Universal Day Diamonds provide another angle or version of what has the potential to manifest on a particular day. All case studies presented so far occurred on exceptional days. They provide excellent material to verify whether Universal Day Diamonds are worth calculating. Three such examples follow. In the UDDs depicting tragic days, look for warnings in the UDD to verify that. For days of celebration or great achievement, look for numbers, patterns and themes that link between diamonds and other branches of numerology to verify that.

If you calculate the Constellations and Magickal Facets for the following UDDs, you will find that they not only verify that UDDs have a place in numerology, they also reveal greater insights about each case's events. Prince Harry's PDD for the day his mother died could not have provided a more perfect example. It was incredibly like its PDD. See below.

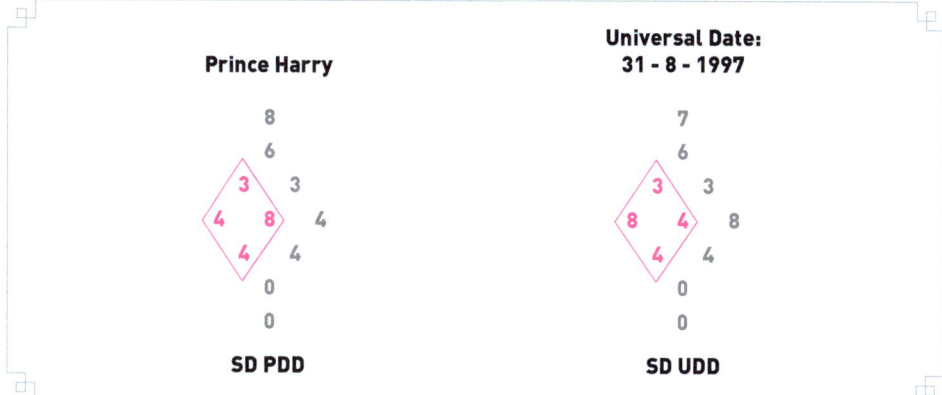

Almost the same can be said for the Irwin family. How many criss-cross links can you find from their PDDs to their UDD for that sad day? Then, how many criss-cross links can you find between family members?

The PDD and UDD on the next page reveal Susan Boyle's life-changing day when she rocketed to fame. It is a marvellous example of when several daunting numbers and Keys auger great achievement, not adversity.

Decade Diamonds & Month, Day, Hour and Minute Diamonds

```
                                          Universal Date:
          Susan Boyle                       11 - 4 - 2009

              4                                  6
              3                                  1
            6   6                              6   4
          2   4   2                          4   2   2
            2   2                              2   0
              0                                  2
              0                                  2

           SD PDD                             SD UDD
```

SUSAN BOYLE'S UDD CONTRIBUTION

Susan's UDD strongly supported her PDD's trends as many of its numbers repeated those in her PDD. Such repetition reinforces the PDD's prospects and increases accuracy when forecasting. First impressions of both ◇s are that Susan had many daunting numbers in each. The **SD PDD's** daunting numbers were four **20s**, three **22s**, two **34s**, **40**, **46/64s** and *six 62s*. The **SD UDD's** daunting numbers were four **20s**, **16**, **21**, five **22s**, **40**, three **46/64s** and three **62s** plus another as the **UDN's Ruler**.

Since both ◇s contained several tens, master and repeat numbers, their type and intensification signified that something momentous, surprising or shocking was likely to unfold that day: happily, it was the former. Their intensification reflected the tremendous pressure, excitement and nervous tension Susan would have been under. But she used their extra powers to deliver a performance that was both spellbinding and surprising. "Plain, average Susan" received a standing ovation. So, it wasn't about the heavy accent on the *paralytic* nature of the **8 of Swords** was it? *It was about its opposite, the **Page of Wands**, coming forward to begin a performance* (**Wheel Ruler 43**); **The Fool**, daring to risk all; the **6 of Cups**, giving and receiving; the **10 of Swords**, the transformation of "Cinderella"! Susan's performance was an unexpected spectacle that not only enchanted and inspired millions (**22s**) but also transformed her life from there onwards (**20s**). Her PDD's constellations and magickal facets were brilliant for the occasion. They are well worth calculating.

The bizarre thing about Susan's ◇s was, although they had many potentially, gloomy numbers, her experience was joyful, fulfilling and uplifting. Then St Joan, as you may remember, had promising numbers yet experienced a horrible death. The clues, as always, lie in the person's **background information** or the unknown. For St Joan it was *her execution day*, for Susan, her *coming out day*.

The following tips provide examples of what to look for when utilising PDDs and UDDs.

INTERPRETATION TIPS

UDDs in their own right are not always useful. To err on the safe side, put up their ruling LDs, PYDs, UYDs and PMDs as the UDD may trigger one or more of them instead of reinforcing its PDD. This practice hones accuracy and timing skills as well as validates forecasts.

Since temporary numbers comprise PDDs and UDDs, they create *TRANSIT* MAPS TO LIFE and act as TRIGGERS TO OTHER ◇s OR MAJOR PERSONAL NUMBERS. Therefore, when studying or planning a significant event, it is essential to locate where links occur from these ◇s to major personal numbers, other diamonds, current dates, hopes and plans or whatever is unfolding in the life. St Joan had six main features that stood out among her personal numbers, her long and short-term ◇s and the day's date. They provide the kinds of signs to look for when investigating past events or conversely planning future events. The points below explain this more fully.

1. There were several repeat numbers in St Joan's PDD that linked to her LD and PMD's Vertical Axes (they link to the Soul via this axis's "spiritual" association) and to the PYD's second cycle. It was during that cycle when her death occurred.
2. Several personal numbers repeated in other ◇s.
3. Transiting numbers activated her major, personal numbers.
4. Links from the current date related to some LD numbers.
5. The UDD made many significant links to other ◇s.
6. Such "traffic" between ◇s suggests May and that day for her demise.

The tips above illustrate how important it is to refrain from analysing ◇s for special occasions in isolation. Going to extra lengths and checking everything out as thoroughly as possible leaves less room for error.

Many of the features mentioned from page 43 to 48 in the previous chapter not only apply equally to PDDs and UDDs but to all long and short cycles. It may pay to revise them.

When a cycle's numbers are isolated from the rest in your journal, take special note of its goal, challenge and rulers. Ask yourself "How can these three numbers help me to figure out the "work" of the cycle? In what way do they relate to my aspirations? What can I cultivate from their positive aspects? How do their negative aspects reflect those in me? How can I transcend them?"

Decade Diamonds & Month, Day, Hour and Minute Diamonds

Chapter 5:
PERSONAL HOUR DIAMONDS

PHN = Personal Hour Number **G** = Goal **C** = Challenge **UDN** = Universal Day Number
PHD = Personal Hour Diamond **R** = Ruler **PDD** = Personal Day Diamond
PHDR = Personal Hour Diamond Ruler **S** = Single **W**=Whole **PDN** = Personal Day Number

ABOUT PERSONAL HOUR DIAMONDS (PHDs)

Personal Hour Diamonds (PHDs) represent **clock timing of events**. They are of particular use when the actual time for an event or the time within a 15-minute time span for an event is either planned for or known. As you can imagine, these Diamonds and their numbers and Tarot Keys are dynamic and very much "alive" due to their very short cycles.

A PHD's numbers *must* link to to all ◇s that rule it or to major personal numbers to act as triggers to them. If not, then its indications must relate to the event. Many examples of triggering from shorter, transiting cycles to ruling cycles and major, personal numbers were provided in previous chapters.

HOW TO CALCULATE A PERSONAL HOUR NUMBER (PHN)

The following formula produces the **Personal Hour Number (PHN)**.

PHN FORMULA: CURRENT HOUR IN REAL TIME + CURRENT PDN

To find the current SD PHN, convert all hourly numbers to **24 hour clock time**. **Then reduce compound hour numbers from 10:00 hours through to 24:00 hours to SDs. For example, 10a.m. reduces to 1**; BUT, 12a.m. reduces to 6 as it equates to 24:00 hours and 24 reduces to 6.

Using 24 hour clock time distinguishes SD p.m. times from SD a.m. times except for 10a.m, 11a.m. and 12p.m. The best way to distinguish the latter is to set up a WN ◇ for them.

Use the following formula and Steps in the box below to create Personal Hour Diamonds. Calculate the Personal Day Number Family (PDNF) first. Then decide if you are creating a SD or a WN Personal Hour ◇.

If a SD◇, use the SD or reduced hour number for the time of the event eg, for **11a.m.** use **2**. For all hours after midday <u>use 24 hour clock time</u> eg, 1pm⇔**1300hrs** use **4**; 3pm⇔**1500hrs** use **6**; 7pm⇔**1900hrs** use **1**; 9pm⇔**2100hrs** use **3**.

If a WN◇, do not reduce the hour number past 9a.m. eg, for **10a.m.** use **10**, for **12p.m.** use **12**.

STEPS AND DIAGRAM FOR CALCULATING SD AND WN PHDs

PHD FORMULA: CURRENT HOUR IN REAL TIME + PHN + PDN

STEPS FOR CALCULATING SD and WN PHDs

1. **SD Baseline:**
   - (a) Select **active SD Hour Number** in **24 hour clock time**; reduce if a WN.
   - (b) Select **current SD PDN** from its PDNF.
   - (c) Add a) and b) for **Personal Hour Number (PHN)**. Reduce to a SD.
   - (d) **Baseline:** Place SD Hour No. first, **SD PHN second** and SD PDN third.
2. Calculate all Goals, Challenges, Cycle Rulers, Constellations and Magickal Facets.
3. Record significant features. Apply "Points to Remember".
4. Interim and WN PHDs if calculated broaden and confirm findings.

Midnight to 1 a.m.—Reduce 24 to 6 for this hour's duration.

Note: DAYLIGHT SAVINGS TIMES—Use 24-hour real clock time.

Each 24–HOUR DAY divides into **4 X 15 MINUTE CYCLES.**

CALCULATIONS FOR EACH 15-MINUTE TIME SPAN:

1st	:	first mini diamond	: 0 mins.—15 mins.
1nd	:	second mini diamond	: 16 mins.—30 mins.
3rd	:	two opposing triangles	: 31 mins.—45 mins.
4th	:	large outer diamond	: 46 mins.—60 mins.

CASE STUDY: LEON and DANA'S End of their Relationship

LEON's SD PHD for 15:00 HRS

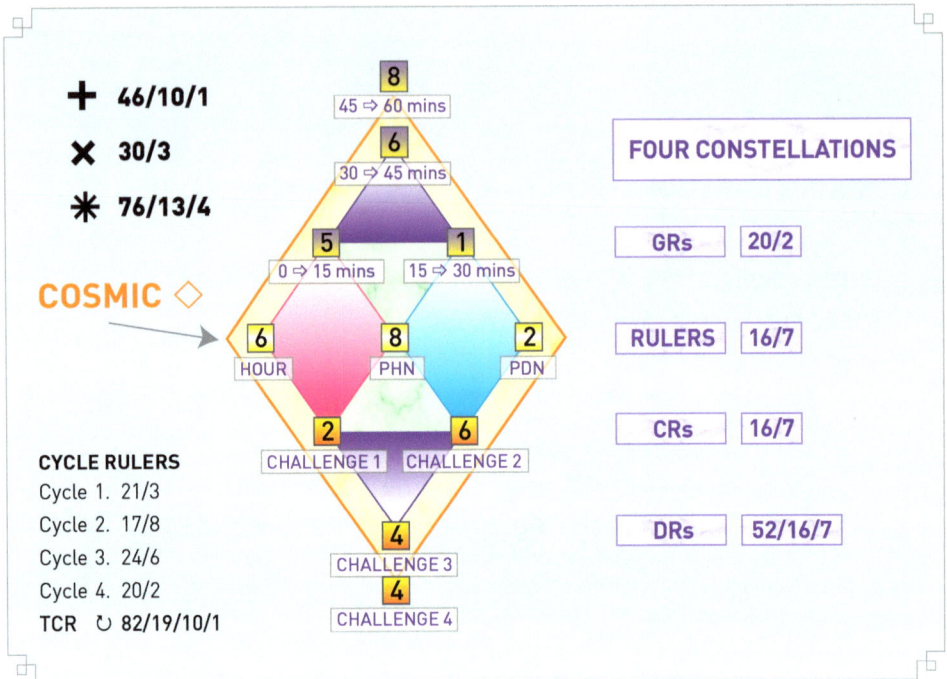

LEON'S SD PHD'S MAGICKAL FACETS: □ 14/5; Grail 22/4; ▲12/3; ▼12/3; ✽'s △14/5; ▽10/1; ✿24/6; ◇20/2

CASE STUDY: DANA AND LEON'S RELATIONSHIP ENDS ON 22SEP2007 ⇨ UDN58/40/22/13/4

This case study recounts a relationship break-up. Since the event is known, number and Keys' aspects in the following reflect the break up of the relationship from beginning to end.

To begin, start with the **day's date.** It had a strong bearing on this event. We know by now that **22** is a number to treat cautiously and there was one as the day's number and another in the UDNF. They, along with two **9s** from the month and year numbers in each ◇, intensified an "endings" aspect. Then **58 and 40**, other UDRs, are also numbers to treat cautiously. Their presence with "emotional" **9s** suggested that the endings would be upsetting.

When **22** is reduced to **4** and paired to **9** of September to make paired **49**, lean towards the prospect of a separation from a male *if* deemed feasible. This aspect of a **49** was noted in previous case studies. A paired **49** was revealed within Steve Irwin's current day's date; it linked to his wife's **49**. In Terri's case, **49's** separation from a male aspect had already manifested because she and the children were holidaying apart from Steve, but the *loss* of Steve eventuated for her on that day. Yet, in Leon and Dana's case, a *separation* was unfolding. **4, 9s, 22 and 40** provide clues to expect some kind of strain on their day.

If this were your day's numbers, would you consider setting up its UDD to clarify your hunches? If so, you would obtain a much better idea as to why the day unfolded as it did……. the UDD is a classic for this event!

Dana and Leon's **PDDs** open this case study because they are essential to what transpired. The active PDD cycle for each person is outlined in their respective ◇s. Study each one to get a "feel" for the day from their numbers, keys, Magickal Facets and Constellations. Search for numbers among them that relate to the event. Practice this before attempting PHDs.

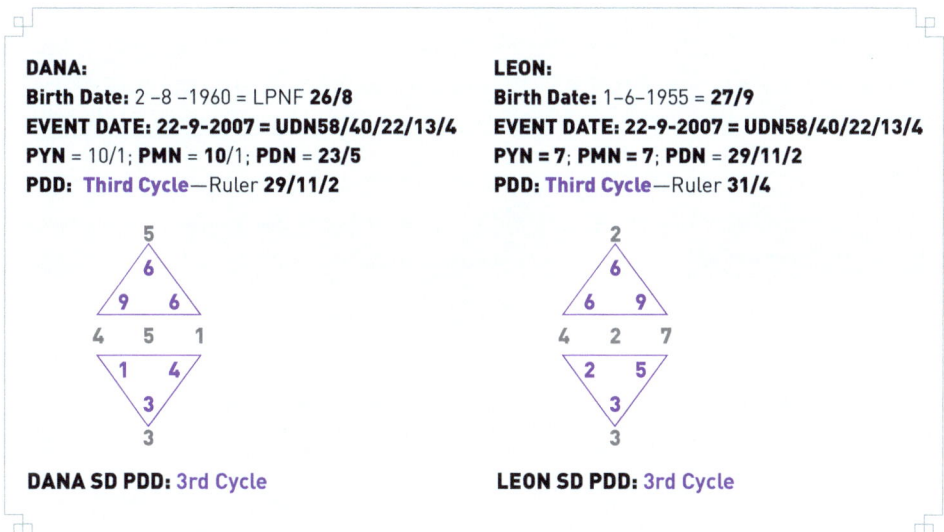

PDDS IN ACTION

Leon

Leon initiated ending his relationship with Dana during the **third, 6–hour cycle** ruled by **31⇨5 of Wands**. This Key is well documented for reflecting tendencies that depict struggle and strife.

Leon's PDD's ♥number "**2**" suggests relationship issues for that day. However, further clues are needed to support this. They are in his *three* **42s⇨2 of Cups** and **57⇨3 of Swords** that link to ♥**2**. Then **6–6–9** forming the Goal ▲ with two **3s** in the Challenge sector combine to reinforce a theme surrounding relationship concerns.

When the Goal ▲ became active, matters of the heart (**6s**) were being brought to an end; **9, 7** and paired **22** being cyclic numbers, supported an endings' hypothesis. **2–5–3** in Leon's Challenge ▼ and **31** as the active Cycle's Ruler, hinted that it would be hard for him to break-up. Paired **57⇨3 of Swords** and **63⇨9 of Swords** indicate anxiety so support this idea. Several **62s⇨8 of Swords** described Leon's plight; he felt trapped and wanted to break free. **26s⇨Page of Wands** signified his need to voice his intentions. ✱ Ruler **55⇨Ace of Swords** indicated the need to be unwavering while carrying out his wishes. **24⇨Queen of Wands** was his Grail Ruler. Using its ending aspect it likely represented Dana's removal as "queen" (a significant female in his life). Then Leon's ↺**84** and its reverse number **48⇨8 of Cups'** moving on aspects, provided a strong clue that the relationship was likely to end.

Dana

Significant links to Dana's LD and LPNs are found in the **PDDRs47/11/2**. They matched her LDRNs and the **PDD's GR26** matched one of her LPNs. Because these are major personal numbers, they made this PDD stand out. Then ♥**5** indicated a day of changes. When linked to her **9–6–6** Goal ▲, ♥**5**'s change aspect and the ending aspect in **9** meant that matters of the heart (**6s⇨Lovers**) would change. When she realised that Leon was ending their relationship, she thought, "How could he not choose me?" (**47's⇨7 of Cups** choice nature—she had *no* choice). She felt too, the injustice (**11⇨Justice**) of being rejected (**2⇨High Priestess**). Then she felt outrage (three **14s⇨Temperance**) at her loss (**45⇨5 of Cups**). Her □ Ruler, **20⇨Judgement**, was adverse for that day. Dana was subjected to a judgement she was powerless to change. The □'s paired numbers did nothing to help. In particular, **64⇨10 of Swords** (also in the ✱'s △) depicted the severity of the emotional impact on her. Devastated (**63⇨9 of Swords** in her ✱'s ▽), she did not want to hear this news (three paired **56s⇨2 of Swords** and ♥**5** relate to hearing or *not* hearing). It seemed to her that Leon was breaking promises (paired **19⇨Sun**) and shattering her dreams of having an idyllic relationship (✱'s Ruler, **29⇨3 of Wands**) with him. His **25⇨Knight of Wands** at the base of his □, linked to her Grail Ruler—he was charged up and rearing to leave! Her heart was breaking (**57⇨3 of Swords**) as she felt both betrayed (**64⇨10 of Swords**) and defeated (paired **59⇨5 of Swords**).

Analysing PDDs first, provides essential background information. Use it to find and confirm themes in their matching PHDs. If they are repeated in the PHDs, then the prognosis is likely to be accurate.

PHDs IN ACTION

Leon began to end his relationship with Dana from **3 p.m.** onwards (**15:00** hours⇨**6**). The three hours it took to end are set out in their three PHDs to follow. Leon's SD PDD for this hour is depicted on page 72 as the example for this chapter. His was chosen because he was the one who initiated the break-up.

EVENT: Leon Announces Relationship's End

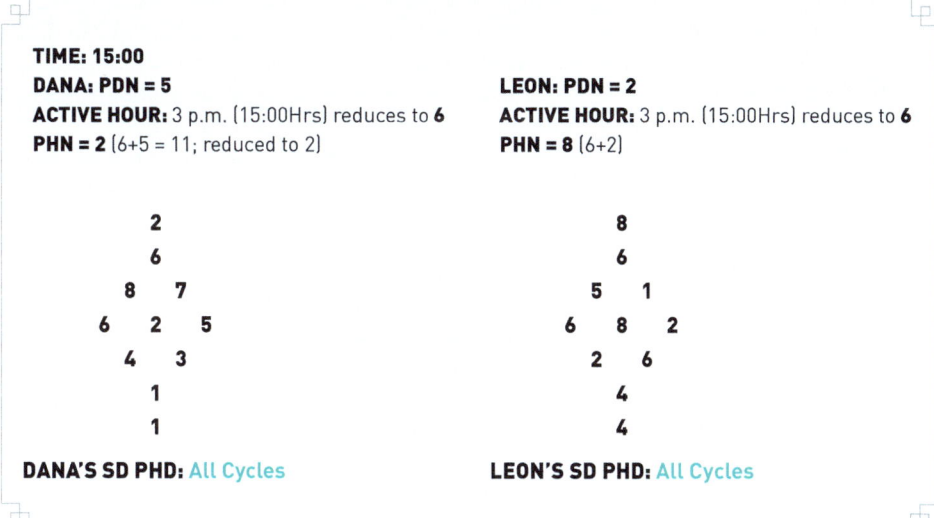

DANA'S SD PHD: All Cycles   **LEON'S SD PHD:** All Cycles

Scanning both PHDs

This hour's ◇s contained two striking features. First was the appearance of **6** for each PHD's active hour number because it links to **Key 6⇨The Lovers**! Nothing could be more apt for this event as affairs of the heart were uppermost during that hour. Second was both ♥numbers. Dana's was **2** (The **Moon** rules this Key) and Leon's, **8** (links to the **Sun** from Leo's rulership of this Key). Did ♥2 represent the victim (Dana) and ♥8, the asserter (Leon)? Leon's Grail Ruler was **22⇨The Fool**. Did it warn of the end of the relationship (*double* **2** **and 2x11 in 22**)?

EVENT: The End Begins

15:00 Hrs: Leon

Leon's ♥8 depicted the courage it took (**Key 8⇨Strength**) to break up with Dana, whilst her ♥2 indicated relationship matters. Three paired **62s⇨8 of Swords** in his ◇ intensified those in his PDD. They highlighted feeling trapped and wanting to break free of the relationship. Paired **26⇨Page of Wands** at the base of his □ signified his need to be clear about stating his intent. Paired **54⇨Page of Swords** in the ✧'s ▽ stood for the news; he was about to cut to the chase and end the union. Paired **15⇨The Devil** adjoined to **61⇨7 of Swords** in his □ reinforced his need to break ties, **15⇨The Devil,** and go his own way (**61s**).

15.00 Hrs: Dana

Dana's **SD G7**⇨**The Chariot** warned of unforeseen, upsetting events. When linked to **64**⇨**10 of Swords** and **57**⇨**3 of Swords**, they are likely to manifest as a betrayal, breakdown and heartbreak. Another strong hint that this is possible is found in paired **42**⇨**2 of Cups**, which is adjacent to paired **43**⇨**3 of Cups**, in her PHD's challenge area. Put together, their signs pointed to a relationship split. Paired **48**, **73** and **78** in the □, reinforce that theory. They implied endings (**78**⇨**10 of Pentacles**), a new direction (**48**⇨**8 of Cups**) and abandonment (**73**⇨**5 of Pentacles**). The Grail contained a **24** and its Ruler was **24** as well. Did they signify Dana as the **Queen of Wands**? Did they warn that something would end due to **24**'s link to death, hence, endings, change and moving on? Because of this connection between **24 to 42 and death**, **42**'s must also contain an aspect of endings. **45**⇨**5 of Cups** was the **PDDR**; it was not a promising omen, as it held a position of power. Its negative leaning helped to clarify this major upset.

EVENT: Quarrel Continues
TIME: 16:00

DANA: PDN = 5
ACTIVE HOUR: 4 p.m. (16:00Hrs) reduce to **7**
PHN = 4 (7+5 = 12; reduce to 3)

```
        3
        9
    1       8
  7   3   5
      4   2
        2
        2
```

DANA'S SD PHD: All Cycles

LEON: PDN = 2
ACTIVE HOUR: 4 p.m. (16:00Hrs) reduce to **7**
PHN = 9 (7+2)

```
        9
        9
    7       2
  7   9   2
      2   7
        5
        5
```

LEON'S SD PHD: All Cycles

16.00 Hrs: Dana

During this hour, several "ending" numbers such as paired **18**, **22s**, **13s**, **41**, **48**, **57**, **58** and **73** diminished the chance of making up. They reflected no ray of hope (**17**). Hence, ♥**3**, really **12**, depicted despondency and a sense of powerlessness instead of joy. Intensified **42s** in the challenge area and **28** known for power struggles indicated the relationship's volatility. **49** and **42** were in the ✿'s △. Linked to many ending trends, they pointed to the loss of a male (**49**) from a couple (**42**). *And*, this △ *adds to* **15**; a number known for relationship severance *if* prevailing conditions support that. The Grail Ruler was **18**⇨**The Moon**. It described Dana's intense emotions. Her ♥**3**, as **12**, depicted her life being turned upside down. Her **PHDR** was a **reverse 64**. It pointed to Dana feeling defenceless, betrayed and "mortally wounded" by Leon's barbs. She felt helpless against the controlling forces he was activating from his intensified **55 and 95/59s**.

16.00 Hrs: Leon

During this hour, Leon's paired **79s** indicated that he was acting out being the "hero". He was trying to end the relationship as gently as he could but maintain his intent at the same time (paired **55 and 59** on the Vertical Axis). The Vertical Axis contained **9s**, paired **59 and 55**; a very strong combination. It provided an unrelenting focus if things threatened to veer off track (**7s**⇨**The Chariot**). Several **72s**⇨**4 of Pentacles** reinforced this firm stand. Leon reached his decision (**11**⇨**Justice** reduced from each **29**). **11, 29** and analytical **27s**⇨**Ace of Wands** (**4** were in his □!) signified his ability to "think on his feet", weigh up the situation and wield **Justice's sword** to finally sever the relationship. The Grail Ruler, another **27**, signified him being wise (**root 9**) yet forceful (**Ace**) as he worked towards initiating a new beginning for himself (**Ace**). The powers from **55's Ace** reinforced **27's Ace**; they reflected his inner strength and resolve. **55** also hinted at drastic change or a major upset.

EVENT: Dana Leaves
TIME: 17:00

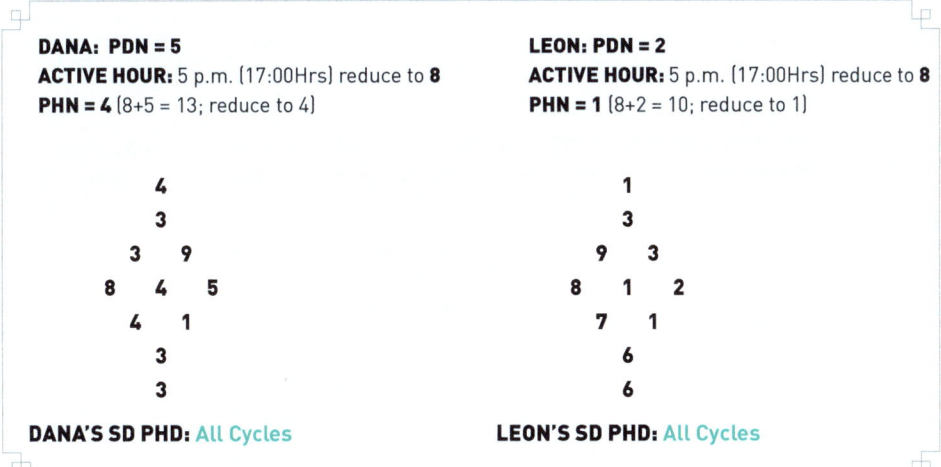

Scanning both PHDs

It was all over between **5 and 6pm**. Did prominent **17s** appearing in both ◇'s and with PHDRs that reduce to **root 2s**, see the couple starring (**17s**⇨**The Star**) in their own "War of the Roses" (conflict aspect of **2**)? **17s** rule Dana's □ and several constellations. Can you see their significance? Did they stand for her dashed hopes and Leon achieving his wishes? Dana held onto the hope of saving the relationship until the bitter end. Did you notice Leon's several **11s**⇨**Justice**, thus **2s**? They would not hold out much hope as single-mindedness is one of **Justice's** aspects. Uncannily, the number of choice, **47**⇨**7 of Cups**, is the top **PHDR** for both ◇s; Leon had made his choice clear leaving Dana no other choice than to go. Perhaps Leon's □ ruler was more telling; it was a daunting **20**⇨**Judgement**. It contained clues that a final decision was likely during this hour and that the realisation for both parties that the relationship was over.

17.00 Hrs: Dana

Dana's many **34s**⇨**8 of Wands** depicted things coming to a sudden conclusion. When **34s** are reversed to make **43s**⇨**3 of Cups** and then linked to **49**⇨**9 of Cups**, they warned of the loss of a lover and a friend. Paired **49** with **15**⇨**The Devil**, **19**⇨**The Sun** and **41**⇨**Ace of Cups** in the second cycle supported anticipating a loss. Negative **14s**⇨**Temperance** in the challenge area not only reflected the dissolution of the union but also frustration and anger. The **39s**⇨**Knight of Cups** depicted shattered dreams. Wheel Ruler **59**⇨**5 of Swords** pointed to defeat. Dana's Grail Ruler was **21**⇨**The World**. It warned of an end and **17**⇨**The Star**, the □ Ruler; ruined hopes and wishes. Two paired **48s**⇨**8 of Cups** and a **45**⇨**5 of Cups** "attached" to the □ saw her leaving with many regrets and a heavy heart (**two 33's root 6**⇨**The Lovers**).

17.00 Hrs: Leon

Leon's ♥**1** in his PHD was surrounded by paired **79, 19, and 73** from his □. Add paired **66** to them to uncover a strong theme of self-ishness in that Leon was being true to himself and his wishes (strongly placed **17s**). They indicated facing (**19**⇨**Sun**) being on his own (**73**⇨**5 of Pentacles** in the □ and ✿'s △ reinforce this). Even so he was left struggling (**31s**⇨**5 of Wands**) with his decision and feelings (**PHC6s and 3s**) when the relationship finally ended (**9** with paired **13s, 16s, 19, 21s and 78** signalled the end). Leon's Grail Ruler was also **21**⇨**The World**. It supported moving on and so did his SD Goal Ruler; it was victorious **7**⇨**The Chariot**!

Footnote: After a few months had elapsed, this couple resolved their differences and are still together.

CASE STUDY:

"TIGER" WOODS— DRAMATIC FALL FROM GRACE

Important clues to this day's events appear in Woods' number families below. The relevant numbers are in bold. The PDD and its PHD for this case study appear on the next page.

- **LPNF:** 139, 127, 118, **64**, 55, **46**, **19**, **10**, **1**
- **PYNF 2009:** **71**, 53, **26**, **17**, 8 Note **71**, one's career; **17**, the number of scandal; **26** the "announcement" number
- **PMNF November:** **82**, **64**, 37, **28**, **19**, **10**, **1** (Matches most of Woods' LPNs)

64, 10, 1 are Wood's Life Path Numbers. Their appearance in the PMNF provides a sure sign to pay more attention to this month as something of note is likely to occur. **64 and 10** provide hints that it might be unpleasant and could be life-changing to boot. **PMN19** suggests something disagreeable to face or face up to. Esoterically, it signifies an opportunity for the renewal of the spirit. Take particular note of **82** in the PMNF. Although not one of Woods' LPNs, it is significant in that a fight broke out between Woods and his wife. The fight relates to **28**'s power struggle aspect; the **2s** in the PHD reinforced war rather than peace.

PDNF 27th NOV: 109, 91, **64**, 55, **46**, 37, **28**, **10**, **1**
Because the day's number is **27** and it reduces to **9**, it means that the PDNF repeats the PMNF. What makes their numbers potentially ominous is that they contain **64, 46, 10 and 1** which belong to Woods' LPNF. When synchronicity like this occurs, the odds are that something significant is likely to happen. With **46** appearing, think of something along the lines of a family disruption and that it will probably force some kind of change within or to the family or its structure. This idea stems from **46** reducing to **10**⇒**The Wheel of Fortune**. Its forced change aspect is actually reinforced due to so many numbers reducing to **10**. **28** is also significant for this event because it reflected the public fight reported to have transpired between husband and wife.

Following SD PDD's Magickal Facets and Constellation Rulers:

□**11/2**; Grail **12/3**; ✥'s △▽ both **11/2s**; ✿**22/4**; +**32/5**; ×**13/4**; ✱**45**; ◇**19/10/1**; ∪**64/10/1**

PD CR **24/6**; PD Baseline **11/2**; PD GR 7; PDDR **42/15/6**; Current Cycle Ruler **19/10/1**

Intensified **9s** tend to evoke confusion rather than focus. Confusion would impair Woods' decision-making faculties (**4s, 7s** and paired **47**) thereby rendering him unable to make good use of his vertical +**54**'s practical wisdom (**54** comes from the ✱'s **45**). This was obvious by his odd behaviours resulting from the fracas and from ingesting a cocktail of medicinal drugs, then driving his car and then crashing it almost immediately afterward. Was this his **Hermit** aspect (hidden **9s** from **18s**) trying to hide from his wrongdoings? Did hidden **16s** from the paired **88s** in the challenge sector signify Woods' brief stay in hospital? Being so rich and famous, which numbers signify specialist doctors? Which ones lies and deception? Would you choose **11s** for his self-centred actions? Do you see a link to Karma in them and his **8s**? The Goal▲Ruler is **6** and the Challenge▼Ruler is **16**. Do you recognise matters of the heart (**6**) and infidelity (**16**) in their indications? What did the Grail Ruler threaten?

Did you notice that Woods' PDD below is a replica of Phoebe's PMD? What similarities do you detect in them; what differences? How many endings' numbers can you find? Did they signify Woods' attempt to end his life to escape facing the shame from his wrong doings? Which numbers depict fame, shame, public notoriety, and an 180⁰ turn-about? Why is the PDD's **TCR↺** so significant? How many numbers signify relationship indications? Which number depicted his reckless actions?

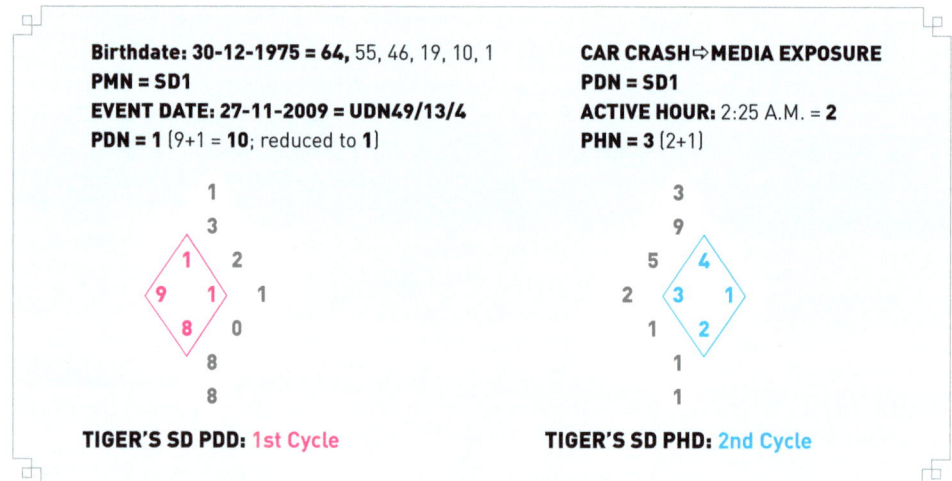

Above SD PHD's Magickal Facets and Constellation Rulers:

□**12/3**; Grail **15/6**; ✱'s △**12/3**; ▽**10/1**; ✿**22**; **+23**; ✕**18**; ✱**41**; ◇**7**; ↺**50/5**

PHCR **5**; PH Baseline **6**; PHGR **21/3**; PHDR**32/5**; Current Cycle Ruler **10/1**

Scan these ◇s to find numbers and Keys that back up what you have already found in Woods' other ◇s for this event. They have many that do.

Then narrow your scrutiny to Wood's **PDD and PHD** to get the following. Note the intensified **1s, 2s, 3s, 12s, and 21s** between them; they make a good place to start. **1s** emphasise matters to do with Woods on a personal level. In the PHD, they are mostly challenges which suggest that whatever transpires is likely to be unpleasant for him. The PHD's current Cycle Ruler was **10**; it indicated *forced change*. When paired to make **11s** (there are three in the PHD), we get Karma in action. **2s** highlight relationship matters. The

Challenge 2 in the PHD pairs to its **Goal 4** to create **42**. This is the number of *love, marriage and union* so it reinforces matters to do with a relationship. However **42** has an ending component if linked to **Path 24** (**24** is **42**'s reverse) on the Tree of Life as this is the Path of **Death**⇨**Key 13**; from it we get **42**'s connection to endings. In this instance, **3s**, and especially ♥**3** in the **PHD**, reflect *love affairs and infidelity*, and of cause, *children*. **12**'s nearly always warn that something about one's life is about to go awry and this was so for Woods. To have **12 ruling the** ☐ only emphasised this likelihood. It also placed a strong negative bias onto ♥**3**. Last but not least, **21s** can also dampen **3s**. But they often signify endings and Woods' game was up due to his wife's proof of his extra marital affairs. The **paired 54** atop his ☐ signified the nasty way events played out. What has been uncovered so far helps to substantiate hardship themes.

The **4th PHD Cycle's Ruling** 7 verified hidden things and bizarre goings on as well as Woods' drug overdose (medicines and drugs are **7** aspects); it links to the **PDD's GR7**. Then we have several paired **18s** in the PDD and **18** ruling the PHD's diagonal ✕. They imply deception and hidden plots and schemes which perfectly fit the nature of what was unfolding at the time besides revealing a compatible theme with the **7s**. (Negative **2s and 3s** are also known for lies and deception but **7s and 18s** are more likely to lie by omission i.e., by withholding vital information.)

INTERPRETING WOODS' PHD'S MAGICKAL FACETS AND CONSTELLATIONS

Baseline Ruler and Grail: Other vital clues to this event are found in the PHD's Magickal Facets and Constellations. Its **Baseline Ruler 6 and the Grail's 15/6** hinted at domestic affairs as well as affairs of the heart. **15 and 6** are both known for their separation possibilities due to **6**'s connection to the Hebrew letter *Zain* that means a *dagger, knife or sword* that *severs* and **15**'s *separation/freeing* aspects.

TCR☋: Perhaps a most telling sign was in the PHD's **TCR☋**. It was ☋**50**⇨**10 of Cups**, a beautiful Tarot Key that would never give the impression of its dire possibilities. We can guess at them when we know that **5** is the number of *change* and has links to **Justice** via the **5th Kingdom** on the Tree of Life whose name is **Severity**. Or, we can intensify what we know of **5** by multiplying it by **10** to get to **50, a tens number**. Tens numbers' energies and forces are raised to higher frequencies. Because of this, they generate greater demands in the form of tests and trials which is why we learn to treat them with caution. There is another reason to treat **50** with caution and that is because it is linked to the Hebrew Letter *Nun* whose number allocation is **50**. But *Nun* is linked to **Death** because it is the Hebrew Letter given to **Key 13**. From this, we are able to understand **50**'s ominous side and to also understand why it signified the Woods family's disintegration rather than that of a happy, united family.

PHDR32: This is a powerful Ruler. **32** corresponds to the **6 of Wands**. The irony is that when in its negative mode it depicts the person *falling from their high pedestal (horse)*. This is another instance of a very positive looking Key having a negative connotation. How can this be? Again, to find the answer we need to use the Qabalah. On the Tree of Life, **Path23** (**32's** reverse), is allocated to **The Hanged Man** and herein lies one clue. When **The Hanged Man** is activated, expect the unexpected and reversals; what is true is false, what is moral is immoral, what appears good is bad and so on. This was so for this event when Woods' seedy past was exposed to all and sundry. His public exposure is evident in ✡**22**. That things came to an abrupt end is noted in **paired 34 and 21** in the active cycle. Not to be overlooked, **Path 32** can be linked to **Key32** as their numbers are the same. However, **Path 32** happens to be the last Path on the Tree of Life. This is significant because **Key 21** is allocated to this Path and **21** was active at the time; both the Key and the Path signify *endings*. To reinforce that a negative outcome may be looming, **Saturn** is **Path 32 and Key21s' Ruler**. This strong theme suggests that something could go wrong; especially when **Saturn** links to careers and reputations; exactly what Woods' lost (**34**)! As **Path 32**, **Keys 12 and 21** and **Saturn** share similar aspects, they explain Woods rapid fall from Grace, the dark side to **Key32⇨6 of Wands**.

WHEEL RULER ✴41⇨Ace of Cups: Here we have yet another promising Tarot Key in a very powerful position that can have dire consequences when and if negative. The clue to this is found in its reverse number, **14**. **KEY14** is allocated the Hebrew Letter *Samekh* which means *prop, support, sustain, reinforce, fortify, bolster, boost* and so on. However, it has other Qabalistic attributes such as *Wrath* which is more to the point as *Wrath* helps to explain **41's** antagonistic traits. It leads us to consider such behaviours as *anger, rage, fury, vehemence and passion*. Woods' wife displayed the latter when she became upset which explains **41's anger side**. This anecdote also serves as a good example for when *the person is the recipient* of another's actions or influence. Another such example is **paired 59⇨5 of Swords**; Woods' wife was the aggressive one and Woods, the defeated one.

Woods' PMD in Chapter 3 and this Chapter's PDD and PHD provide us with very good examples of how the intensification of energies and forces build over time and then manifest when the right conditions come together. By their example, we gain an understanding of the importance of setting up the sequence of ◇s that relate to an event. We also gain some understanding of how to treat them if they appear in our own numbers.

Chapter 6:
Personal Minute Diamonds

> **PMinN** = Personal Minute Number
> **PMinD** = Personal Minute Diamond
> **PMinDR** = Personal Minute Diamond Ruler
> **PHN** = Personal Hour Number
> **SD** = Single Digit
> **WN** = Whole Number

ABOUT PERSONAL MINUTE DIAMONDS (PMinDs)

Personal Minute Diamonds (PMinDs) fine-tune each minute of the day by condensing them into four, 15-second cycles. Their numbers and Tarot Keys provide vital guidance when the actual *moment* of an event is known or planned.

Although timing events to this extent is seldom required, PMinDs nevertheless come into their own for special occasions or moments in time such as: time of birth, moment of saying, "I do"; an inaugural ceremony; important appointment; signing a contract; a personal achievement; receiving an award; an operation and so on—this is where and when they shine. Not only can PMinDs be used for these purposes but they can also be used to find the right time to launch or establish something. Alternatively, they can be used as a tool to validate or rectify the birth time.

The following formula produces the Personal Minute Number (PMinN) from adding the current minute to the Personal Hour Number (PHN). Remember to work in **24 hour**, *real* clock time. For example, Jessica Watson crossed the finish line at **1:53** p.m. Australian Eastern Standard Time (AEST) after battling strong head winds and heavy swells for several hours which caused her to arrive at the finish line hours after the estimated time. As this is a SD PMinD, we convert the **53** of the **53** minutes to **SD8**. Then we take the PHN from her PHD which is its ♥**5** and then add **8+5** together to get **13** then reduce to get ♥**4**.

So here we have an example of a SD PMinD for this event with a baseline: **8(actual min. 53 reduced) + ♥4 (PMin.N) + 5 (PHN) = Rulers: 17/8**

To be able to appreciate the PMinD's numbers, Jessica Watson's ◇s for her truly remarkable feat are set out from her LDs to her PMinD. No WN ◇s are

Decade Diamonds & Month, Day, Hour and Minute Diamonds

included except for her WN LD. Enthusiasts may wish to calculate the others to study their numbers. References are made to conspicuous Magickal Facet and Constellations' numbers and Keys. Although all are not shown, most of the calculations are done for each ◇. They begin on the opposite page and continue on page 86.

PMinN FORMULA: CURRENT MINUTE + ACTIVE PHN (REAL CLOCK TIME)

STEPS AND DIAGRAM FOR CALCULATING SD AND WN PMinDs

PMinD FORMULA: CURRENT MINUTE + PMinN + PHN

STEPS FOR CALCULATING SD and WN PMinDs

1. **SD Baseline:**
   - (a) Select active SD Minute Number or reduce if a WN.
   - (b) Select current SD PHN using 24 hour clock time.
   - (c) Add a) and b) for Personal Minute Number (PMinN). Reduce to a SD.
   - (d) **Baseline:** Place SD Minute No. first, SD PMinN second and SD PDN third.
2. Calculate all Goals/Challenges, Cycle Rulers, Constellations and Magickal Facets.
3. Record significant features. Apply "Points to Remember".
4. Interim and WN PMDs if calculated broaden and confirm findings.

Note: **DAYLIGHT SAVINGS TIMES**—*Use 24-hour real clock time.*

Each MINUTE divides into **4 X 15 SECOND CYCLES.**

CALCULATIONS FOR EACH 15 SECOND TIME SPAN:

1st	:	first mini diamond	:	0 secs.—15 secs.
1nd	:	second mini diamond	:	16 secs.—30 secs.
3rd	:	two opposing triangles	:	31 secs.—45 secs.
4th	:	large outer diamond	:	46 secs.—60 secs.

SD PMinD: JESSICA WATSON SAILS INTO THE RECORD BOOKS

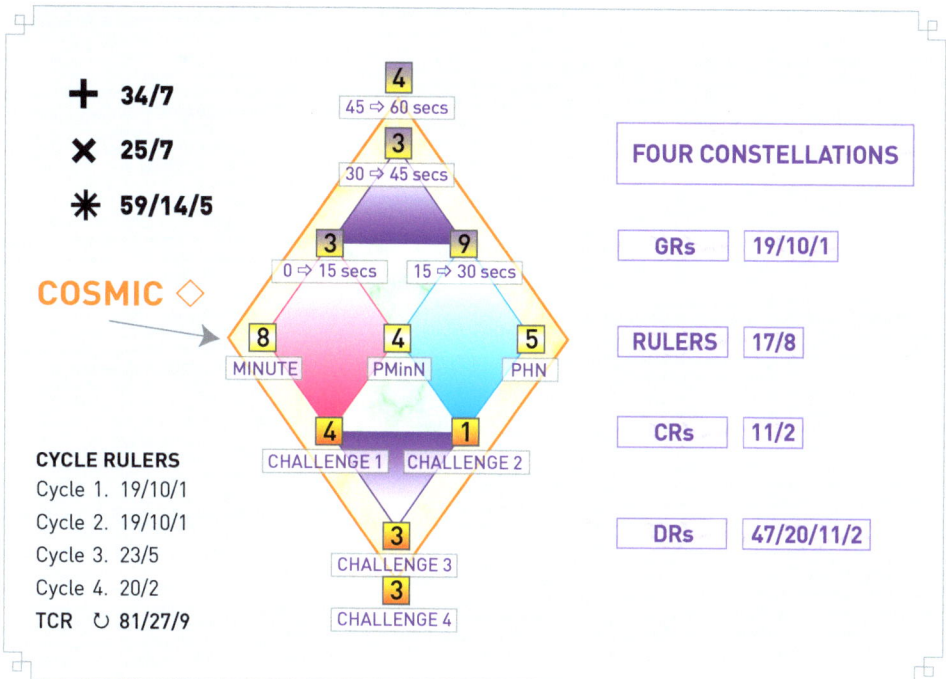

CASE STUDY: JESSICA WATSON—16 years old

Youngest person to sail solo around the world unassisted
Event: Crossed the finishing line from sailing around the world solo
Event Date: 15–5–2010 ⇨ UDNF: 50, 32, 23, 14, 5
Current Age: 3 days off 17
Birth date: 18–5–1993 ⇨ LPNF: 135, 128, 117, 54, 45, 36, 18, 9

2010 PYNF: 53, 35, 26, 17, 8
MAY PMNF: 58, 40, 31, 22, 13, 4 (Add **5** to each PYN)
DAY15 PDNF: 73, 55, 46, 37, 28, 19, 10, 1 (Add **15** to each PMN)
PDN: 1
Active Time: 1:53 p.m.
Active Hour: 13:00 = **SD4**   PHN: 5 (4 +1PDN)
Active Minute: 53 reduced to **8**   PMinN: 4 (8PMinN+5PHN)
PMinD Baseline Calculation: SD Min8 + **SD PMinN4** + SD PHN5

Jessica Watson set new world records when she courageously sailed around the world *solo, non-stop and unassisted* at the incredible age of 16. Interpretations for this event reflect this truly inspiring achievement.

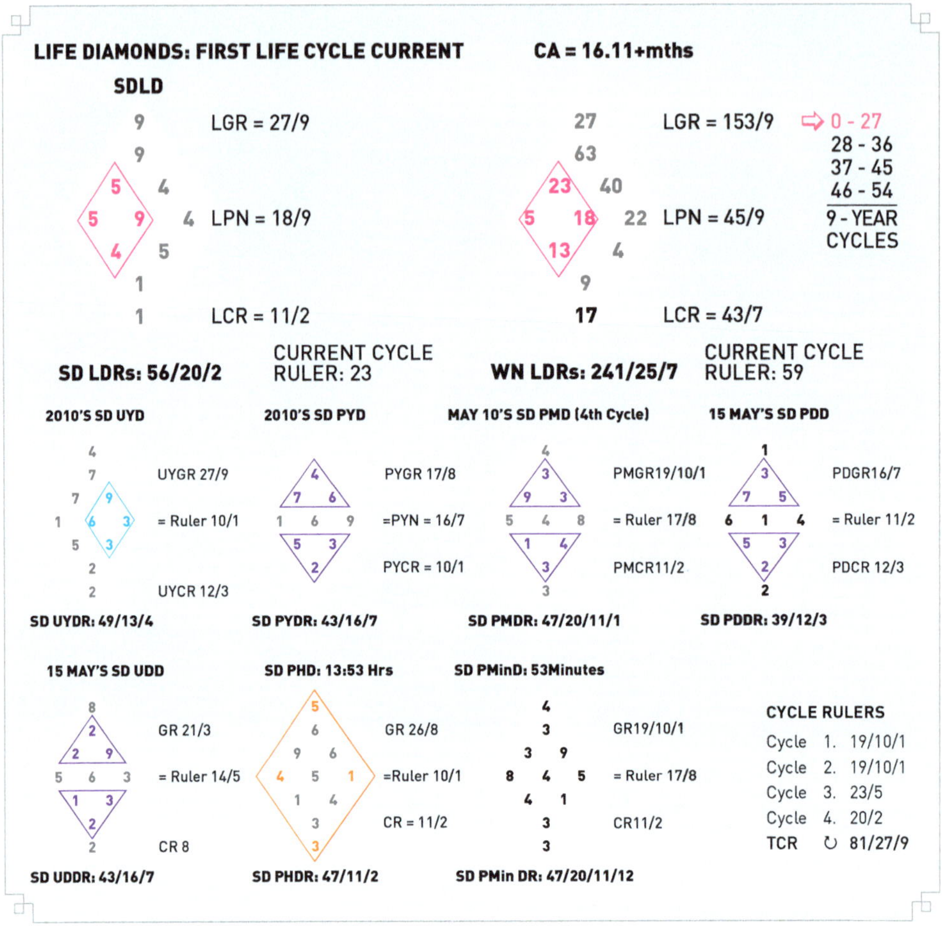

Decade Diamonds & Month, Day, Hour and Minute Diamonds

LIFE DIAMONDS: FIRST LIFE CYCLE CURRENT   CA = 16.11+mths

SDLD

- LGR = 27/9   LGR = 153/9 ⇒ 0 – 27
- LPN = 18/9   LPN = 45/9   28 – 36
- LCR = 11/2   LCR = 43/7   37 – 45
                                  46 – 54
                                  9 - YEAR CYCLES

SD LDRs: 56/20/2   CURRENT CYCLE RULER: 23   **WN LDRs: 241/25/7**   CURRENT CYCLE RULER: 59

2010'S SD UYD
- UYGR 27/9
- = Ruler 10/1
- UYCR 12/3

SD UYDR: 49/13/4

2010'S SD PYD
- PYGR 17/8
- =PYN = 16/7
- PYCR = 10/1

SD PYDR: 43/16/7

MAY 10'S SD PMD (4th Cycle)
- PMGR19/10/1
- = Ruler 17/8
- PMCR11/2

SD PMDR: 47/20/11/1

15 MAY'S SD PDD
- PDGR16/7
- = Ruler 11/2
- PDCR 12/3

SD PDDR: 39/12/3

15 MAY'S SD UDD
- GR 21/3
- = Ruler 14/5
- CR 8

SD UDDR: 43/16/7

SD PHD: 13:53 Hrs
- GR 26/8
- =Ruler 10/1
- CR = 11/2

SD PHDR: 47/11/2

SD PMinD: 53 Minutes
- GR19/10/1
- = Ruler 17/8
- CR11/2

SD PMin DR: 47/20/11/12

CYCLE RULERS
- Cycle 1. 19/10/1
- Cycle 2. 19/10/1
- Cycle 3. 23/5
- Cycle 4. 20/2
- TCR ↻ 81/27/9

Activated Cycles are marked in colour except for the PMinD as the exact second for the time of crossing the finish line was not published.

Life Diamond's 1st cycle Rulers— SD 23/32; 5/50: WN 59/95; 14/41; 9/90

UYD's 2nd Cycle Rulers—21/12; 3/30; □24; Grail30; ✿33; ◇10; ✳67; ↻83
PYD's LAST Cycle Rulers—27/72; 9/90; □21; Grail27; ✿27; ✳61; ↻70
PMD's 3rd Cycle Rulers—23/32; 5/50; □17; Grail21; ✿23; ◇20; ✳59; ↻81
PDD's 3rd Cycle Rulers—25/52; 7/70; □20; Grail21; ✿25; ◇13; ✳42; ↻70
UDD's 3rd Cycle Rulers—19/91; 10/1; □15; Grail21; ✿19; ◇18; ✳61; ↻72
PHD's 4th Cycle Rulers—13/31; 4/40; □20; Grail25; ✿29; ◇13; ✳62; ↻77

PMinD's Cycle Rulers—It could have been any cycle judging by the numbers. I favour Cycle 1 or 2, Cycle 1 for its leaving a way of life behind (two **48s**) or Cycle 2 because it contains her **LPNs: 45/9**.

PMinD's Magickal Facets and Constellations: ☐17; Grail21; ✧23; ◇20; ✶59; ☾81

At the young age of 16, Jessica Watson became the youngest person to circumnavigate the world when she crossed the finish line in Sydney Harbour, Australia, at **1:53 p.m. on 15th May 2010**. However, the actual time down to seconds was not made public. This is unfortunate, as we cannot plot which cycle in her PMinD was active then. However, it is so nice to have this information to confirm the use of these ◇s.

POINTS OF INTEREST

LPN: The first thing that struck me about Jessica's **LPN45** is that she uses it in very positive ways. This is not someone who "cries in her cups" as the **5 of Cups Key** depicts. Rather, this inspiring, young lady uses what she has rather than what she has not. For example, Jessica has dyslexia and has overcome it to become very successful (Sir Richard Branson is another successful dyslexic). She is a shining example of a person who is determined to see the glass half full instead of half empty.

COMMON 39s: Note the recurring presence of **39** in the 2010 UYD; '09 ⇨'10 PYD; PMD; PDD's PDDR; UDD and PMinD. It symbolised Jessica manifesting her dreams.

☾**70s⇨2 of Pentacles** appeared as the **PYD** and the **PDD's 3rd Cycle Ruler.** Key **70** beautifully portrays Jessica's battle with herself, her skills, the seas and the unknown. She encountered heavy seas that tore a hole in her mainsail during her last two weeks rounding Tasmania. She also encountered heavy swells on the last day when returning home. Note the challenging waves in the Key's background. Also note the little boats doing their best to remain afloat and continue their journey despite the heavy going. Now note the person doing their best to stay calm and in control of a demanding, tricky situation. Not only did Jessica have to juggle poor weather conditions, she also had to navigate her way through a flotilla of well wishers, on air TV cameras, media shouting to her across the water and helicopters buzzing overhead, all to welcome her on her last lap home.

17/71s are present in all ◇s except for the UDD. **17** ruled *three* of the PMinD's ✶'s number-lines. Now that was significant! It is important to have high profile **17s** in the ◇ to establish a "star or fame" possibility. Then **71**, its reverse, provided the recognition and accolades from her peers and the public for her outstanding feat.

So much more could be elaborated on but it is best that you do the work at this advanced stage. Familiarise yourself with Jessica's background information first, and then study the ◇s in relation to it.

Details of another two brave, very young, solo sailors follow. Background information about them is on the internet. They not only make excellent case studies on which to practice fine-tuning ◇s but also to compare the three solo sailors together. Other solo sailors are listed on the internet, as well.

JESSE MARTIN, an Australian, was the youngest person to sail *solo, non-stop and unassisted* around the world in 1990 setting off when only 17, returning when 18. It took him 328 days, Jessica 210 days. Jesse's birthdate is **26 August 1981**. Jesse set sail from Port Phillip Bay, Melbourne on the **8th December 1998**. He crossed the finish-line on the **31st October 1999**. It is very worthwhile doing his ◇s not only for this event, but also to compare them with Jessica's.

ABBY SUNDERLAND, a Southern California 16 year-old, is the latest hero to attempt a solo voyage around the world. She set sail from Los Angeles on **23rd January 2010**. However, bad seas disabled her boat on **10th June**; she was rescued at **7:45 p.m. (AEST), 12th June**. *This is an approximate minute, time*. However, the PHD can be done, then choose either the 2nd or the 3rd cycle for the event according to the numbers' suitability. Abby's birthdate is **19 October 1993**.

Another case study for PMinD practice is Michael Jackson's time of death.

MICHAEL JACKSON'S untimely death presents an excellent case study to practice on, even for a PMinD. His details, taken from the internet, are: **Birthdate: 29-8-1958**; **Death: 25-6-2009**; **Time of Death: 14:26** (officially pronounced dead from cardiac arrest). Reports say that breathing stopped hours earlier—the call went out at **12:22 p.m**. but his doctor had tried to resuscitate him earlier than that. Does this indicate that breathing ceased sometime during late morning? If so, this presents good practice for determining the real time of death.

To Conclude this Section

The main aim behind the study of all ◇s is to grow and develop our "*self-knowing*". The next main aim is to acknowledge that Divine Guidance is eternally present and available to us via our numbers and Keys when we use them in this vein. The object of condensing life cycles is to fine-tune that guidance and make it current. Then the self-instructive, self-directional, self-knowing aims of this science can be extracted from our numbers and Keys and then purposefully activated. This hard won skill comes from much dedicated study and practice.

PART 2

WINDOWS TO THE FUTURE

Chapter 7: Personal Year Tarot Spread

LPN = Life Path Number
PY = Personal Year
PYN = Personal Year Number
PYNF = Personal Year Number Family
PYD = Personal Yearly Diamond
SD = Single Digit
WN = Whole Number
UYD = Universal Year Diamond
UN = Universal Number
UY = Universal Year

A PERSONAL YEAR'S WINDOWS OF OPPORTUNITY

Instead of creating Diamonds from Years, Months and Days' respective number families, we learn to create simple Tarot spreads from them. As with their corresponding Year, Month and Day Diamonds, these Tarot spreads not only help us to understand and learn from our past but also how to apply what we have learnt to gain further insights from numerological configurations that depict current and future trends.

The main difference between Tarot spreads that represent a Year, Month and Day and their matching Diamond is ….

- **Diamonds** provide an **in-depth, detailed account** of their time spans.
- **Tarot spreads** provide an **overview** of their time spans.

From the above, you may get the impression that these new Tarot spreads are not worth bothering with, as they appear to lack depth and meaning. Although they may seem to fall short when compared with their companion Diamonds, their different perspectives on a year, month or day *extend and validate* their matching Diamonds' projections. To have a divinatory tool that provides additional information that reinforces what their Diamond predicts provides us with a definite advantage. It not only opens up other parameters to consider but also builds greater confidence when interpreting current or future Year, Month or Day trends.

You will find these new Tarot spreads' calculations and layouts very simple to do. For this reason, they provide us with a particularly handy tool to use to confirm whether their corresponding diamond's indications appear favourable or unfavourable.

These Tarot spreads are not fortune-telling spreads. This is because they are derived from a *mathematical premise*. Hence, their mathematical derivation puts them on a par with occult science, not mysticism. Since each spread is derived from a person's numbers, their indications can be counted on (pardon the pun!) as a mathematical basis eliminates much of the mystical approach's speculation factor. However, and as always, accuracy depends on the skill of the interpreter.

Each Tarot spread is derived from a Personal Year, Month or Day *personalised* number family. Their instructions were introduced in Part 1. (Appendix 3 lists their formulas.)

For the Personal Year Tarot Spread, the Universal Year (UY) or calendar year for a specific point in time is used as part of its calculations. Using UY calculations means that the **Personal Year (PY) Tarot spread begins on the 1st JANUARY and ends on the 31st DECEMBER**. This follows the same principle used for when a Universal Yearly Diamond begins and ends. It is best to calculate both guidance tools together, as they supplement each other. The best times to do this are prior to or close to each new year's commencement.

To begin learning to work with yearly Tarot spreads, calculate two or three prior to the current year. They will show you how they represented past events. This practice teaches how to interpret current and future trends. Another approach is to set up spreads for significant years. Since your memories of them are likely to be sharp, they serve as excellent teaching tools.

Detailed instructions on how to calculate a Personal Year Number Family's Tarot spread follow.

HOW TO CALCULATE A PYNF'S TAROT SPREAD

These calculations are based on YEAR 2007; Birth DAY **27**; MONTH **6**.

STEP 1:
CALCULATE the PYNF as per Chapter 3 from Step 1 to Step 6.

STEP 2:
FIND the hidden yearly number
   2007 (use full **year** number)
   27 (use full birth **day** number)
   6 (use full birth **month** number)
ADD: <u>20**40**</u> ⇨ Root 6

Note: This total either reduces to a compound number or a single digit. Eg, if **15** emerged before **6**, it is used as part of the *PYNF*. It takes second lowest position in the PYNF series, which would then place it in the Tarot spread's **TOP ROW.**

Do not miss this additional step because if **2040** is split and paired thus: **20** and **40**, they can be read separately as **20/2** and **40/4**. Eg, **20/2** is universal or generic in nature therefore not influential in a personal sense. As **40** *changes each year, it is personal*, therefore influential. **40** and its **root 4** add significant indications to their year. Treat them as "surrogate PYNs". (Refer to *Yearly Diamonds—Your Soul's Yearly Maps to Life's* Chapter 11 for treatment of **40** as a number, then as a Tarot Key.)

STEP 3: COMPILE 2007's PYNF—60, 42, 24 and 6
Check that each number within a number family reduces to the same root digit.

STEP 4: FIND the PYNF's "MISSING" NUMBERS
Find any missing numbers within the **PYNF's** sequence by **adding 9** to each **present** number. **Begin with the root digit**. If the next higher number in the sequence is missing, **15** in this case, you have found a **missing** number, and subsequently, its Tarot Key. Stop at the highest number. Do not proceed further. On occasions two or more *consecutive*, missing numbers appear in a sequence. If so, include them. (St Joan of Arc's Personal Day Tarot spread in Chapter 9 does this.) For this example, all missing numbers in the PYNF sequence are in bold and underlined: 60, **<u>51</u>**, 42, **<u>33</u>**, 24, **<u>15</u>** and 6.

STEP 5: LAY OUT 2007's TAROT SPREAD
- **Top Row:** Present Numbers—**60, 42, 24** and **6**
- **Bottom Row:** Missing Numbers—**51, 33** and **15**
- **Convert** these numbers to their corresponding Tarot Keys
- **Assemble** the Tarot Spread

HOW TO INTERPRET A PERSONAL YEAR'S TAROT SPREAD

Once the **PYNF** is calculated and present Keys sorted from missing Keys, the Tarot spread is laid out and scanned for impressions and clues. Consult both the number and its Key's keywords to ascertain as much as you can from their meanings. Use several resources to enrich findings.

- View the top row's Keys as signifying ideas, things and plans that seem clear in the mind.
- View the bottom row's Keys as subtle urges, influences and desires that are vague or unmanifest.

The unusual thing about the missing numbers and Keys is that they seem to be more significant, powerful or intense than those in the top row. They seem to depict yearnings or things that are brewing just beneath the surface or just out of reach. More often than not, it is not until they are brought to conscious awareness, that what is struggling to manifest and the meaning of the number and Key that represents what it happens to be, becomes clear. Only then, can we understand these elusive Keys' meanings and ways we may use them.

S.O.S.: 2007 PERSONAL YEAR TAROT SPREAD

PRESENT NUMBERS AND KEYS

6₀   42   24   6

6 of Swords   2 of Cups   Queen of Wands   The LOVERS

MISSING NUMBERS AND KEYS

5₁   33   15

King of Swords   7 of Wands   The DEVIL

This was my Tarot spread for **2007** but it began in earnest on **18th December 2006.** (This premature phenomenon is explained in Chapter 10.) I received a phone call that day from a female relative who was seriously ill and in need of immediate help.

My Tarot spread's windows for 2007 showed the new fields of experience I was about to be catapulted into; they depicted "rescuing" a family in dire straits (**60⇨6 of Swords**). **60's** inherent serious nature as well as being a ten's number reflected the urgency of my relative's, family situation. This calamity brought us together (**42⇨2 of Cups**). I became hers and her family's carer

(**6**) and took charge (**24**⇨**Queen of Wands**) until her health improved. This situation challenged my "authority" and wits (**51**⇨**King of Swords**) besides my ability to meet and overcome obstacles (**33**⇨**7 of Wands**) as well as not be manipulated by her guile (**15**⇨**The Devil**). This situation reflected classic **6** traits such as: obligations, duties, responsibilities and day-to-day adjustments. Yet, **5's** traits, still in operation, merged with them (**5** indicated these sudden changes to my life and the need for *adaptation;* a **5** trait). This state of affairs perfectly matched the new **2007 PY6** numbers and Keys **waxing** in strength and the old **2006 PY5's waning** in strength.

PYNF's and their Tarot spreads also serve to demystify why, when two people who have the same SD PYN, do not share exactly the same experiences. If their spreads were laid out, their Tarot Key's placements in the top and bottom rows would graphically reveal why, just as any differences in their numbers and Keys in their YDs would reveal why. The Tarot spreads pinpoint more clearly where same and different experiences are sure to occur when comparisons are made between spreads that are based on the same root digit. *(The same applies to Personal Month, and Personal Day Tarot spreads that follow in the next two chapters.)*

Around **November or December** is a good time to calculate the next year's Tarot spread and copy it into a journal. As you study each number and its Key, imagine different scenarios for them. Write them out and review them from time to time to test and update your forecasting skills.

If setting up your Tarot spread for the first time, a good plan is to construct one for at least one year beforehand. As we all learn best from the past, knowing what happened then greatly facilitates interpreting the new year's windows of opportunity.

Important Note

Sometimes the numbers and/or Keys' symbolism may be daunting because their nature evokes negative thinking such as with the **6 of Swords**⇨**60, 7 of Wands**⇨**33** and **The Devil**⇨**15** Keys in the spread on page 93. This is a common reaction and perfectly normal. The **6 of Swords** and **7 of Wands** clearly depict some type of struggle. **The Devil** can signify people and things that are toxic in our lives besides our temptations, weaknesses, guilt and fears. Its discrimination aspect from its **root 6** serves to recognise such side-tracking aspects so that they can be sorted out. The **5** in **15** helps us to *interpret*, the **1** to *concentrate* on a particular thing and root **6** to *distinguish*. When these aspects are integrated, we actually have the wherewithal from **Key 15's** attributes to fix things that are detrimental, wrong or not going to plan. This is a Tarot Key's function: to provide clues that help us to fix our problems.

The aim when faced with such numbers and Keys is to draw on what we know or can find out to determine what might go wrong or needs correcting. This exercise prepares us for what might eventuate and forearms us at the same time. However, do not fall into the trap of dwelling on the negatives or allowing self-fulfilling prophesies to come true. Given your circumstances, formulate possible scenarios in your mind of what might come to pass and then devise practical strategies to offset negative possibilities; this is a wiser, healthier, more positive approach.

For instance, when **60, a tens' number** appears, sacrifices, obligations and duties rank high on its attributes' list. Therefore, it alerts you to the possibility that you are either already in or entering a type of "proving ground" that will most likely upset your comfort zone while it lasts. Typical areas in which these upsets might occur are matters concerning: the home, family, parenting, children, work or health. The important thing is that there *is* a way out of **60's** "trials"; it may just be a matter of time or timing along with making right decisions at the right time. If **60** rules a long cycle it is more likely to signify that the period of discomfort or hardship lasts a lot longer—sometimes, right up to the end of its cycle.

It is important to calculate each year's numbers and not take for granted that they will increase by one each year. Year **1999 and 2000** provide an excellent example. They are only one year apart but there is an enormous divide between their makeup. That difference dramatically alters their number families from one year to the next. "Tiger" Woods Tarot spreads for 2009 and 2010 that follow provide such an example. Although not as stark in contrast as years 1999 and 2000, the changes in the structure of these two spreads is easy to see.

"TIGER" WOODS' 2009 PERSONAL YEAR TAROT SPREAD
PRESENT NUMBERS AND KEYS

7_1 5_3 2_6 1_7 8

3 of Pentacles   Knight of Swords   Page of Wands   STAR   STRENGTH

MISSING NUMBERS AND KEYS

6_2 4_4 3_5

8 of Swords   4 of Cups   9 of Wands

Compare this Tarot spread with Woods' Personal Yearly Diamond in Part 6, Book 2. For further practice you may wish to set up his matching UYD.

2010: "TIGER" WOODS' Tarot Spread

PRESENT NUMBERS AND KEYS

7²   54   45   1⁸   9

4 of Pentacles   Page of Swords   5 of Cups   MOON   HERMIT

MISSING NUMBERS AND KEYS

63   36   27

9 of Swords   10 of wands   Ace of Wands

Calculate Woods' 2009⇔2010 PYD and 2010 UYD and then compare them with 2010's Tarot spread. Bear in mind that its top row represents what Woods is mostly aware of, is planning or acting out. See how well it reflects what has been publicised about him so far.

Brief readings for 2010's top row's Keys:

4 of Pentacles: Woods will use its aquisitive trait to fight to hold on to what he perceives as his. Hopefully this will be to protect his wife and children and not just be about his money and material possessions. **Page of Swords:** hopefully he will use this Key to tap its practical wisdom attributes and find the right solutions to his problems. **5 of Cups:** this Key might indicate that he truly regrets what he has done. **The Moon:** its psychological implications might indicate that Woods could consider this type of help to understand and better himself and so initiate the voluntary, self-change aspect of this Key. **The Hermit:** Woods becomes more mature and wiser from his transgressions. Also, **The Hermit** may reflect that he appears more reclusive at times.

Brief readings for 2010's bottom row's Keys:

View the bottom row's windows as "foggy and blurred" in the shadowy recesses of the conscious mind. One reason could be that ideas and things not yet clear are working their way into the conscious mind. This may be due to embryonic plans, desires, hopes and wishes floating in the ethers until time and circumstance synchronise, making conditions right for them to materialise. Or, they could be indicating elusive degrees of unrest, avoidance behaviour or denial because whatever is vying for expression is being suppressed.

What might be anticipated from this row's Keys follow: **9 of Swords:** worry and anxiety. Possible bad dreams and disturbed sleep. Possible medical or hospital procedures. Women in his life, on his mind and threats they pose to his well-being and reputation. Treachery. **10 of Wands:** working hard to make up for his wrongdoings. Mending his tattered reputation. **Ace of Wands:** searching for insights and ideas that help him to atone for his transgressions in the eyes of his wife, family, sponsors and public.

SUSAN BOYLE: (1–4–1961)
2009 PERSONAL YEAR TAROT SPREAD

This Tarot spread was active during 2009 when Susan Boyle suddenly rose to fame for her singing ability. Note the particularly dynamic nature of each one of her Keys. Is it any wonder that she became an overnight success?

PRESENT NUMBERS AND KEYS

34   16   7

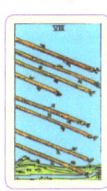 

8 of Wands   TOWER   CHARIOT

MISSING NUMBERS AND KEYS

25

Knight of Wands

SUSAN BOYLE'S 2010 PERSONAL YEAR TAROT SPREAD

Susan Boyle's 2010 Tarot Spread is expanded to include each Key's, *reverse Key*. They are displayed in sepia tones below. These Keys are: **Keys53** and **71** in the top row and **Key62** in the bottom row. They make an enormous difference to her spread when included. This is an excellent technique to use to uncover more clues about a year's directions and to improve accuracy when forcasting.

PRESENT NUMBER AND KEY AND THEIR REVERSALS

35   53   17   71   8

9 of   Knight of   STAR   3 of   STRENGTH
Wands   Swords   Pentacles

MISSING NUMBERS AND KEYS AND THEIR REVERSALS

26   62

Page of   8 of
Wands   Swords

When perusing the spread:
- Which Key keeps the spotlight on Susan?
- Do you see her going from strength to strength?
- Do you have concerns re her health?
- Which Keys signify that?
- Which Key signifies achieving her hopes and wishes?
- Which Key depicts travel?
- Which Key represents being recognised for her gift?
- Which Key coming to grips with her desires?
- What other configurations would you set up to verify success or any reservations you might harbour?

KEVIN RUDD'S 2010 PYNF: 60, 51, 42, 33, 24, 15 and 6

This is the year when Kevin Rudd, Australia's then Prime Minister, was thrown out of office. Note the threats to his office by Keys 51 and 24 in the bottom row. They depict the "King" (Rudd) being threatened by the "Queen"—Julia Gillard his deputy Prime Minister who became Prime Minister by "default". His PMNF and PDNF details are found on pages 105 and 108, respectively.

TOP ROW:

60	42	33	15	6
6 of Swords	2 of Cups	7 of Wands	DEVIL	LOVERS

BOTTOM ROW:

51	24
King of Swords	Queen of Wands

MICHAEL JACKSON'S 2009 PERSONAL YEAR TAROT SPREAD

Jackson's numbers present an excellent case study for practice. His details follow.

Birthdate: 25–6–1958
Date of Death: 25–6–2009

- Which Key depicts his cardiac arrest?
- Which one working hard to achieve a dream?
- Which one a threat to life?
- Remember to set up his matching UYD and PYDs as these tools work in sync with one another.

CHAPTER 8: PERSONAL MONTH TAROT SPREAD

> **UY** = Universal Year   **LPNF** = Life Path Number Family   **PM** = Personal Month
> **UM** = Universal Month   **PYNF** = Personal Year Number Family   **PMNF** = Personal Month Number Faimily
> **YD** = Yearly Diamond   **SD** = Single Digit   **WN** = Whole Number

A PERSONAL MONTH'S WINDOWS OF OPPORTUNITY

Personal Month Number Families (PMNFs) form the basis to Personal Month Tarot Spreads. They are calculated by adding the current month number to each number in their PYNF. When their numbers are converted to create a monthly Tarot spread, their Key's reveal its possibilities and opportunities. These spreads are most useful if time is of the essence and quick clues to a month's prospects are required. They are also useful to corroborate a PMD's indications or to validate a special future event or one from the past.

HOW TO CALCULATE A PMNF'S TAROT SPREAD

Preparation
- Calculate **current PYNF: 57, 39, 21, 12 and 3**
- Current month for analysis: **(JULY)**
- **Add 7** of **JULY** to **all** numbers in the PYNF
- **Do not reduce month number if Oct, Nov, Dec**

Create the PMNF and then its Tarot Spread

Step 1: **Present numbers: 64, 46, 28, 19, 10 and 1**—convert to Keys
Step 2: **Missing Numbers: 55** and **37**—convert to Keys
Step 3: Assemble JULY'S Tarot spread—**Top Row: 64, 46, 28, 19, 10** and **1**
Step 4: Assemble JULY'S Tarot spread—**Bottom Row: 55** and **37**

HOW TO INTERPRET A PERSONAL MONTH'S TAROT SPREAD
JULY 2004: FAMILY RIFT

Although this example is taken from my experiences, its numbers may be used for comparison for all those who share the same PMNF, or have, or will experience it at some time. This is due to us all experiencing these numbers or part thereof simply because their cycles rotate continuously.

PRESENT NUMBERS AND KEYS

64	46	28	19	10	1
10 of Swords	6 of Cups	2 of Wands	SUN	WHEEL	MAGICIAN

MISSING NUMBERS AND KEYS

55	37
Ace of Swords	King of Cups

Interpretations

Before proceeding with your interpretations, begin by recapping what the current life cycle from the Life Diamond (LD) and yearly cycles from the Personal and Universal Diamonds' cycles are depicting. Then figure out the Personal Month Tarot spread's prospects in relation to them. Make sure that what you intuit ties in with your current circumstances, hopes and dreams or to whom the spread belongs. Then, settle on plausible outcomes. Check out the matching PMD for essential timing triggers that may be present in any of its weeks. Do this by looking for a week that might reflect what the spread is portraying. If one does, this week could be the one to reveal timing options.

This was my Personal Month Tarot spread for **July '04**. It mirrored several numbers in my LPNF, namely **55, 37, 19, 10** and **1**. These powerful links to my LPNF meant July was likely to be a significant month. **Keys 64** and **46** in the spread triggered **64/46** in my LD's □. The importance of these two numbers in anyone's LD, PYD or UYD is explained in Chapter 12. As missing **55** was an exact match to my top LPN, it warned that personal tests and trials could be anticipated; Destiny issues were at work (**10**). This month would have its highs and lows (**10**) and very likely produce a catalyst to a life-changing event as **10s** indicate forced change. Such events are often disguised as a crisis.

Armed with this fore-knowledge, I searched for signs that would alert me to what might unfold given my current levels of awareness, current circumstances and current plans.

64's warnings were clear. I knew that I would be at risk in areas such as dealing with compulsive, obsessive behaviours, health, finances and family situations and possible backstabbing. A serious family upset was the more likely option as difficulties in family relationships had been brewing for a long time and tension was mounting. Having both **64** and **46** in the top row of the spread indicated that I was conscious of this. A deep family rift did occur from my son's (**37**) betrayal (swords in **Key64**). His false accusations ultimately caused our separation (**55**). They triggered the potential for heartbreak in the **PYN57** for that year.

The clues to this crisis were mainly found in **64/46** and **55** and the **10s** that appear when these numbers are reduced. **55** warned of evil forces. **10s** meant that my Wheel of Life was about to turn. It took the form of severance (**55**⇨**Ace of Swords**) and dissolution (**64**⇨**10 of Swords**) of family ties (**46**⇨**6 of Cups**). **19/91** and **28/82** provided further clues. **19/91** triggered my **PYN3**. Together they signified facing parent (**19**) and child (**3**) issues. **28/82** represented the power shift between us. The **Wheel of Fortune**⇨**10**, in the top row, reflected our unstable relationship. In many respects, the stage was set for missing **55** to manifest as a family rupture. It meant that a sudden reversal (**55** with **PYN12**) in family matters (**64/46**) was definitely "on the cards" for that month. *(For those with these numbers at a different stage in life and in different circumstances, expect different matters and outcomes to eventuate. They could be to do with health, property, or affairs of estate or a family business, or contracts or promises or new beginnings. We saw stark differences occur in the way numbers operate when "Tiger" Woods' numbers in Chapter 5 were the same as Phoebe's in Chapter 3.)*

Missing numbers, known for their intensity, indicated that the **Ace of Swords**⇨**55** and the **King of Cups**⇨**37** meant encountering *their* specific kinds of *negative trends* according to *my* circumstances *at that time*. Given that my family situation was tense, this made it easy to surmise that **55 and 37** types of negative probabilities, *which were relevant to me*, were likely to manifest. This negative tendency was reinforced when **57** and **12** were two of my **PYNs**. Besides being major *name* numbers, **37** was one of my **LPNs**. Acknowledging these links to major numbers, my task was to figure out their applicability and power and the possible extent of their negative scope. I needed to recognise their signs at work during this period so that steps could be put in place to offset, change, transform and transcend them for the better, if possible.

However, all was not gloom and doom as several, really good things occurred during that month. They mainly came from **37⇨King of Cups, 19⇨The Sun** and **1⇨The Magician**. They indicated that if I was ready, it could be a perfect month for publishing. Creative writing, teaching and lecturing were other possibilities. Much writing was achieved and a successful workshop was presented on this very topic to the now disbanded Victorian Association of Numerologists in Australia.

The Wheel of Fortune's⇨10's natural, evolutionary attributes promised growth from the month's experiences. Growth in maturity, understandings and wisdom were gained from the endings, new beginnings and forced changes experienced. As time wore on, I understood what had been set in motion by the Wheel's appearance for that month; I saw it as Soul Forces in action because the spread contained my LPNs. Although quite painful at the time, hindsight helped me to see that the Wheel cleared the way to continue this work by "removing" my son and his family's disturbing influences from my life.

July's PM Tarot spread was extremely relevant in that it perfectly described my situation and experiences at that time. Its missing numbers and Keys, and reversed numbers and Keys, played a pivotal role in helping me to understand the purpose behind the events that transpired.

NOVEMBER 2009'S PERSONAL MONTH TAROT SPREAD:
"TIGER" WOODS—Family Crisis

The numbers below are "Tiger" Woods' PMNF for November 2009 when he fell from Grace.

TOP ROW:	82	64		37	28	19	10	1
BOTTOM ROW:		73	55	46			

This cameo demonstrates that when two people have several of the same numbers activated, they are likely to have similar encounters. Compare Woods' numbers and his experiences with mine. Although our lives and circumstances are totally different, we shared some things in common.

The first thing that might strike you is that Woods' LPNF: **64, 55, 46** and **19, 10, 1** was contained in his PMNF; differences occurred in their inclusions and placements. This was the month when he activated his self-ruin (**64**).

Like me, Woods also experienced a personal (**1**) and a family crisis (**64** and **46**) when his Keys for November 2009 matched his LPNF. He was forced (**Wheel of Fortune⇨10**) to face (**19**) issues of rejection, abandonment and being shunned (**5 of Pentacles⇨73**). These were some of the consequences that resulted from his betrayals to his wife, call girls and sponsors, as many turned from him. Then we saw the radical change (**Ace of Swords⇨55**) that being exposed as a fraud made to Woods' credibility. A snide aspect of the **6 of Cups**⇨**46** is linked to incest so I guess this might stretch to include sex addiction on this occasion. Otherwise, **46** indicated a dysfunctional family. At the time, we saw the axis of power shift (**82** and **28**) from Woods to his wife and jilted lovers.

To demonstrate parallel experiences between people who bring up the same types of numbers, **73, 55 and 46** were in Woods' and my Keys and we both experienced being abandoned, shunned and rejected. Jessica Watson's Personal Day Tarot spread in the next chapter provides us with an example of the same numbers depicting a positive outcome but not without its unique, stress factors that pertained to her.

This comparison between Woods and myself demonstrates how the Challenges in our Tarot spreads indicated similar forms of hardship. It also shows how reliably the numbers and Keys reflect what is in us and that their consistent reiteration validates their predictive basis.

When you recognise a PMNF presaging a significant month for whatever reason, the best way to judge its trends is to erect its PMD and then compare it with its Tarot spread. From that standpoint, you are better able to judge the month's trends. However, if your preparation seems inadequate, calculate the PYD, the UYD, the LD and more, if necessary. Going to extra lengths provides a better chance of being correct in your forecasts.

PRACTICE:

1. JESSICA WATSON'S Tarot Keys for MAY 2010 when she completed her solo, circumnavigation of the world are below. Note how **58** in the top row depicts overcoming problems, great accomplishment and time for a well earned rest. In fact, all of the numbers in the top row suggest accomplishment that grows from struggle.

TOP ROW:	58	40	31	22	13	4
BOTTOM ROW:	49					

2. KEVIN RUDD'S Personal Month Tarot spread for **JUNE 2010** when he was deposed as Prime Minister:

TOP ROW:	66	48	39	21	12	3
BOTTOM ROW:		57		30		

TOP ROW: Key12 indicated a reversal and **Key48** a new direction with some regret. **Key21** pointed to an ending. Was it the end of a dream (**Key39**)?

BOTTOM ROW: Key57 Signified Rudd's devastation at being thrown from office (**Key30**).

Chapter 9: Personal Day Tarot Spread

LD = Life Diamond
CA = Current Age
PY = Personal Year
PYN = Personal Year Number
S = Single   W = Whole

PYD = Personal Year Diamond
YG = Yearly Goal
YC = Yearly Challenge
YG/C = Yearly Goal/Challenge
P = Personal

YGR = Yearly Goal Ruler
YCR = Yearly Challenge Ruler
YDR = Yearly Diamond Ruler
TCR = Top Cycle Ruler
U = Universal

A PERSONAL DAY'S WINDOWS OF OPPORTUNITY

Personal Day Tarot spreads excel when a significant event occurs. They also excel when planning for any type of special event in the future. Working with short-term highly personal, cyclic numbers such as these provides the opportunity for witnessing numerology and Tarot *in action.*

The day of St Joan of Arc's tragic death is used once more to illustrate, in this case, an example of how to work with a PDNF's Tarot spread. Compare her PDD with it for that day (Chapter 4) to see how their numbers link to each other. This is excellent numerological practice.

As before, ruling number families such as the LPNF, PYNF and PMNF are set up before the Personal Day Number Family (PDNF) is calculated. When the PMNF is ready, simply add the calendar day's number to each of its numbers to get the day's PDNF from it.

Decade Diamonds & Month, Day, Hour and Minute Diamonds

St Joan of Arc was burnt at the stake on 30th May, so 30 is added to each number in her PMNF.

HOW TO CALCULATE A PDNF'S TAROT SPREAD

Birth Date: 6-1-1412   **Event Date:** 30-5-1431= 44/ 8

Preparation
- LPNF ⇨ **33, 24, 15** and **6**. (6+1+14+12⇨**33**; 6+1+5+12⇨**24**; 6+1+5+3⇨**15** ⇨ **6**.)
- PYNF for 1431⇨**52, 16** and **7**
- PMNF for MAY⇨**57, 21, 12** and **3** (**ADD 5** to each PYN above)
- PDNF: Add 30 to all PMNs above—**do not reduce**

Create the PDNF and then its Tarot Spread

Step 1: **Present** numbers: **87, 51, 42, 33** and **6**—convert to Keys
Step 2: **Missing** numbers: **78, 69, 60, 24** and **15**—convert to Keys
Step 3: **Assemble** current DAY'S **Tarot Spread** —Top Row: **87, 51, 42, 33** and **6**.
Step 4: **Assemble** current DAY'S **Tarot Spread**—Bottom Row: **78, 69, 60, 24** and **15**.

(All of these numbers are in St Joan's LD which makes them act as powerful triggers to it **only if** prevailing conditions and circumstances support the occasion.)

HOW TO INTERPRET A PERSONAL DAY'S TAROT SPREAD
30TH MAY 1431: ST JOAN OF ARC—BURNED AT STAKE

PRESENT NUMBERS AND KEYS

87   51   42   33   6

King of Swords   2 of Cups   7 of Wands   LOVERS

MISSING NUMBERS AND KEYS

78   69   60   24   15

10 of Pentacles   Ace of Pentacles   6 of Swords   Queen of Wands   DEVIL

BURNED AT THE STAKE

Now that the windows to this day's ill-fated event are in place, compare them with its PDD's numbers. **69, 60, 33, 15** and **6** are strong in the PDD and Tarot spread. Having checked them out, now look for *major* back-up signs from other ◇s that link to this spread. Among them, **15/6** rules St Joan's LD and PMD's baselines and is present in the day's spread. **87/78** appear in her UYD's Grail and □ and her **PDD↻** was **87**; they, too, are in the spread. Her UYD's Grail **33** matches her LPN and it is in the spread. These are reinforcing signs so they can be relied on to mark a significant day in the life.

Before excluding **87** from the reading because it goes beyond Tarot's range, look up its keywords from Appendix 1 of *Life Diamonds*. Although **87** is large and does not have a corresponding Tarot Key, it does have a rightful place in this spread as a contributor to the day's indications. **87's** relevant keywords for this event validate some of what took place; eg, cruel treatment, treachery, sedition and treason; therefore, it is significant.

78, although a missing number and **87's** reverse, is significant from the perspective that it sometimes infers an end to life but usually, an end to a phase in life. Then, by a stretch of the imagination, **33's⇨7 of Wands**, could reflect St Joan being valiant (*Valiant* is this Key's actual title!) to the bitter end. The **Devil Key** implies facing one's worst fears. I have read for people when it appeared in this position. They were nervous or anxious or suffered the loss of a family member or someone close. However, it needs to be made clear that an actual death is not as common as one might think. This is due to **The Devil** being a member of *all* **root 6** number families. Whether it is present or hidden, it mostly represents what we are creating that is not for our Highest Good hence, reflecting our private hells.

The **Devil Key** depicts when we attach or bind ourselves to someone or something. Yet in Kevin Rudd's **Personal Year Tarot spread** for **2010** we have an example of when the **Devil Key** depicted *letting go* of something; he was forced to *let go of office* (letting go being the *opposite* to binding to or attaching to something; usually something one desires. Take out the **Devil Key** and look at its picture).

To move on to Rudd's **Personal Day Tarot spread** for the **24**th **June 2010**, it had very telling numbers and Keys for what transpired. Two numbers and their Keys stand out in the spread. One pair is **63** and its **9 of Swords Key**. (See over page).

Decade Diamonds & Month, Day, Hour and Minute Diamonds

My keywords taken from *Life Diamonds* for **63** are very apt for the occasion. They are *at the mercy of controlling women; malicious attacks from women; persecution*. **Key63**'s picture on the **9 of Swords** graphically shows Rudd's "nightmare". Then, **81** and its reverse **18s**' keywords from *Life Diamonds* are *deception, treachery and tragedy*. From **Key18** you get *hidden enemies* and *secret plots and schemes*.

24TH JUNE 2010: KEVIN RUDD—Political Assassination

TOP ROW: 90   72   63   45   36   27   9
BOTTOM ROW: 81   54

The amazing thing about **JUNE 24, 2010** was that Rudd's PDD's ✶Ruler was **87**—the number of treachery. it was the day of his political assassination by his party members and **87** was St Joan's top PDN for her day of execution; note the similarities.

Yet another amazing thing was that the Universal Day Number Family for the 24th JUNE 2010, was: 60, 51, 42, 33, 24, 15, 6 which was exactly the same as Rudd's 2010 PYNF! See page 99.

27TH NOVEMBER 2009: "TIGER" WOODS—Day of Reckoning

Incredibly, "Tiger" Woods' **2009** PMNF and PDNF for **27th November** produced extended versions of his LPNF and PMNF. The shaded numbers below are his actual LPNs. Those that made up his Tarot spread for that day follow.

TOP ROW: 109   91   64   55   46   37   28   19   10   1
BOTTOM ROW: 100   82   73

When we see such amazing synchronicity between Woods' LPNF, PMNF and PDNF, we realise why that month and day were so outstanding in his life. It also brings to our attention the significance of transiting numbers and their power to trigger major personal numbers when they match up. For example, Woods' **LPN64** contains the potential for *self-undoing* or *self-ruin*. The likelihood of triggering its negative aspects intensifies when a build-up of wrong-doing has taken place. The extent of what transpires depends on the intensity of this build-up against major personal numbers. What happened to Woods is a good reminder to us all. It demonstrates what can transpire when we are forced to face the consequences of our wrongdoings.

However, given different circumstances, this might have been a day of great triumph.

And we have an example of such a triumph! It is …….. **Jessica Watson**.

15TH MAY 2010: JESSICA WATSON—Day of Victory

TOP ROW: 73 55 46 37 28 19 10 1
BOTTOM ROW: 64

Jessica's family of "ones" was ideal for this day's events. It showed that the day was all about Jessica and her amazing accomplishments.

TOP ROW:

73 was perfect in that it represented Jessica single-handedly accomplishing her dreams. One only has to recall her weary, solitary figure standing on the deck of "Ella's Pink Lady" as she inched her way to the finish line in those trying seas to recognise the lone, steadfast aspects of this number. **73's** abandonment aspects were also evident. They manifested when Jessica abandoned the sea and her boat when she stepped onto land for the first time in months.

55 depicted the radical change to Jessica's life that day. This was due to becoming famous for her unprecedented achievement and for being no longer at sea.

46 signified reuniting with her family and the accolades from all and sundry.

37 reflected that Jessica had the potential to become wealthy from her heroic feat but she chose not to exploit that avenue.

28 had to represent her dominion over the sea and her ability to negotiate many challenges successfully on her arrival home.

19 depicted success, status and many things to face on that memorable day.

10 signified changing fortunes because of her efforts and fame.

1 represented her single-handed victory.

BOTTOM ROW:

64's "ruin" aspect indicated that something "threatening" about the day was likely to occur. Hence, some form of possible defeat or spoiled plans should be thought of and factored into the spread's considerations. As it turned out, strong head winds and lumpy seas were the main problem. Hence, some of the day's plans were ruined (**64**) by them because Jessica's arrival time was delayed for several hours. But, isn't it interesting to note that **46** (**64's reverse**) signified her anticipated family reunion.

This concludes our study of Year, Month and Day Tarot spreads and how they may be used to enhance their matching Diamonds' meanings.

Chapter 10:
The Personal Month Grid

PY = Personal Year **PM** = Personal Month **SD** = Single Digit
PYN = Personal Year Number **PMNF** = Personal Month Number Family **WN** = Whole Number
PYNF = Personal Year Number Family **PMG** = Personal Month Grid **F** = Family

The Personal Month Grid (PMG) receives a "new look" in this chapter. The Grid is compiled by placing each month's PMNF in consecutive rows. When the Grid is set out, an obvious pattern and order emerges within its matrix. It shows how our monthly numbers are based upon a system of rotating cycles that have repetitive features. Their repetitive nature fits them well for predictive purposes. Subsequently, they make a handy adjunct to Personal Year and Personal Month projections. A PMG Worksheet is provided at the end of this chapter which can be photocopied for personal use.

The PYNF provides the platform from which a PMG is constructed. It is calculated first and then each PMNF is created from it. Instructions for PYNF calculations were provided in Chapter 2; Appendix 3 also displays them.

When ready to construct a PMG, place the PYNF above it as a handy reference point. This is illustrated on the sample PMG shown on the next page.

Some people have more numbers and others less in their PYNFs so their PMNFs reflect this. Hence, the worksheet provided at the end of this chapter may need to be modified to suit these variations. Regardless, remember to leave a blank box at the end of January's row (some years require two). This provides spaces for extra numbers that appear when PMNFs grow longer in latter months. (See May's row for when this begins to occur.)

HOW TO SET OUT A PMG

Calculate January and February's PMNFs. Insert them in the grid. Their pattern and order quickly reveals that *adding 1 to each row's numbers thereafter* is all that is required to complete it. By the time October is reached, 10 is already added to the highest PYN (**50**). Hence, **60, 61 and 62** appear at the beginning of October, November and December's rows. If these month's numbers are reduced, they repeat January, February and March rows. Reducing them would prevent obtaining additional directions for October, November and December from **60, 61 and 62**.

PYNF: 50, 41, 32, 23, 14 and 5

MONTHS	PYN 5: PERSONAL MONTH NUMBERS						
JAN	51	42	33	24	15	6	
FEB	52	43	34	25	16	7	
MAR	53	44	35	26	17	8	
APR	54	45	36	27	18	9	
MAY	55	46	37	28	19	10	1
JUN	56	47	38	29	20	11	2
JUL	57	48	39	30	21	12	3
AUG	58	49	40	31	22	13	4
SEP	59	50	41	32	23	14	5
OCT	60	51	42	33	24	15	6
NOV	61	52	43	34	25	16	7
DEC	62	53	44	35	26	17	8

PERSONAL MONTH IDIOSYNCRASIES

Examination of the PMG above reveals certain idiosyncratic patterns. The easiest to spot is that **September** *repeats* the **PYNF**—except for **59**. Another is that the first three months' PMNFs *reappear* in the latter three months except for **60, 61 and 62** at their front.

September and October provide yet another idiosyncrasy. September represents *endings* as the **9th** month. October represents *completion* from its **10** along with *new beginnings*, which arise from its root **1**.

It is only when PMNFs are set out sequentially, that these idiosyncrasies become plain to see. They illustrate how our numbers are based upon rotating, repetitive cycles. Their rotating, repetitive nature illustrates that they are based upon a sound, mathematical premise of forewarning that facilitates preparation for future possibilities. Certain months indicate times during the year that best suit initiating, consolidating or modifying actions. They are explained in the following.

The New Year

January, February and March are *initiating* in nature. Since they contain the impetus to get the new year's energies and forces underway, this is a good period to start things.

March through to August is the period when *consolidation* of what was set in motion during Jan/Feb/Mar takes place. This period provides a firm foundation upon which the year's plans are unfolded and then developed.

October, November and December are *modifying and finalising* in nature due to repeating January, February and March's numbers. So, this is the period to create opportunities that modify and change things as this is the best time to go back over the year to reflect on and evaluate how well things have progressed to that point. Successes can be savoured and built on while failures are learned from and rectified. The finalising nature of this period allows sufficient time to tie up loose ends and prepare for the next year's trends. **Due to *not reducing* October, November and December's 10, 11 and 12 to their root digits**, a higher octave number appears at the beginning of their month's number family. These additional numbers create extra means or tools with which to work during the latter months of the year.

Repeat Patterns

January and October's numbers of the current year actually introduce the *next* year's PYN family. Therefore, the very first sampling of the next year's influences arrives as much as twelve months early! The new year's energies and forces begin to filter through more noticeably when October *reintroduces* them. This idiosyncrasy exemplifies how we are forewarned and prepared long in advance for the changing of an energy field and what it brings.

November and December also have a role in forewarning and preparing for the incoming year's trends. This is due to January and February repeating their numbers in the following year.

As mentioned, **September's PMNF repeats the year's PYNF**. This phenomenon broadcasts that by September each year, the full strength of the personal year's numbers is now waning. It also broadcasts that this is the time to check how well the year's work is progressing.

Merging Years

Because **November and December's** numbers are *repeated* in **January and February's** numbers of the next year, they merge the old year with the new. What is experienced during these "overlapping" four months is a simultaneous, twofold process that sees the old year's numbers waning in strength while the new year's numbers wax in strength. During November and December the new year's influences are definitely filtering through and into these months while the old year's energy field is losing power as it leaves them. January and February, on the other hand, see the new year's numbers strengthen as the old year's numbers weaken. They peter out altogether by the end of February providing an excellent example of being eased into and out of a particular numeric, field of experience.

A Cycle within a Cycle

Another merging pattern commences each **September** and ends at **February's** close of the subsequent year. When these six months are singled out and their numbers closely examined, they indicate that there is an indisputable underpinning of cyclic change that specifically ends one phase at September, whilst October, subtly yet effectively, ushers in the new cycle. This is an ingenious way of attuning and preparing us for new numbers and their specific areas of experience that carry us over from one year's energy field to be developed further in the next. Having this knowledge provides us with the opportunity to exercise three courses of action at this stage of the year. They might be to *stay attuned* to goals or *modify* them or, decide to *begin something new*.

The old year's influence is completely gone by the end of **February** when **March** ushers in the pure essence of the new year's numbers.

USING THE PMG AS A FORECASTING TOOL

To observe these graphic patterns, photocopy three PMG worksheets. Use them to set up the year before, the current year and the year ahead. Also make blank copies to set up significant PMG years for study purposes. Use them to learn from studying their patterns what happened then, to read future directions by. Can you pick when initiating, consolidating, modifying and finalising phases occurred among them?

Identical shading is used to highlight "twin" months that repeat each other's numbers (Jan/Oct; Feb/Nov; Mar/Dec.) and the month, which repeats the PYNs (Sept.).

If you include missing numbers in the Grid, highlight them to distinguish them from present numbers. Remember that "missing" numbers are likely to be more potent than "present" numbers. This appears to be due to being more in our subconscious; hence, the struggle for manifestation. These subtle differences between present and hidden or missing numbers affect the ways in which they are expressed, therefore, interpreted. Give them more emphasis when interpreting them.

Besides the above, use a different colour to highlight where any major personal numbers appear. These months are when significant events are likely to happen. Examples of this follow.

PARALLELS—ACCIDENTS AND EVENTS

Parallel Accidents

What appears to transpire is that some encounters, experiences, events or circumstances met with during January, February and March often recurs under the same or similar guise during their "twin" months: October, November and December. Hence, foundations for being able to predict the future from what is remembered from January, February and March's happenings can be established.

Two isolated yet related incidents to follow provide an example of parallel accidents that occurred during January and October's "twin" months. This anecdote recounts a young, single mother's experiences.

The mother's **PYNF** for **2007** was: 66, **57**, 48, **39**, **30**, 21, 12 and **3** (numbers in bold type were her missing numbers). **3** is underlined because it gave a sure sign that children would play a significant role in her life that year (a ♥3 does the same). Her **PMNF** for **January** was: 67, *<u>58</u>, 49, **40**, **39**, 22, 13 and 4.

On **January 23rd**, her son suffered a spiral fracture to his tibia and fibula when he catapulted over the handlebars of his friend's scooter and landed heavily on the concrete guttering beside the road. Later that year, on **October 24th**, her daughter broke her wrist while playing on the monkey bars at school!

This example demonstrates the importance of not forgetting to include ruling numbers when interpreting their counterparts. The most important number for those events was **PYN3**. It is highlighted for these occasions because **3** is not only ruling each month's number family, which makes it significant, but also relates to children as well as mothers. Hence, matters involving the mother and her children are sure to stand out during those months of the year. What was also interesting about these two incidents was that both children were happily playing at the time of their accidents (having fun is a typical **3** attribute!).

However, **January and Octobers' PMNFs** produced their own "telling" number. It was hidden *<u>58</u> in the mother's PMNF's grouping for those two months. 58's links to hospitals and forms of confinement were the clues. Either the mother would go to hospital for tests, be hospitalised or, visit someone in hospital; the latter was so in each case. Caring for her children while convalescing caused **58's** confinement aspect to manifest each time. This was especially so in her son's case as his leg took several months to heal.

Sometimes, this ability to tie together similar events that occur during correlating months can be taken further. I have found that future forecasts may be derived from as far back as November and December of the *previous* year because their numbers are repeated for January, February and October, November of the following year. Go back as far as November of the previous year for the mother and the daughter who broke her wrist was hospitalised for a deep cut to her wrist due to falling on broken glass. This accident occurred during *November 06*. When you do the maths, you will find that **hidden 58** appeared in the mother's PMNF for that month, as well!

Parallel Events

This example of paralleling events is subtler. They began when a young man was released from prison early **November 2003** (**PMNF: 47, 38, 29, 20, 2**). During mid **January 2004** (**PMNF: 38, 29, 20, 11, 2**), he began reverting to his old ways. Come **October 2004** (**PMNF: 47, 38, 29, 20, 11, 2**), due to his poor choices (**47**—decision-making badly affected by alcohol and drugs) and deception and lies (**29**), he broke the law (**11**), was sentenced (**20**) and returned to prison.

TIP: PMG's are convenient self-help tools and worth taking the time to calculate. Naturally, the best time to erect them is each January. The benefit from doing this is that once the PMG is calculated, each month's PMNFs are set up and ready for creating all twelve Personal Month Tarot spreads throughout the year.

NB: Spaces have been left on the PMG WORKSHEET on the next page for you to draw shapes to represent the TAROT KEYS and write their numbers in them as well. It is also a good idea to label each Key as shown below.

EXAMPLE:

PRESENT NUMBERS AND KEYS

10 of Cups   6 of Wands   King of Wands   Hierophant

MISSING NUMBERS AND KEYS

Ace of Cups   Temperance

WORKSHEET:
PERSONAL YEAR & MONTH TAROT SPREAD + PMG

TAROT SPREADS FOR: _____ DATE: _____

PERSONAL YEAR NUMBER FAMILY for _____(year)

PRESENT   KEYS /NUMBERS

MISSING   KEYS /NUMBERS

PERSONAL MONTH NUMBER FAMILY for _____(month)

PRESENT   KEYS /NUMBERS

MISSING   KEYS /NUMBERS

PERSONAL MONTH GRID for _____(year)

PYNF:

MONTHS	PYN___: PERSONAL MONTH NUMBERS					
JAN						
FEB						
MAR						
APR						
MAY						
JUN						
JUL						
AUG						
SEP						
OCT						
NOV						
DEC						

Part 3

PERSONAL DECADES

Chapter 11:
INTRODUCTION TO DECADES

YD = Yearly Diamond   **PMG** = Personal Month Grid   **PYD** = Personal Yearly Diamond

INTRODUCTION TO DECADES

What is presented in this section shows a way to not only become aware of the myriad pieces (mouse or micro view) of life's jig-saw puzzle but also to make its broader picture clearer (eagle or macro view). PYDs and shorter-term diamonds provide the "mouse" view while Decades and other long-term cycles provide the "eagle" view.

Decades are new to numerology and because they are new, they require in-depth treatment to explain their idiosyncrasies. Hence, this section's chapters are devoted to introducing them, their unique characteristics and their diamonds. Each chapter highlights how to apply their special features to daily life.

Decades emerged as the by-product of an intense study of PYDs. The intent behind this study was two-fold. One was to obtain a deeper understanding of PYDs and the other, to obtain knowledge of future trends and directions. Nothing prepared me for the revelations that resulted from that curiosity.

These revelations initially stemmed from wondering what would be uncovered if decade sequences of PYDs were set out in rows. I began the first row at year 0 and finished at year 9. Each row thereafter followed suit continuing on until the final row of PYDs for the years **90 to 99** was complete. It was only when this layout was finished that I recognised decades as a branch of numerology in their own right.

Perhaps the most awe-inspiring revelation of all was to uncover a main matrix upon which a large portion of the countless ways we can choose to live out our lives is made known. Its matrix, in a simple, mathematical format, reveals our Soul's requirements for an incarnation in great detail. The genius of such a layout is in having a visual of the Soul's agenda that progresses yearly. My conclusion from this study is that each lifetime is preordained and that numbers can be used as one means to relay that information to those who wish to know the true purpose of their earthly destiny.

Ascertaining this may send the message that there is no way of changing what has been "set in place" prior to birth. On the contrary, *we, the Personality,* are given the reins to our destinies on earth in that, we have a duty to find out, by trial and error, what has been programmed for us to achieve, and to hopefully be victorious in achieving it by life's end. Each of us has our own unique contribution to make and it is up to us to find out what it is and how to go about accomplishing it. Our personalised matrix supplies us with ways of doing so.

One way to explain this is to imagine that what was preordained is like a recipe; like all recipes, changes can be made to them at will. We *can* and *must* make changes to our recipes because the main point of earthly existence is to be self-directed. Therefore, we have the power within to manipulate our "ingredients" and learn to *improvise, improve and master them* in order to evolve, incarnation after incarnation. Only we have the power to do that. Only we can change *us*, things and directions, stymie or accelerate our growth, be materially inclined or spiritually inclined—we have that scope, that power and those options as well as the free will and the creative, autonomous intelligence to exercise them in ways *we* choose. So, by making changes to our recipe's ingredients, flavours or look, we have exercised our free will; we have stayed within our life plan (recipe) but made modifications to it (free will) to improve ourselves, thereby, become more.

Emergence of a Fixed Agenda

When a full set of PYDs is assembled its decade idiosyncrasies and cyclic pattern and order is plain to see. (This is similar to how the PMG's pattern and order became plain.) Their features, *individualised* to suit each person's incarnation, reveal a large portion of the "fixed agenda" or "recipe" to be followed throughout the course of each decade within a lifetime. Hence, a layout of decades reveal year by year and decade by decade that our lives from beginning to end are geared to a preordained, cyclic agenda; a cyclic agenda that uniquely reflects our Soul's requirements and consequently this life's "Plan".

Emergence of a Timetable

The patterns that emerged throughout each decade were also geared to a "timetable". The idea of a timetable was aided by the knowledge that all cycles have a beginning, middle and end and that *time is the underpinning factor* to their unfolding. Hence, a decade's sequential, cyclic nature provided the clues that they contained set timetables. This meant that decades may be used for pinpointing when endings, beginnings and times in between are likely to occur. Such use facilitates keeping the Life Purpose on track.

Emergence of a Preset Destiny

As numerology is just one esoteric science that reveals the Soul's proposed goals for an incarnation, it suggests that each matrix' maze contains hidden clues and guidelines that tell us what those goals are and how to get from "A⇨Z". The word *guidelines* itself, implies that they are *suggested*, therefore open to revision, modification and change. This is due to their inbuilt provision for autonomy. It all narrows down to how well we manage and apply our intellect and autonomy and whether or not we are able to fulfil our destiny as the Soul's guidelines are very much subject to *how we interpret and live by them.*

Hence, a PYD/decade matrix depicts a linear yet upward, spiralling progression from "A⇨Z". It unfurls from a preset agenda (what), to a timetable (when), to a destination (where), to their interpretation (how).

Predictive Basis to Our Numbers

As already stated, all decade sequences of YDs are founded upon the basis of repetitive, cyclic pattern and order which fits them for predictive purposes. Familiarity with their cycles' idiosyncrasies refines forecasting skills.

Cosmic Origins to Our Cycles

It is my belief that **Key10⇨The Wheel of Fortune**, explains the macrocosmic origins behind the regulatory, involving, evolving, sequential, rotational, cyclic nature of our numbers. This unfolding, developing premise, whether cosmic or made personal, makes predicting the future possible from what occurred in past cycles. Paul Foster Case describes this aspect extremely well in his book: *The Tarot—The Wisdom of the Ages*.

Awareness of an Earthly Assignment

Assuming that our matrix represents our Soul's agenda for this incarnation, it may be perceived as revealing our "earthly assignment" when used to describe our earthly sojourn from beginning to end.

Special Turning-points

Each matrix contains our unique pathways. These pathways with their goals and challenges not only behave in predictable ways but by means of their cyclic timetables bring about beginnings, middles and endings. The element of time brings the element of change to a cycle's agenda or pathway—something like changing trains to reach a new destination. Such turning-points open up new options, scope, encounters and experiences. They ensure continuous, evolutionary growth. Although times of change within decade cycles are easy to detect when laid out before us, special mention is made of them because they depict gateways in time; times when significant moments or periods in life are best planned for and not missed.

Many examples throughout the following chapters draw your attention to such pivotal periods within decade cycles. Data such as this is hard to ignore, as these times usually signpost important turning-points or life-changing years. This is the vital information that a decade matrix contains. Right use of its information, clues and guidlines helps us to demystify our Destiny and take full advantage of such times.

Cyclic Rotation of Numbers

Three basic things occur as decade cycles rotate. Firstly, we get the opportunity to *re-engage* with numbers and patterns as old number fields are sequentially rotated. They are repeatedly impressed and imprinted on us in this manner. Secondly, we are introduced to new ones. Thirdly, we strengthen and refine character and skills with repeat contact. It is from this repetitive, cyclic contact that we inch our way towards mastery of *all* numbers and Keys and their combinations and self-initiate our evolution. This hard won skill results from lifetimes of exposure to their influences, from acquainting ourselves with their qualities and from experimenting with their modes of operation. Such learned familiarity from aeons of contact, experience, trial and error enables self-directional skills to develop to levels of mastery.

Developing Informed, Self-Help Skills

In order to prepare the way to make informed life choices, learn as much as you can about the cyclic nature of your decades and their numbers eg, take note when new numbers emerge in the matrix. Acknowledge that when they do, they signal that new fields of experience are filtering in. Also seek out where and for how long a number's field of experience is being reinforced via repetition. These are important signs that tell you that you have that amount of time to complete an "assignment". To facilitate grasping such opportunities, become familiar with those numbers' traits and their many avenues of expression. This practice enables you to take advantage of their gifts, possibilities, options and scope to get much more from them.

Use past experiences as guides when "old" numbers resurface. Anticipate that similar encounters might occur when they return. Also anticipate that you may be "tested" in the fields of expression that the "old" number represents. At the same time allow for "*something new*" to sprout and grow even if an "old" number field is repeated. Do this with the knowledge that you are multi-dimensional and capable of growing many aspects of yourself simultaniously and that numbers represent endless possibilities, chance and change besides evolution being at their root.

Also, look for and locate where and when major personal numbers appear within the matrix. Triggering of major personal numbers signals special times when you can become more closely attuned to your destiny. Expect their attributes to be mildly or heavily intensified when this occurs.

TIP: Calculate one full decade matrix with its attendant Decade Diamonds for an entire lifetime. This invaluable data is no doubt best laminated or kept in a special notebook. However, it may be in your best interests to work your way through to Chapter 15 before you do.

Chapter 12: Decade Idiosyncrasies

LPN = Life Path Number	**YD** = Yearly Diamond	**DD** = Decade Diamond
PYN = Personal Year Number	**YG** = Yearly Goal	**DG** = Decade Goal
CA = Current Age	**YC** = Yearly Challenge	**DC** = Decade Challenge
LD = Life Diamond	**YG/C** = Yearly Goal/Challenge	**DR** = Decade Ruler
SD = Single Digit	**WN** = Whole Number	**DG/C** = Decade Goal/Challenge

DECADE IDIOSYNCRASIES and PATTERNS

This chapter begins the study of decades and the major roles they play in our lives. Their unique, idiosyncratic patterns commencing with the year of birth are highlighted in this chapter.

Each new decade begins on the anniversary of each **10th, 20th, 30th to 90th birthday**. Hence, *only* **P**YDs relate to decades. Many sequences of PYDs in decade format follow that display noteworthy points within their pattern and order. Once their emerging pattern and order is noted and acknowledged, there is no denying that decade cycles represent a Grand Plan and that our lives unfold in a *purposeful manner* according to that Plan. It is based on a repetitive, sequential introduction of numbers from 0 to 9.

This organisation from 0 to 9 reflects the order that prevails in Creation. It stems from the ancient doctrine that the Master Builder geometrises and has arranged all things throughout the universe according to measure, number and weight. Hence, the properties of number manifest through all that exist …. *including us.* This relativity to us becomes plain as the "Divine" nature of the pattern and order in our decades is revealed throughout this chapter. This is not surprising when all numbers from 0 to 9 represent successive stages in every cycle of evolution. And this is so whether they represent the macro scale of the cosmos or the micro scale of a human being.

1. YEAR of BIRTH'S EXCEPTIONAL PYD—AGE 0

A LPN1 is used to show the exceptional nature of a PYD's first year of life. Its pattern is truly extraordinary no matter which LPN is used. The most outstanding feature in it is to notice how indelibly the LPN is impressed, imprinted and impacted on every baby for its first year of life—even the PYN matches the LPN! To appreciate fully your own pattern at birth, calculate your first year's PYD including its PYN. Then you may wish to consult Point 13.

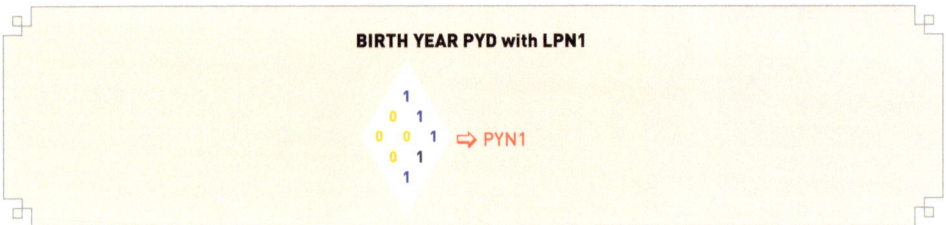

2. INDELIBLE IMPRINTING—SINGLE DIGIT YEARS from 1⇨9

The array of PYDs from **1 to 9** below, display a **LPN1's** new patterns when age one is reached. In this decade the ♥number begins a sequential introduction of each number from **1** through **9** via the *current age*.

This **0 to 9** ♥number **pattern** is established from birth. Then it repeats over and over again as each successive decade rotates this ♥number pattern throughout life.

Note below how each new age holds a commanding position in its PYD by replicating itself three times within the first cycle. This triple impression clearly demonstrates how important it is to become accustomed to a number's specific qualities, attributes and fields of expression during the initial cycle of our lives. To see visibly this actual concentration of energies and forces compressed within the first 4-monthly cycle shows how important it is for us to be fully sensitised to their influences and traits. To see them "purposefully" reinforced leaves no doubt in our minds that we are subject to a Divine Plan. This is evident when we see that this process only occurs in the first two decades of life during our most impressionable years when we learn primarily through imitation and repetition!

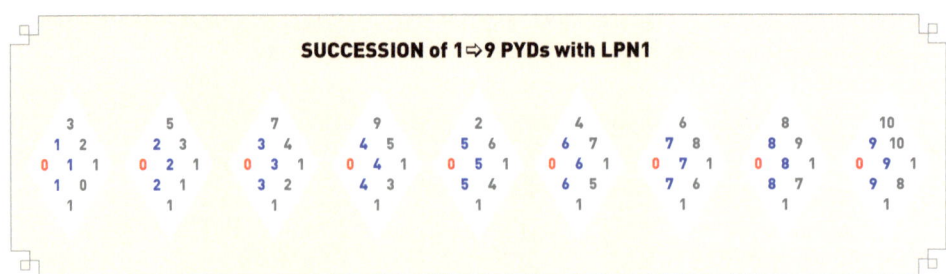

3. INDELIBLE IMPRINTING—10s' DIGIT YEARS

When **10s' age** numbers commence each new decade, i.e., ages **10, 20, 30 to 90**, its **10's digit** reigns for its decade; we have **ten's 1 first**, then **2, 3, 4, 5, 6** and so on. **Each ten's number determines the tone of its decade.**

10s' age PYDs are unique in that they *reverse* the pattern established in the first decade of life. Their **10's age** number not only begins the numerical sequence from 0 to 9 over again but also indelibly *grounds* its attributes at the beginning of each decade by replicating itself three times in the first 4-monthly cycle which is similar to the 0 to 9 year decade, on the previous page. Not to be outdone, the LPN does likewise. It creates a dominant pattern by replicating itself three times in the second 4-monthly cycle for those years. What we take from this is that a **LPN's influence is never overridden by transiting numbers.**

This triple pattern shows us yet again how important a new number's field of experience is by being intensified via a repetitious, sequenial process that ensures an indelible imprint. The constant engaging, re-engaging and reinforcing of numbers in this rotational manner, ingeniously facilitates becoming acquainted with a new number's energies and forces. Yet we can simultaneously remain in touch with the enduring powers of the LPN since it retains its permanent place on every PYD's baseline.

During these exceptional years, the PYN also increases its powers by replicating itself in the third Goal position. Witnessing how these three important personal numbers indelibly imprint **10s' age years** validates their significance in our lives.

To witness this regulated, systematic, decade patterning, proves just how important a role numbers play as self-help tools for directing our lives. By their purposeful repetition and placements, we not only become accustomed to their new vibrations but also have ample time to adjust to each new number's qualities and attributes when they arrive at important junctures in our lives; we are not suddenly exposed to them without having had some experience via prior exposure.

This stepping up of energies and forces from decade to decade may be likened to progressing through the "school of life" as we advance from one level of accomplishment to the next; it is no different to college years demanding more than junior years.

The beauty and simplicity in the *sequential introduction and reinforcement* of each number as we progress and ascend through each successive decade, and through each successive year within a decade, assures us that a Divine Intelligence maps out our destinies; that everything is ordered and proceeding according to Its Divine Plan. It is only when a full PYD/decade matrix is calculated that this Order, this Plan and successive exposure to each number's field of experience can be appreciated fully for what each represents. The sequence of 10s' ages below, displays this pattern and order.

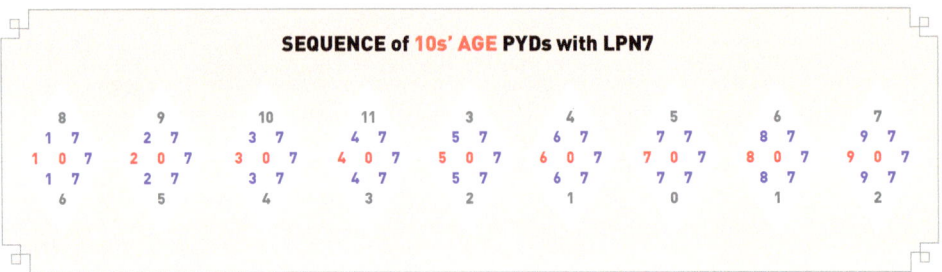

4. ♥0 PYDs

Once a 10's age year is reached, its ♥0 at the hub of its PYD may be likened to a portal that provides access to all that its new decade is about to "deliver". Is it not surprising then, that greater output and greater expectations accompany these years, especially when they generate master and tens numbers? Not only that, their top PYDR Ruler and ✱Ruler are the same and the Inner □ Ruler and the Grail Ruler are the same. These outstanding features impress on us just how important these years are when we arrive at them.

Using **Key 0⇨The Fool** enables us to understand that when a new decade arrives, we are standing on the precipice of the abyss of greater possibility. This explains why we sense deeply within our being the burgeoning promise of becoming more at these times. We feel this because we know that we are about to face unknown potential and opportunities stretching before us that take us beyond heights previously reached. Therefore, each new decade marks a milestone in life (mountain experience—evolution—transcendence). Its sequentially, rotating numbers ensure growth via the new fields of exploration and experience that they open up. Such regulatory changes to our numbers cause us to discover, cultivate, nurture and so develop an understanding of unknown aspects about ourself, things and our environment. This newness at the beginning of each decade metaphorically takes us down the mountain into the valleys below (valley experience—involution—immersion). Awareness of these evolutionary and involutionary aspects within decades explains why travel or life-changing decisions, happenings or events are often activated during ♥0 years.

Part 3 **Personal Decades** Chapter 12 Decade Indiosyncrasies

The **Wheel of Fortune**⇨**Key10** reflects this mountain/valley journeying in another way; it represents cosmic and personal involutionary and evolutionary cycles. When personalised, each **10s' number** and its Key depicts that our "Wheel of Life" is about to rotate once more. Each rotation widens, broadens and deepens our scope for involutionary and evolutionary growth. ♥**0** years and **The Fool Key** mirror these aspects in their unique ways. However, we can project involutionary/evolutionary aspects into any of our Keys that reduce to a **10** or has a **10** on the front or face of its Key; this is so wherever or whenever they appear (see below). The **1** in the **10** represents new learning (ignorance in the pursuit of knowledge—valley experience) and the **10** represents the culmination of learning (understanding, wisdom and transcendence gained from the knowledge—mountain experience).

When a new decade begins, its ♥**0** exerts a powerful influence on its surrounding numbers because it creates repeat tens and master numbers when they are paired to it. Tens and master numbers greatly increase these PYD's frequency levels due to having the potential to take us or force us above and beyond present levels of attainment. Tens numbers provide the impetus for that while master numbers provide the potential to cultivate higher degrees of *mastery*. These qualities develop from the decade's options and scope as humanity, spirituality, maturity, wisdom and greater competence are instilled.

5. INDELIBLE IMPRINTING—UNIT 9 YEARS

As with 10s-ages, those ending in unit **9** produce their own unique patterns. Note their marked similarities when compared with one another.

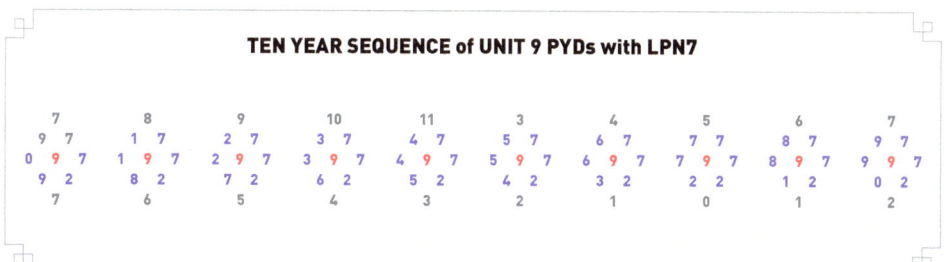

TEN YEAR SEQUENCE of UNIT 9 PYDs with LPN7

7	8	9	10	11	3	4	5	6	7
9 7	1 7	2 7	3 7	4 7	5 7	6 7	7 7	8 7	9 7
0 9 7	1 9 7	2 9 7	3 9 7	4 9 7	5 9 7	6 9 7	7 9 7	8 9 7	9 9 7
9 2	8 2	7 2	6 2	5 2	4 2	3 2	2 2	1 2	0 2
7	6	5	4	3	2	1	0	1	2

Considering that we are given much help to become accustomed to new fields of experience at the beginning of each decade…..then, why not at its end? To see the 10's year's PYGs repeat in each **unit 9** year shows us that we are given a golden opportunity to review and complete the work of the decade, before moving on and up in life. Again and again, "Divine Grace" allows us time to round off the old and prepare for the new by not catapulting us from one decade's vibration into the next—time is allowed to tidy-up, finish off, adjust and prepare.

As with **unit 0** years, there is no doubt that **unit 9** years are also significant. Their PYDs are even more powerful if major personal numbers or the LD are triggered by them. Furthermore, as **0's** nature can be forceful or extreme, **9's** can, too. These innate characteristics provide us with another reason to pay special attention to their PYDs.

♥0 and ♥9 PATTERNS for LPN2

To expand on Points 3, 4 and 5, ♥9s lift ♥0 year's Goals, PYGRs, PYNs and PYDRs to higher frequencies in readiness for the next decade's commencement. This is evident in their Ruler totals. ♥9s also signify the wisdom gained from the decade's experiences as one reflects on it. Hence, its connection to **Key9⇨The Hermit** and why this Key signals attainment, completion and the end of a cycle. Its ending contains within it the seed for understanding as the new cycle that follows brings renewal within it. Many similarities arise in their PYD's numbers and Keys as shown below.

The Keys and the PYDs below display the strong links that exist between **FOOL⇨0 years**—the "Eternal Youth" and **HERMIT⇨9 years**—the "Ancient One". In their unique ways, each one signifies attainment as well as preparation for new learning and accomplishment. Note how the Goals remain the same in their PYDs. What was begun in the **0** ends in the **9** to culminate and begin again in the next **0** (really, **10**).

AGE 50–BEGINNING 6th DECADE   **AGE 59–END of 6th DECADE**

7. INNER □s in 10s' and 9 YEARS

No other numerological aspect or construct can compete with the power of **10's and unit 9 Inner □s**. Although challenging, the number of tens and master numbers paired from them usually mean that greater achievements are won from the extra potential and demands that underpin their **□'s** possibilities. Their **□s'** idiosyncrasies for these two exceptional years are explored further using the example on the previous page.

- Paired **52s** will never appear again as the **□'s** top numbers for a **LPN2**.
- Paired **52** only appears *once in a lifetime* as the **□'s** bottom number for a **LPN2**.
- Paired **55** on the **□'s** *left* side never appears *in this position* again.
- Paired **22** and **27** on the **□'s** *right* side *repeat* here **every tenth year**. (See Point 11.)

To appreciate fully how infrequently the above idiosyncrasies occur, a full set of PYDs from 0 to 99 needs to be calculated. Only then does the weight of a **□'s** numbers become plain; only then can the power that its numbers exert on its years be appreciated fully. Once the rarity of their appearance is acknowledged, we can comprehend why a **□** provides a brilliant starting-point from which to begin our interpretations with great confidence!

Other than these exceptional years, and due to number-pairing techniques, the **□'s** numbers appear many times in other positions throughout PYDs, Magickal Facets and Constellations. But, they do not enjoy the strength and power of the **□'s** positions unless they happen to replicate a major personal number or intensify other numbers by repetition.

8. OUR MOST PERSONAL DECADE'S RARE FEATURES

Our most personal decade occurs when the **10s' digit duplicates our SD LPN**. It not only marks the arrival of possibly *the most personal decade* in our lifetime but has within it the only PYD that has a **triple digit baseline** that spawns **triple zero challenges**. A **30's** decade with its **LPN3** shown below, displays this rare PYD. See its **triple 3 baseline** in the **fourth PYD** below. As it appears once only in a lifetime, it is quite possibly *the pivotal year* to be experienced. See Point 16, also. **Note the triple 9 PYD.**

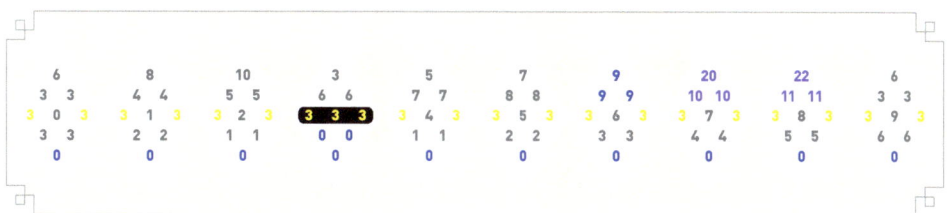

More of this decade's unique features are outlined below.

- **Triple 9 goals** are unique to this decade; they herald gain with loss.
- **Master numbers** appear above and below each baseline; they raise hopes, capabilities, skills and demands.
- **The third challenge is always a zero**.
- **Paired tens' numbers** are created from the **zero challenge**; they create greater opportunities, optimism and increase types of stress levels.
- **Paired master and tens numbers** always increase prospects, aims, choices, intensity levels, burdens and despite the added strain, joy from achievement. Since they appear in every, successive PYD throughout this decade, they explain its unique nature.
- **Repetitive SDs** are prevalent therefore, expect their traits to be intensified.
- **The first PYD for this decade always contains a rare Inner ◇**. This is due to all four SDs being **3s** which limit the ◇'s capacity to produce several paired numbers. In this PYD, only one kind of a paired number is possible and that is **33**. **33** repeats *six times* in this PYD's ◇; even the Grail contains a **33**! This phenomenon only occurs in ♥0 year's PYDs.
- Each ◇ contains top and bottom paired master numbers.
- The numbers in the ◇s at the beginning and end of this decade contain paired **33s** never to appear here again.
- Paired **33** on the ◇'s *left* side will not appear here again.
- The ◇'s *right* side's paired number *repeats* here every **tenth year**. (Explained further in Point 11.)

9. THE PYD's ♥ NUMBER and the WHEEL of LIFE

The ♥number of every PYD is the only number that changes on a PYD's baseline during an entire decade. And, it is the *only number* that can be paired to every other number in its PYD.

Pairing the ♥number to all other numbers in a PYD creates invisible pathways to and from it. These pathways create a sacred symbol; an "Eight-pointed Star". They relate to the eight spokes of the "Wheel of Life" on the Wheel of Fortune Key. When viewed in this context, the ♥number is the hub of each PYD's "Wheel".

These associations explain why ♥numbers have greater powers—somewhat like the numbers that make up Inner □s, they also set the "tone" of their PYDs. Consequently, their PYD's trends may be confidently predicted in broad terms according to their nature.

- ◆ Jamie Oliver's ♥1 is a very good example of this phenomenon. When he turned 21 and 1 was at the heart of his PYD, everything centred around what he could and could not do. His 1 shone forth, bringing his *individuality* to the forefront. This was pivotal, for it was the year when he was "discovered", appearing on worldwide television networks. (His PYD and Decade Diamonds are introduced in the next two chapters.)

- ◆ "Tiger" Woods' ♥3 for 2009 signified major themes such as the birth of his baby boy, celebrations, infidelity and misery.

- ◆ St Joan of Arc's ♥9 for 1431 represented the end of her life.

10. A PYD and UYDs' CA CYCLES are GENERIC

Although CA cycles are common to everyone for each age, they produce countless variations that hinge on equally countless, personal factors. When we studied Jan's personal outcomes for her 39th CA cycle in *Yearly Diamonds*, it provided us with an excellent example of a first time mother's experiences. But this is *not* what all women experience when they turn 39. Eg, Nicole Kidman was married for a second time, just 5 days after turning 39. To cite another example, we have the little five-year-old girl, Sophie Delezio, well known to Australians, who was almost killed by the car that hit her while on a pedestrian crossing when returning home from school. Her CA cycle was active at the time and this is a *rare occurrence*; even for a 5 year old's generic cycle. Her experiences were very different to those of 5-year-old Tom's in Chapters 4 and 8 of *Yearly Diamonds*. However, what they shared in common was the *severity* of their experiences; Jan and Nicole shared *joyful* experiences.

The above explains why we cannot assume that the same events and experiences will occur for everyone, during matching, active, CA cycles. Even though the CA cycle is essentially generic, the mere fact that it is y*our own CA personalises* it. Important background information always provides the keys to interpreting these cycles. Clues stem from your hopes, plans and current circumstances but must be combined with what your ◇ suggests. Background influences that are unique to you are not generic and this is why they bring *exclusivity* to your CA cycle.

For CA cycles, the golden rule when forecasting from them is to never lose sight of the person's age, gender and prevailing circumstances along with any other relevant data. However, *always* allow for the unknown and unexpected as they sometimes dramatically affect how a CA cycle manifests.

The best way to get to know how generic or CA cycles operate is to research what you and others shared during the same CA cycle. Then again, the best way of all is to find those who have the same LPN as you.

11. THE PYD'S 2nd CYCLE *REPEATS* EVERY TENTH YEAR

Each time the same ♥number returns every tenth year, the second PYD's numbers are the same as ten years prior. This is due to the LPN on the baseline never changing.

Because this cycle's format is strictly *personal*, it is not generic like the first cycle. What needs to be borne in mind when interpreting it is that parallel experiences might occur when it is reactivated. That being so, let past experiences and the fact that a new reality is brought to this ten-year cycle be your guide. Eg, in the PYDs shown below for **returning ♥6 years**, their recurring second cycle numbers offer renewed options and scope to establish (**Goal 4**) a new sense of self besides something new (**Challenge 1**) upon its return. Interpret this cycle within the context of how you are utilising your options on each return, given your greater age and maturity levels and current awareness.

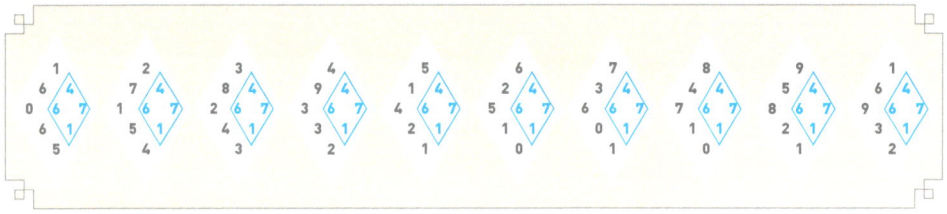

12. INTRODUCING the DECADE DIAMOND (DD)

DDs only apply to PYDs and only four numbers complete it.

The DD is the "missing" fourth cycle that would surround its PYD from the beginning of every following **tenth year** (**♥0** year) to its **unit 9th** year if included. DDs are extracted from the PYD's baseline when each 10s' age is reached. They have their Goals (DGs), Challenges (DCs) and Rulers (DRs), too. Unlike all other PYD cycles **its numbers never alter** during this time, which may be why it was omitted in the PYDs I found when reading a book about them back in the 1980s (See *Yearly Diamonds* Preface). The next chapter provides other possible reasons for their being left out.

If included, the DD's composition surrounding a **PYD's 7th year** is shown on the next page. Its **0, 1, 1 and 1** composition indicates how the **LPN1** is indelibly imprinted on the Personality *throughout* its first **ten** years of life; **not just for the first year as shown in Point 1**. This phenomenon is highly significant for those seeking rhyme and reason about their existence from a Personality/Soul point of view.

Part 3 Personal Decades Chapter 12 Decade Indiosyncrasies

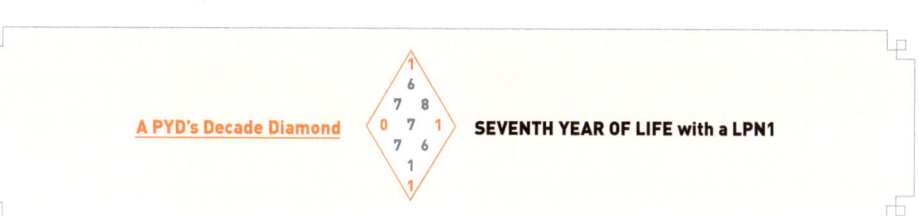

13. A DD's GOAL (DG) and CHALLENGE (DC)

The 10s' age at the beginning of the decade in conjunction with its LPN, creates a *perpetuating* PYG and PYC. It creates a duplicate, fourth PYG/C pair if included. Because these numbers remain constant throughout the decade, this makes them appear "redundant" in a PYD. However, the next chapter refutes that.

A forties decade with a **LPN5** is used below to display the ten-year long **DG9** and **DC1**. See how they repeat at the top and bottom of each PYD's Vertical Axis. Because the **DG/Cs** for this decade are **9** and **1**, their attributes *continuously* underpin their decade. Therefore, when interpreting the decade from them, anticipate that fitting trends such as endings and beginnings in the form of leadership possibilities, new and old ideas, aims, experiences, habits, relationships, things and projects, etc, will be subtle, yet noticeable developments throughout its reign.

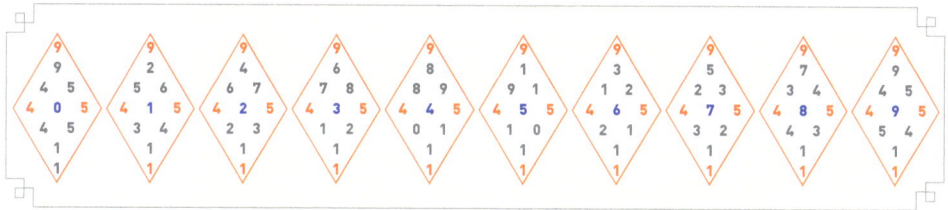

14. The DD's RULER (DR)

Simply add the four DD's SDs to get their Ruler. The DD's Rulers for the above PYDs are **19/10/1** (**4+5+9+1**). Chapters 13–15 introduce and explain DDs and their rulers.

15. 10s and 9 AGE YEARS' VERTICAL AXES

We know that these years produce distinctive patterns. However, two more appear when their auric envelope i.e., their Decade Diamond is placed in position. Then we see a master number emerge at the top and tail of their PYDs' Vertical Axes. They provide another reason why these two years seem more outstanding. The PYN's influence is actually trebled for these two years, just like the tens' and LPNs are. To illustrate this idiosyncrasy, PYDs for the fourth decade (thirties) with a **LPN 5** are shown on the next page.

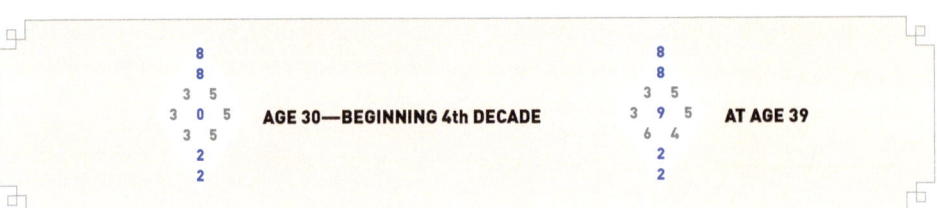

16. ZERO CHALLENGES

Zero challenges do not appear in PYDs as often as we might think. When they do, they seem quite clear in the ways that they operate. They have the potential to be expressed for either productive or counterproductive purposes. Consult the *Life Diamonds'* Appendices 1 and 3 for zero (**0**) or **The Fool Key** interpretations. Also refer to Points 4 and 6 in this chapter.

When the CA 10's digit duplicates its LPN, dual challenge zeros emerge. (See below.) However, zero Challenges also emerge when matching digits occupy a PYD's baseline. This occurs at ages **11, 22, 33**, etc. or for when the CA ♥number matches the SD LPN eg, CA 47 with LPN7 (baseline: **4**–7–7). However, when all baseline numbers are the same, all challenges are zeros. This was made clear in Point 8.

Zeros always increase their paired numbers' powers hence, their cycles and ◇'s frequencies as well. Eg, **4** paired to **0** creates **40** and **40's** influences are much more powerful than **4's**. This is why tens' numbers operate similarly to master numbers.

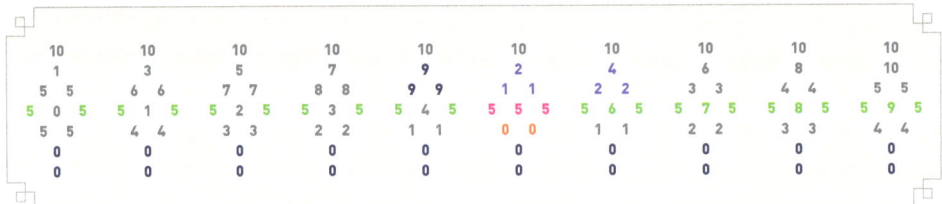

17. THE ♥6 YEAR

A subtle phenomenon that is common to all decades, appears when a **♥6-year** is reached. It may be experienced as feeling mildly driven to get on with completing an aim, a project or simply mundane matters during its year. The sixth year seems to trigger this. It brings in a slow build up of pressure and/ or demands that gather momentum during the last four years of the decade's cycle. It is so subtle to start with that it is usually ignored until a point is reached when its influence becomes obvious. Now that this has been brought to your attention, view each **♥6-year** as having a slight "pressure cooker" effect when your sense of "obligation and duty" becomes awakened; a "**6 thing**". Perceive it as a pressure that steadily builds until ♥**6 year's** stimulus becomes more urgent by ♥**9's** year when "the urge to purge" is keenly felt. This impulse often flows over and into the early part of the ♥**0 year** that follows immediately after. This allows more time to rid the new decade of detrimental encumbrances. More on ♥**6-years** is found in Chapter 15.

18. IDEAS for FURTHER INVESTIGATION

The following ideas offer food for thought. Other years than those mentioned also have the potential to be significant during decade cycles. They are the years when the 10s' digit or ♥number or any age's reduced total is the same as the LPN. These notions might explain when and why an added emphasis or intensity causes that number to have greater impact then.

- ◇ Eg, if the **LPN** is a 7, look for ♥7 years when the CA *ends* in 7.
- ◇ Look for ages that *begin* with 7 (seventies' decade).
- ◇ Check any age that *reduces* to 7 (**16, 34** or **52**).
- ◇ This notion quite possibly extends to **Goal 7s, Challenge 7s** or **Ruling 7s** in a **DD**.

PRACTICE TIPS

To be able to appreciate fully what has been covered so far, calculate your decade sets of PYDs in rows from year 0 to year 99 (you may wish to wait until you have read Chapter 15). On completing this task, you will have your unique, grand matrix at hand that represents a major template of your Soul's requirements and directions for this lifetime. Closely observe its regulated, pattern and order with the awareness that this is your self-revelatory, matrix, a "tailor made", comprehensive, holistic guide to this lifetime's unfolding trends.

To make good use of this tool, study PYDs already experienced first, as we learn best from the past. Then find numbers among them that represented outstanding events. Also, find those that reflected recurring or paralleling events. From this review, learn to recognise that when certain numbers and/or groups of numbers reappear, they *consistently* describe same or similar themes, encounters, options and potential. Familiarity with past PYDs' numbers' consistent performances increases a forecaster's ability to interpret future PYDs.

Train your eye to detect outstanding features within your grand matrix. Any PYD that signals something of note, whatever it is, is likely to transpire at some point during its year. Highlight it or its parts that attract your attention.

Also be on the lookout for repetitive number *groupings*. As they reveal likely *themes,* advanced, forecasting skills are developed from them. These skills also lead to recognising when a particular number within a grouping alters the group's or ◇'s tone or intensity levels. More accurate forecasting develops from these skills and those that find synchronistic links from PYDs to other configurations and major personal numbers.

As you study your matrix's template, are you able to recognise which numbers, groups of numbers or number patterns consistently present favourable possibilities? Are you able to recognise those that warn of hardship? Did you spot which patterns indicate your "seasons" such as beginnings, plateaus and endings. They signal times of instigation, consolidation, modification, success and tests. Which numbers act as triggers for initiating phases in life? …for ending them? … for extending them?

When major personal numbers appear within a PYD's patterns, which ones alert you to focus on your Soul's requirements? Which ones indicate Karmic or Destiny opportunities? Do you expect to have intense experiences and/or important events take place or important decisions to make during those times? Do specific elements of your Life Path become clearer or are they triggered then?

This point is of particular importance. Learn to look for the same numbers or thematic numbers that carry on from one PYD to the next. They often emerge in different places in subsequent PYDs (or UYDs). *Being repeated is a special indication. It means your work in their specific fields of experience is not yet over. By their repetition, you know that. And, you know you have whatever extra time is allocated to remain in their fields of influence to hopefully get "the work" done satisfactorily.*

The outstanding feature of a matrix's cyclic, PYD/decade pattern and order is the way that its visual display reveals a large part of an incarnation's spiritualisation process in graphic detail. It marks our special gateways in time making them much easier to find and follow. Its unfolding pathways continually open up new opportunities, new options and new scope. But, perhaps most remarkable of all, is that its rotating numbers and patterns prove that our evolution is Divinely mapped out for us.

Most of the points regarding PYDs may be applied to UYDs.

Chapter 13: Decade Diamonds

> DD = Decade Diamond
> DG = Decade Goal
> DC = Decade Challenge
> DR = Decade Ruler
> N = Number   S = Single
> CA = Current Age
> P = Personal
> U = Universal
> Y = Yearly
> W = Whole
> LD = Life Diamond
> YD = Yearly Diamond
> LDR = Life Diamond Ruler
> LPN = Life Path Number
> LPNF = Life Path Number Family

ADVENT OF DECADE DIAMONDS (DDs)

My need to know why Personal Yearly Diamonds (PYDs) did not have four goals and challenges as their parent Life Diamonds (LDs) do, led to the advent of **DECADE DIAMONDS (DDs)**. As explained in the previous chapter, research revealed that PYDs actually do have a fourth Goal and Challenge that make an outer diamond. Being left out seems to be due to the fact that if put in, their numbers repeat in this position for all ten, successive PYDs from 0 to 9 irrespective of which decade the PYDs are representing. This repetitive, "auric" pattern gives them the illusion of being "redundant"; they are for PYDs but have great significance when seen as a numerological configuration in their own right. When acknowledged as such, I assure you that these numbers are not redundant, for they produce **Decade Diamonds**.

If included in a PYD, the DD's four numbers would surround it like the Cosmic Diamond does in LDs, UYDs, PMDs to PMinDs. Because its cycle is long term, it produces long-range, *general* forecasts as LDs do. Although a DD's numbers are "invisible", they can be imagined as "auric envelopes" that contain extra, meaningful data that is there in the ethers for us to utilise.

Once put to use, a DD's *auric* or *background* influences can make a difference to the way we plan our lives because they provide us with a general sense of where our individual Destinies are heading. Their beauty is in their simplicity, hence their directness. We can take advantage of their attributes to show ourselves, in a nutshell, how to remain in touch with our Soul's Purpose.

As mentioned in the previous chapter, **DD's only apply to PYDs.**

Why? **Because DDs commence on each birthday's successive 10th year.**

To begin the study of DDs, this chapter introduces SD DDs first. To interpret them, their numbers and Keys are best kept separate from their PYDs after which they are compared with major, personal numbers and other numerological configurations. Only then can their composition, significance and meaning be judged in accordance with what they represent in the grand scheme of things.

When the SD DD is drawn and set up separately from the PYD, place its ruler/s in its centre. Then consider its composition and envisage its guidelines as *overall* and *general* since they take ten years to unfold. Connect their guidelines to current achievements and aspirations. Also, reflect on how they can be used to attain future plans, hopes and wishes that are in line with what you perceive to be your Soul's requirements.

Each number's field of influence, whether a SD or a paired, compound number, is to be perceived as indicating *unfolding, developing qualities and skills.* These terms imply gradual growth and progress which helps to understand a DD's numbers basic nature. They mean that a DD's numbers take much longer for their attributes and trends to be shaped into desired character traits and hoped for outcomes. Therefore, a SD DD's main purpose is to be instrumental in exposing specialised areas of growth that are likely to manifest within its long-term projections. Use the symbolic images of the DD's Tarot Keys and other skills you may possess to broaden insights and understanding of its promise.

Keep the DD's long-term, unfolding nature uppermost in mind while interpreting its numbers and Keys. Apply the same basic interpretation principles and techniques to them as you would for other ◇s. Although their calculation and structure are simple, their guidelines are profound and accurate. If you are unable to find numerological indications that explain certain circumstances, episodes or events, I suggest that you consult DDs. In all probability, you will discover that they provide the answers you are seeking. Failing that, consult other branches of numerology or astrology—the answers may be found there, from meditation or simply from living life.

If you have just entered a decade, review how the DDs of the previous decade unfolded. This provides a platform from which forecasts are formulated that endeavour to get the most from your current DDs indications. To assist with this, tips and keywords pertaining to DDs and their components are provided in this and the next two chapters.

When a DDs' numbers and/or Keys appear to contain potentially negative tendencies then, as often mentioned, cultivate positive ways of working them. Know that whatever they bring to your awareness, no matter how challenging, they provide you with the means to find and do what is necessary to create and mould your destiny from the wisdom gained from their proving grounds in the past. If you can hold the thought that you are bigger than any of your problems, you are already on your way to creating success.

As with LDs, the greatest feature of a DD's numbers and Keys is that there is ample time to prepare for what they indicate. There is also ample time to improve on and update predictions especially if a new decade has just been entered or, is in its early years. If the opposite is the case, use the time pending to make enlightened decisions as to how to make the best use of what is left of the decade. Then, calculate the next decade's ◇s and begin preparing in advance, for what they indicate.

Also, check out shorter cycles that are in sync with your DDs. Their more specific directions and triggers help you to achieve its "assignments" and "destinations". Triggers always provide clues as to when things are likely to unfold or materialise during their term. Or, they might disclose when the best times occur to initiate, consolidate, modify or complete certain things. Synchronicity between short and long cycles greatly assists forecasting for when promising and/or challenging times seem likely.

HOW TO CALCULATE SD DDs

Decade Diamonds are constructed from **two** numbers; they have Goals, Challenges and Rulers but no Magickal Facets or Constellations. The two numbers used to construct the DD's baseline are:

◇ the **ten's number** extracted from the Current Age's 10's digit,
◇ a **Single or Whole Life Path Number** to create a SD or a WN DD

A DD's COMPOSITION

◇ A 10's digit, a Single or a Whole LPN.
◇ 1 Goal, 1 Challenge and Ruling number/s
◇ Four long-term SDs (unless WNs are used)
◇ Possible twelve compound numbers from pairing SDs
◇ Hidden numbers from paired numbers' reductions

STEPS FOR CALCULATING SD DDs

1 Calculate the **LPNF** and **CA**
2 **Baseline:** CA's 10's digit —space—SD LPN
3 **DECADE GOAL (DG):** CA's 10's digit + SD LPN
4 **DECADE CHALLENGE (DC):** CA's 10's digit - SD LPN
5 **RULERS:** Add all four numbers—write Rulers in centre of each ◇

CASE STUDY:

JAMIE OLIVER'S ("The Naked Chef") DDs for his TWENTIES

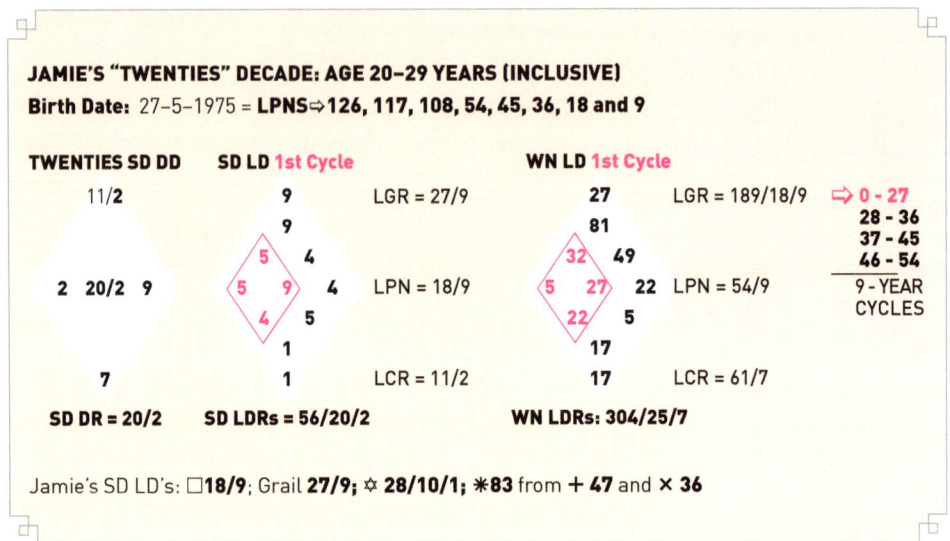

JAMIE'S SD DD'S NUMBERS

Special attention needs to be paid to all DD numbers as they are all significant; even the LPN holds a permanent place on its baseline. However, the DD's **10's number and Rulers** set the decade's "tone". **Goals** signify what is being striven for; **Challenges** what might thwart attempts to achieve them.

To begin your study, extract the SDs, paired and hidden numbers, Rulers and Keys from the SD DD. Then check the decade's numbers and Keys against Jamie's LDs and major personal numbers to establish if there are any links to them. This exercise helps to obtain a clearer perspective of what there is to work with and where to place emphasis. One way to do this is set out below.

SD DD

11   20   2
WN GOAL   DD RULERS

- SDs ⇨ **2, 2, 9** and **7**
- PAIRED NUMBERS ⇨ **22, 27/72, 29/92** and **79/97**
- HIDDEN NUMBERS ⇨ **4/40** from **22**; **9/90** from **27/72**; **11/2/20** from **29/92**; **16/61** and **7/70** from **79/97**
- RULERS ⇨ **20/2**
- LINKS to LDs and B/date ⇨ **2s, 4s, 7s, 9s, 11s, 16, 20, 22s** and **27s**.

INTERPRETING JAMIE'S SD DD

As a DD's numbers and Keys are active for ten, long years, we have ample time to acquaint ourselves with their possibilities. The best way to work them to our advantage is to study their attributes in detail, make notes and then figure out how best to apply them to our lives. Because they are with us for a long time, we have access to a broader range of aspects, hence ample scope thus more opportunities. This greater diversity should then be factored into the interpretations to consider. The following interpretations for Jamie's DD are more detailed to reflect these features because DDs are new.

Background Information

During Jamie's 21st year, a female TV director was searching for new ideas and material around which to create a trend-setting TV, cooking show. His unabashed, youthful exuberance, and his exceptional skills as a chef, caught her attention. At the same time, his DD's numbers and Keys were in sync with his SD and WN LDs. Their indications were such that they would support such an opportunity if her offer suited Jamie.

SD Interpretations for 2, 2, 9 and 7

For this decade, **2** used in broader terms represents learning to interact with others. Accordingly, this would include personal, social, business and work areas as well as any negotiations, agreements or contracts. **DG11** has similar traits as it can be used to administrate and maintain balance in one's affairs. **7** has analytical properties and **11** weighs and measures. They work well together when one considers that the decade's emphasis was mostly centred on enterprise. To be able to activate the *"Victory"* aspect of **7** would depend on how well Jamie can activate his **LPN9** potential. It puts at his disposal visionary aspects that enable him to initiate endings, break new ground, think ahead, think big and grow wise from his experiences.

We saw Jamie use his **2s** and **9** to seek ideal (**9**) partnerships and relationships (**2**) in areas that cover all kinds of unions and connections such as friendships, marriage (Jamie married "Jools" in 2000), business partnerships and associates. They were also used for networking (**9**) among political circles (**2s**). Late in the decade, Jamie successfully worked the political arena to petition British Parliament against the junk food culture in order to get schools to serve nutritional, cost efficient meals that schoolchildren enjoyed eating. Because of his efforts, school menus changed from junk food to healthy food. As **7** sometimes depicts the people, Jamie used this aspect of **7** to reach out to them. When he merged **9's** global aspect with his **2s** and **7** he created what grew to become a global enterprise (paired **27/9**). It brought with it global exposure (paired **22**) and "hero" status (paired **79**).

Number-Pairing Interpretations

22, 27/72, 29/92 and 79/97 make up this decade. Jamie used **22** and **27's** initiating aspects when he dared to take a new path. Perhaps he sensed this in his numbers' gifts. Some were that he could choose to serve the masses, reach a milestone and/or run a large enterprise or become engaged in one. He chose to use **27's** enterprising and **29's** lucrative traits to commence a career in TV. It gave him global exposure (**97**) and brought him before the masses (**22**). Money, prestige and a burgeoning career grew from his choices and work ethics.

Many numbers in this decade link to powerful numbers in Jamie's birthdate and LDs. If these were an aspirant's numbers, they would show the aspirant that they were being presented with an opportunity to firstly get in touch with and then cultivate and nurture those aspects within themselves. They also show that "timely events" are likely to occur. However and as always, success depends on the aspirant's "readiness".

For example, the **27s** in Jamie's twenties' numbers constantly trigger his **WN LD♥27** and fourth **WN LG27**. That powerful link meant that he had the potential to achieve something monumental if he was ready, willing and able to make the most of this opportunity. If one has talent, is prepared to be greater than their challenges and is willing to "pay the price", this gives everything a better chance to turn out in the way one hopes.

Jamie was ready. He had put in the hard yards in his father's English pub since the early age of *eight*. So, at **21**, he was already highly regarded as a chef. Jamie was due rewards for his labours (**29**). Not only had he put in the work but he had also developed high principles (**LPN9** and **29**) by then. This was plain to see in his deeds, sacrifices, high degree of commitment, success and strongly developed sense of humanity.

We saw Jamie's unique qualities at work during the course of his TV shows; school lunch programmes and especially, in "*Fifteen*". *Fifteen* was a visionary training scheme (really nice use of his **9 and 27**) to train disadvantaged youth in the catering industry. He gave them the chance to become world-class chefs. This is an excellent example of a person using the "hero" aspect in their paired **79/97** combination, their **7's** protector and influence aspects, their **2's** compassion aspect and their **9's** idealism aspect. Jamie lived and demonstrated **9's** highest aspects as a "Way**shower**" to those less educated or fortunate throughout this and into the next decade. (Apart from his ♥ and LP numbers having **root 9s**, his birth potential to be a Way**sharer** as well as a Way**shower** is further supported by the three supporting **9s** to be found in his SD LD's Vertical Axis!)

When working out a DD's directions, factor in negative as well as positive aspects because a decade is a looooong cycle. Hence, a large range of positive and negative probabilities has the chance to manifest eg, in Jamie's case, **29's** negative qualities such as broken promises, betrayal and deception had ample time to unfold and he did not escape them—a hate campaign was mounted against him. This was largely due to overexposure and the public's perception that Jamie personified a conflict of interests. Consequently, Jamie endured death threats and smear campaigns that tarnished his hard won reputation. This is the "bad news" aspect of his **LPN54** manifesting. Also, the threat of falling from Grace was present in the *hidden 16*, which appears when you add **LPN9** to **DC7** in his SD DD. Are you able to see in them, the people (**DC7**) challenging (hidden **16**) Jamie's integrity (**9**)?

Decade Ruler (DR) Interpretations

Each **DR** represents the total of all numbers in their tiny ◇s. For example, **DR20** is comprised of **tens' 2**, a **LPN9**, a **DC7** and a **DG11/2** (the latter is a SD/interim combination). **Tens' 2, DC7 and DG11/2** are the new numbers for this decade. They and their Ruler receive most attention, because LPNs hold their position on a DD's baseline throughout life. However, these three, cyclic numbers' individual fields of experience and possibilities are **channelled through their Ruler**. *They, and their Ruler, determine this decade's new fields of options, opportunities, learning and scope that facilitate ongoing development.*

Jamie's **tens' 2+LPN9+DG2+DC7DD** are ruled by an analytical, judicious, onerous **DR20**. It reduces to a sensitive, diplomatic **DR2**. Jamie drew very heavily on the unflagging nature of his **20** throughout the entire decade in order to accomplish the enormous targets he set himself. He was bubbly, enthusiastic, optimistic and passionately positive about everything he did; there were no half measures and little rest for him! **DR20** "charged" its components (the numbers that made up **20**) with greater stamina during this extremely productive time. It enabled him to channel enormous energy into his projects. (Apparently Jamie worked extremely long hours with little sleep for many years, which is, a typical, **20** trait.) Another **20** trait is that Jamie would make important decisions during the decade that would have significant long-term consequences on his life and his Life Path.

A major keyword for **20** is *realisation*. Realisation implies that Jamie could become more self-aware and activate or fulfil certain aspects of his Life Purpose during this decade especially as it is one of his LDRNs. It signalled that he would probably experience some gruelling times. Yet, the paradox in **20** is that, if Jamie put in the hard yards to achieve his dreams, then the "gruelling" he endured would not be perceived by him as a hardship. To achieve **20's** spiritual requirements one must go beyond previous limits. This was made more likely if the **DR20** and its numbers reflected high profile numbers in his LD. On the other hand, he could use **20's** *judgement* aspect to evaluate his efforts or, conversely, others would. (Jamie faced harsh judgements from his fans when they accused him of double standards relating to certain products and food chains that he was promoting at that time.)

Because **20** mainly signifies elevated consciousness, growth or movement from one situation, phase or virtue to a higher one, Jamie had the option to make the most of its reign for lofty purposes. Jamie did that even at this early stage in his life. He not only stood ready to reap rewards from past works (good Karma⇨**11**) but to use them as a platform from which to reach higher and farther than before. But **DR20** warned that these rewards would come after many tests and trials and much hard work. It also warned that he would find himself in positions of making life-altering decisions in matters that would test his mettle and stretch him beyond previous limits. The result of these decisions would close some doors and open others which would have far-reaching consequences.

As all rulers are the sum of their parts, **DR20's** numbers and Keys that compose it, describe how **20** is "coloured" by their specific traits and trends in the way it manifests. So, expect to see various elements of **ten's 2, LPN9, DC7** and **DG2** tinged with **20's** traits or vice versa. **20's** "job" is to absorb, harness and merge their properties into itself and then disperse them as one. Their combined traits make **20** either stronger, weaker, livelier or unchanged. So, all Rulers are modified by their parts. Eg, a car's parts and condition define its performance levels just as we are defined by the state of our minds, emotions, bodies and health. Hence, a Ruler's parts alter its mode of operation. Although an advanced skill, it makes positive and negative inclinations easier to detect hence, forecasts more accurate.

A simple example of how to employ this concept is to consider each number's traits. They have the clues that tell us how **20** and **root 2's** directions are likely to unfold. If they are favourable numbers, they will temper **20's** naturally, harsh leanings and if not, they will exacerbate them. The best forecasts are obtained when appropriate keywords are selected that take into account Jamie's nature, status and background as well as the numbers' composite attributes. However, **20** and **2** have the overriding influence in the final analysis. So, for this decade, imagine that **20** provided Jamie with the opportunity to raise his abilities and station in life and this is what he set out to do. Then you have a clue as to how he could use this Ruler's components to achieve that. Eg, paired **22, 7 and 9's** aspects channelling through **20** depict the high-minded, service-oriented ways (**79**) in which he built up a large enterprise (**11 and 22/4**) as well as becoming a worldwide (**9**) popular (**22** and **7**) figure. He not only achieved that, but also set a high benchmark for the youth of the day to aspire towards, by demonstrating that right intent and hard work pays.

If Jamie's LDs were not consulted, you would not be aware that his SD LD Rulers were being constantly triggered therefore, activated, by his twenties' DD. This oversight would detract from the significance and meaning of Jamie's **DD's SD2s** as well as the strength of his **DR20**. Subsequently, their emphasis could neither be properly weighed nor measured; nor could they be properly interpreted and timed without the LD's additional information. The same may be said for his PYDs, UYDs, PMDs, numerology Tarot Spreads and so on.

Awareness of these links makes both **DR20** and its **root 2** high profile numbers. By triggering Jamie's **LDR20/2** and **LCR11/2**, this was the right time to develop and practice negotiating, contractual, diplomatic, and decision-making skills. It was also the right time to develop his caring nature. We saw this when he took up the challenge of lobbying (political aspect of **2 or 29**) for healthier school lunches. He used the fame aspect of the decade's paired **22** (public notoriety) to contribute to the greater good (**97**). He used **11** for his educational programmes, **9** for passion, sharing and mentoring and **22** for organising the provision for meaningful employment for down-and-out young people. Then Jamie used **DR and LDR 2** for the perfect opportunity to exercise his relationship/interactive skills. They were not only exercised in the workplace; they were also exercised in his role as a loving husband and father and with those close to him.

However, due to their position in the DD, **Challenge 7** and **Goal 11** provided significant clues that warned Jamie that he would be encountering situations that have potentially, powerful Karmic implications. Observing this, it would pay him to be forthright in his undertakings otherwise he would accrue or attract bad Karma even though his intentions may be honourable at the beginning. The fact that **7** is a **Challenge** provides the Karmic clue. Because a **7** aspect is to possess the potential to *influence others* it tests Jamie's intent re his transparency and credibility. To note how **7's** influential aspect was so prominent in Jamie's plans throughout those ten years, it would be a great oversight if this and the importance of the karmic implications were missed by the interpreter, especially if this were an aspirant's numbers. **Goal 11** reinforces this as it has Karmic implications no matter where it is placed. Soulwise, the decade's results would be weighed against success and failure i.e., accrued good and bad works, attitudes, behaviours, efforts and activities and of course, integrity.

Decade Determinants

All DDs explain the mystifying themes manifesting in the background of our lives during their subtle reign. Being the custodian of many significant clues or signs as well as being new to numerology, the following points summarise their salient features.

DDs Bring to Light

- the unfolding nature of our numbers in accordance with our Soul's Purpose
- progressive life-stages within the Soul's grand plan for our evolution
- progressions of the LPNF
- major keys behind the unfoldment and development of innate potential
- major keys that seed new ideas, impulses, stimuli and urges to grow
- major keys that open up new situations, encounters and events
- major keys that open up new areas in which to develop and test new qualities, skills and talents
- major keys that open up new areas of experience, learning and growth
- major keys that further individual gifts, prospects, options and challenges
- major keys that further character development
- major keys that provide the opportunity to master specific number or Key's aspects
- major keys that provide the opportunity for advancement, consolidation, modification or closure
- times when fame and fortune or the reverse are likely
- opportune or *right* timing

DDs' Special Considerations

- the time of life they address
- their long-term, enduring nature, which allows a broader range of their aspects to be utilised and manifested
- their unique directions
- concordance with major personal numbers and other branches of numerology/astrology

As we become adept at using our DDs for self-revelatory, self-directional purposes, they assist us in achieving much of our decade's potential on Personality and Soul levels.

Chapter 14:
Whole Number Decade Diamonds

DD = Decade Diamond	**CA** = Current Age	**LD** = Life Diamond
DG = Decade Goal	**P** = Personal	**YD** = Yearly Diamond
DC = Decade Challenge	**U** = Universal	**LDR** = Life Diamond Ruler
DR = Decade Ruler	**Y** = Yearly	**LPN** = Life Path Number
N = Number	**W** = Whole	**LPNF** = Life Path Number Family

WHOLE NUMBER DECADE DIAMONDS (WN DDs)

In this chapter, the study of Whole Number DDs (WN DDs) is undertaken to broaden the scope of a SD DD's findings. You will find that a WN DDs' range of personalised numbers and Keys accurately describe life experiences that other numbers cannot account for; this makes them very worthwhile adjuncts to other branches of numerology.

In addition, it is essential to grasp that since *all* DDs' numbers occupy the background of our lives, their trends cannot be triggered *unless and until* they are known for what they represent. Only then can their signs be *consciously* integrated with other numerological indications.

Begin to find a decade's signs by calculating a Life Path Number *family* (LPNF). The second number on all WN DD's baselines is taken from one of its *whole* numbers. As your LPNF is unique to you, its WNs *individualise* your DDs. Hence, generalities from SDs bow to precious details obtained from WN DDs as they produce a truer, more precise description of a decade's purpose.

CASE STUDY: JAMIE OLIVER

Numbers to use from **JAMIE OLIVER'S LPNF** are **9, 18, 36, 54 and 126**. (Appendix 3 lists steps for LPNFs)

All of Jamie's LPNs define specific facets of his Life Purpose. Therefore, each LPN provides him with a particular field of learning via experience that is vital to enable him to accomplish this lifetime's requirements. The following demonstrates how Jamie utilises his LPNs.

Jamie uses **LPN9's** empathy, sensitivity, warmth and its service orientation for others. When coupled to **LPN54**, his *practical* wisdom that develops from logic and reason tempers **LPN9's** emotional, extremist, perfectionist qualities. This practical wisdom is seen and heard coming through his **"26"**— extrapolated from **LPN126**—when he feels he has something important to convey. Then **"12"**, also taken from **126**, is seen in the unique ways that Jamie approaches everything and the way he expresses himself. **"21"** (**12's reverse**) signifies Jamie striving to better himself (bettering oneself is also a powerful aspect of **LPN18**), make his world and the world at large better and thereby make his mark (**21**) on it in some way. How he goes about it will be unique as that is a **12** trait. Note how these aspects align with and expand on what can be read into Jamie's **LPN9**.

Not to be missed, **LPN36** adds the potential for success from earnest endeavour. It also has the potential for being able to shoulder large responsibilities. However, it has a warning aspect and that is that its bearer is likely to overreach and take on more than they can handle.

The "antidote" to **36** is to learn to delegate. This aspect of **36** is at work when we observe how Jamie trains his staff to ultimately take charge of their areas of responsibility.

Reverse **63** from **36** can suggest a high degree of nervous energy but also has a beautiful healing, comforting, caring side to it; it is capable of impulsive or random acts of kindness and generosity and it can drive its bearer to try to minister too much to others to the point of self-neglect….but Jamie has **18**, the number of self-initiated change. It helps him become aware of the error in his ways when he goes to extremes.

Each LPN targets specific fields in Jamie's life to encounter and explore. When used to calculate his sets of DDs, Jamie can depend on each set to provide him with ongoing, updated signs while in force that alert him to what his unique Paths in life are. His numbers show him his unique fields of learning for those points in time. Although specific in nature, they provide him with *general* directions to follow because their cycles are so long. Their purpose is to be used by him to uncover and stay in touch with his unfolding destiny.

Part 3 Personal Decades Chapter 14 Whole Number Decade Diamonds

Steps for calculating WN DDs are found in the box below.

> **STEPS for CALCULATING a SET of SD and WN DDs**
> 1. **SD DD's baseline:** CA 10's digit—space—SD LPN.
> 2. **WN DD's baselines:** CA 10s' digit—space—WN LPN. Work from second lowest to highest LPN, until all WN LPNs are used.
> 3. Calculate SD and WN **GOALS** (DGs) and **CHALLENGES** (DCs). Do not reduce.
> 4. **RULERS:** ADD all four numbers—write unreduced Rulers in centre of each DD.
> 5. **HIDDEN NUMBERS:** Obtained from WN reductions and their reversals.

Jamie Oliver's complete set of personalised DDs are below. Note that his first DD shows a combination interim and SD DD. Also, note that the Rulers for Jamie's interim DD are **29/2** and the Rulers for his SD DD are **20/2**. This **29** naturally intensifies the paired **29** from the SD DD's baseline thereby giving it more power. It also helps to understand why enterprise was so uppermost during the decade. This type of emphasis is what you are seeking when additional calculations are put up. Repetitive numbers, "new" numbers, or ones that change the "strength" of another number are others to look for. To get such important details is one reason why supplementary calculations are important as they add clarity and verification to your pool of data.

JAMIE OLIVER'S SET of "TWENTIES" SD and WN DDs

```
    11/2           20            38            56           128
2   20    9    2   56   18   2  110  36   2  164   9   2  380 126
    7             16            34            52           124
```

Insights from Jamie's Twenties' DGs

Jamie's set of **DGs** for his twenties is: **2, 11, 20, 38, 56** and **128**. Take special note of how the 10's digit (**2**) intensifies Jamie's **DG2s** *and* **DR2s**. This intensification factor is a *natural* occurrence because he has a LPN9. This phenomenon occurs for all people who have **LPN9s**. Some are able to achieve great things or have memorable experiences whilst others are not; it all depends on their maturation levels, states of readiness, skills and destiny.

Jamie's **SDs** and **11** and **20** were dealt with in the previous chapter. However, the appearance of *interim* **WN DG11** in the first ◇ was very significant because Jamie was so keen on educating others about cultivating good eating habits; teaching and education are two of **11s** major aspects.

Decade Diamonds & Month, Day, Hour and Minute Diamonds

WN DG38's creative, enterprising aspects were seen at work when Jamie channelled his business acumen and culinary expertise (**8**) through imaginative cooking (**3**). He activated the media aspects of **38** via his TV shows, advertising and self-promotion. **38's** wealth aspect manifested as he rapidly grew in stature and rich from his labours. The **"Queen" aspect of 38** was also evident, as Jamie grew in status. This was apparent when his industry honoured Jamie with a prestigious award. It was also evident when he met the Queen of England when she honoured him with an MBE in June **2003**; he also served a meal to England's then Prime Minister (Tony Blair) and distinguished guests. The latter shows how a Queen (or King) Key has the potential to connect to royalty or prominent figures in real life.

WN DG56 undoubtedly tested Jamie's patience when his plans went awry at times.

Split and pair **WN DG128** to create **12** and **28**. **12** depicted Jamie's life reverse during the second year of the decade when he was thrust from private life into the public eye. It also represented the sacrifices he made to achieve his dreams. **28** indicated business dealings, power struggles (**8** part of **28**) and lucrative contracts. **28** also provided valuable experiences in the art of negotiation and diplomacy (**2** part of **28**).

On a personal note, the first thing to do when working with **DGs** is to remind yourself that you are working with powerful, background numbers that indicate specific life directions covering a long period of time. They provide definitive guidelines. From them you are able to recognise specific areas of potential, points of attainment and likely pitfalls in relation to what you envisage as being in sync with your plans for the future. If you have made projections in accordance with what you anticipate and believe you can attain by harnessing the promise in your numbers, and things do not turn out in the way that you hoped, you will have learnt a lot! The knowledge gained this way can be put to better use for decades that follow. It all helps to learn to get better and better at reading your aspirations into your numbers and Key's positive and negative possibilities. Correct projections enhance your ability to create successful outcomes as long as you remain practical, flexible and resourceful and true to your capabilities.

Insights from Jamie's Twenties' DCs

All challenges represent areas in life where corrective measures are central to fixing whatever impairs aspirations and growth. They also pinpoint areas and things in one's nature and life that cease to be useful or are detrimental to one's well-being. Jamie's set of DCs indicate this. They signify this decade's "proving ground" where life's problems are solved. They help him to know what is likely to challenge him personally as well as what could challenge his ability to achieve his goals. Jamie's DCs for his twenties are: **7, 16, 34, 52** and **124**. It is common for changes to occur in DC families when WNs are introduced but Jamie's **DC family of 7s** remained true.

Jamie's DCs' combined traits and trends provided clues to what might impede his aspirations. **7** pointed to tests in the areas of: what Jamie said; his dealings with the public; his ability to cope with the unknown and unusual; his ability to remain on track; his ability to protect his integrity, himself and his family and finally, his ability to gain Personality control. **16** warned to remain honest, to deal with the unexpected and to balance public and private life. **34** warned of making on the spot decisions; acting too quickly and forcefully; getting things done under pressure and the need for right timing. **34's** test was to avoid premature decisions and actions. **52** signified the potential to shoulder responsibilities; hone perceptive powers and shrewdness in affairs. Split and paired **DC124** creates <u>**12**</u> and <u>**24**</u>. **12** warned of stalemates and unexpected reversals. **24** warned of possible stress or pressure when travelling; to exert his influence with care; that executive and administrative pressures were likely and to meet his wife and family's needs (Queen number) despite such pressures.

Insights from Jamie's Twenties' DRs

Jamie's set of DRs for his twenties are: **11, 20, 56, 110, 164** and **380**. All of Jamie's DRs belong to the **"2 family"**. Each ruler represents the sum total of all numbers derived from its tiny diamond. Apply the advanced techniques for Jamie's rulers given for **2, 11** and **20** in the previous chapter. They are not repeated here.

DR56 guaranteed impasses and things not always going to plan or plans being thwarted and things having to be repeated. But **56** also provided Jamie with the opportunity to develop sound powers of reflection, greater sensitivity and intuition. Note how these aspects mirror similar **12** themes.

DR110 split and paired creates <u>**11**</u> and <u>**10**</u>. **11** is intensified. Being intensified further explains Jamie's focus on entrepreneurial and educational themes. **10** indicated dealing with many ups and downs and forced change. It also signified gain as in becoming wealthy. Fascinatingly, the poverty aspect of **10** was projected into his *"Fifteen"* programmes when he elected to help disadvantaged individuals find work and restore their sense of purpose.

DR164 creates daunting <u>**16**</u> and <u>**64**</u>. **16** demands complete honesty in all dealings and predicts pleasant repercussions if adhered to or unpleasant repercussions if strayed from (instant Karma, sometimes!). **64** warned of "self-ruin" if double standards are lived by. This manifested as death threats, smear campaigns and family upheavals that resulted when Jamie promoted food chains and products which the public knew he would neither purchase nor use. But **64** depicts a "new dawning" and can represent the "butterfly syndrome"; we saw Jamie emerge as a super star soon after he began this new career path.

Decade Diamonds & Month, Day, Hour and Minute Diamonds

38 and **80** from **DR 380** indicated wanting the best in every way. It also represented the media (**38**) showcasing his skills. The mastery aspect of **80** indicated the potential for "polishing" his trade and becoming recognised for his craftsmanship. Consequently, Jamie became extremely wealthy via his skills. Was the wealth aspect of **38** amplified by the zero in **380**? Did that, plus the wealthy **King of Pentacles (WNDG56 reversed⇨65) + The Wheel of Fortune + the Queen of Cups**, contribute, as a group, to depict his meteoric rise to fame and subsequent wealth?

FAMOUS PEOPLE'S PROMINENT DECADES

The following brief, DD examples depict famous and infamous men and one woman, in their prime. They include Winston Churchill, Adolf Hitler, Osama Bin Laden, Saddam Hussein, Alan Bond and Susan Boyle. Beginning with Britain's Prime Minister during his WW2 years, how many similarities between their DDs can you find?

SIR WINSTON CHURCHILL (British Prime Minister 1940–1945)
Birth Date: 30–11–1874 = LPNF: 133, 124, 61, 52, 43, 25, 16, 7

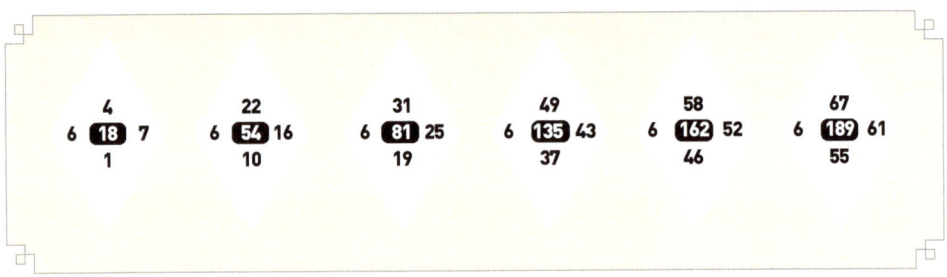

WINSTON CHURCHILL was in his sixties during his first term as Britain's Prime Minister. **Ten's 6** promised added responsibilities and discerning powers; 7, the ability to influence to create order from chaos and to orate; **4**, powers of command and **1** literally, powers of the Magician! **DR18**, however, warned of enemies, plots and schemes, deception and tragedy. Paired **64** warned of betrayals, ruin, death, failure, disaster and destruction; it reinforced **18**. But **64** also saw Churchill "emerge" as an inspirational leader; the "butterfly effect" again. Paired **74** reinforced **SD4**. Winston expressed **74** and **7** as being the people's protector. Paired **47** indicated the choices he had to make from many; paired **17** his hope for victory (**7**), rise to fame and ability to solve serious matters; paired **16** being under attack and paired **61** his retaliation against the Germans via tactical measures.

Churchill's WN DDs for his sixties also show his struggle (**DG31**); humanitarianism (**DG49**); ability to go within to find answers and to deal with death and destruction (**DG58**); instil an aura of solidarity (**DG67**); face his enemies as a leader (**DC19**) and be a powerful force for good (**DC55**).

He drew on **35**'s determination (extracted from **DR135**), to use its power to never give in to what appeared to be an indefensible position. **26**, taken from the **62** in **DR162** indicated his oratory capabilities (**26** and **LPN7**) besides his potential to find his way out of what held him and his country "trapped" (**62**). But he was victorious in the end (**7**). **DR54** reflected his capacity to deliver practical wisdom when most needed. **89/98** drawn from **DR189** indicated the "super powers" he was able to summon from within to carry out the enormous task set before him. Note the powerful nature of the numbers that comprise **DR189**'s DD. They stood for autocratic, omnipotent, unstoppable, tactical qualities.

ADOLF HITLER:
German Chancellor 1933–1945; Dictator 1934–1945

Birth Date: 20–4–1889 = LPNF: 131, 122, 50, 41, 32, 23, 14, 5

	1			19			37			55			136	
5	**11**	5	5	**47**	14	5	**101**	32	5	**155**	50	5	**398**	131
	0			9			27			45			126	

When he began World War 2 at **50**, **ADOLF HITLER** entered a powerful **DG10/1** and **DC0** combination. He had three very significant numerological coincidences occurring then: the first, his turning **50** matched his **LPN50**. The second, that when he turned **50**, his own special decade began. The third outstanding coincidence was that Hitler also entered a **PY10/1**, that year. These converging personal indicators moved him onto his LD's crowning **LG30** and **LC22**—two numbers that can reach their full potential for good or evil in the hands of a national leader—the consequences of which are well documented.

Compare Hitler's numbers with Churchill's. Both SD DDs are ominous—Hitler's the more so, as he had the force for good or evil in paired **55** (two more appear in his WN DDs thereby intensifying them thus orienting them towards being negatively expressed). Paired **50s** (**50** also appears as his **WN LPN**) depicted the havoc he wreaked, destroying social mores and countless families. Paired **51s** saw him as the "cruel king" and paired **15s** as the devil incarnate as well as his addictions to power and drugs. He literally inflicted hell on others due to his depraved mind and warped, social views (**DR11** and the **5s**). **15, 51** and **55** are present in **DR155**. This DR's composition, its components plus the SD DD's potential for negative expression are ominous. They gave out a strong warning.

Another point of interest in Hitler's numbers is to note that his **DRs** belong to the **2 family**; he used them for war, not peace. Hitler's DRs are Churchill's DCs. Did this mean that Winston's were more powerful because they were holding challenge positions? (This question stems from a challenge's apparent added power when exerted to transform its negative potential i.e., to strive for peace rather than war; it was challenging Churchill to achieve that.) Now see how Hitler's DC's and Churchill's DRs belong to the **9 family**. Did Hitler's **DC9s** forecast his end and Winston's **DR9s**, reaching the pinnacle of his career—an end to the war and restoration of peace?

Adolf Hitler, along with all others engaged in forcing their narrow beliefs of what God's Truth is onto others, epitomise Voltaire's wise words—"*He who believes in absurdities, commits atrocities.*"

And this could well be applied to the next despot, as well.

OSAMA BIN LADEN
(Founder of Al-Qaeda terrorist organization infamous for "September 11" attack on the U.S.)

Birth Date: 30–7–1957 = LPNF: 113, 104, 95, 59, 50, 41, 14, 5

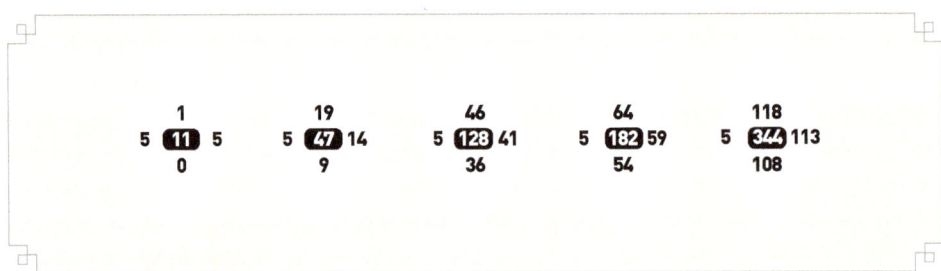

OSAMA BIN LADEN has the same root **LPN5** as Hitler. This gives them identical 9-year cycles and PYDs for each year. But, Bin Laden's personalised LPNF differs from that of Hitler, which is why their WN DDs are found to differ. Further, Bin Laden's **LPN** is **59**, not **50** as in Hitler's case; hence, Osama Bin Laden's **LPN59** may be even more formidable than Hitler's was? When negative, **59** depicts ruthless aggression, scorn, victimisation, revenge and evil-speaking.

What concerns me is that Bin Laden has entered the same period as Hitler's when he spiralled in power. Having now reached his fifties, Bin Laden has triggered his *personal decade*, which is ruled by a powerful **11/2**—the same decade and PYDs as those of Hitler when he began WW2. It is interesting to note that after years in hiding, Bin Laden unexpectedly made a public appearance on TV issuing new threats just before 11SEP07. His new SDLD

Part 3 Personal Decades Chapter 14 Whole Number Decade Diamonds

fourth cycle's ruler is **16**; its matching WNLD cycle's Ruler is **73**. These are powerful numbers. There is no sign of weakness in Bin Laden's numbers unless unforeseen factors such as betrayal or insubordination and/or poor health undermine him. Perhaps his weakness lies in his ego? his rage (**14 from 59**)? his reluctance to heed advice? or his proneness to betrayal (**64**)?

It is worthwhile setting up the PYD sequence for these two despots in their rise to power. Start Bin Laden's from 44, his age at the time he orchestrated the September 11, 2001 attack on America's World Trade Centre (Twin Towers); which led to wars in Afghanistan and Iraq. (Their PYDs are identical so only one set needs be calculated but their UYDs will differ due to changes in year numbers.) Then set up Bin Laden's 50s decade as this is the decade he has now reached. When you compare Bin Laden's numbers against those of Hitler, you will have a better understanding of his powers for his fifties decade.

SADDAM HUSSEIN (Iraqi political leader; became president: 1979)

Birth Date: 28–4–1937 = LPNF: 88, 79, 70, 52, 43, 34, 16, 7

Saddam Hussein led Iraq to war with Iran 1980–90; annexed Kuwait International War Crimes Tribunal leading to Gulf War of 1991); Guilty of crimes against humanity and executed: 30–12–2006 = 50/5

```
            4              22             40             58             94
    6  18  7       6  54  16      6  108  34     6  162  52     6  270  88
            1              10             28             46             82
```

Compare the DD similarities between Hussein and Churchill. His personal numbers follow, providing an excellent example on which to practise your skills.

- **LPNF: 88**, 79, 70, 52, 43, 34, 16, 7
- **PYNF 2006: 58**, 40, 22, 13, 4 (□ 18/9; ✿ 23; ✱ 72 from 36+36)
- **PMNF DEC: 70**, 52, 34, 25, 16, 7 (□ 19/10/1; ✿ 23; ✱ 66 from 33+33)
- **PDNF30th: 100**, 82, 64, 55, 46, 37, 10, 1(□ 30/3; ✿ 39; ✱ 65 from 33+32)
- **SD DDR = 18/9; SD DG/C = 13/4 over 1**

Time-line: After becoming president (17–7–1979); Hussein used chemical weapons (17–3–1988) against the Kurds killing in excess of 5000 people; Iraq invaded Kuwait 3–8–1990; the Gulf War began 17–1–1991; Kuwait liberated by international forces 28–2–2001; Saddam's sons Uday and Qusay executed 23–7–2003; Saddam captured 14–12–2003 and executed by hanging 30–12–2006.

Here are the DDs of another man in his prime who ran a different kind of international warfare—that of competitive sport—**ALAN BOND**. This case study depicts the time when Bond won the prized America's Cup yacht race.

ALAN BOND: Entrepreneurial Businessman

- Birth Date: 22–4–1938 = **LPNF: 83, 74, 65, 47, 38, 29, 11, 2**
- Event—America's Cup Won: 26–9–1983 = **UDNF: 137, 128, 119, 56, 38, 20, 11, 2**

- **PYNF 1983: 128, 119, 47, 38, 29, 11, 2** (□20/2; ✡29; ✱55 from +25; ✕30)
- **PMNF SEP: 137, 128, 56, 47, 38, 20, 11, 2** (□13/4; ✡15; ✱37 from +20; ✕17)
- **PDNF 26th: 163, 154, 82, 73, 64, 46, 37, 28, 10, 1** (□10/1; ✡18/9; ✱33 from +21; ✕12)

Note that Bond's LPNF, PYNF, PMNF and UDNF belong to the "2 family". Also note the prevalence of 11s in his ◇s on the next page.

	6		15		33		51		87	
4	**15**	2	4	**37**	11	4	**91**	29	4	**145**	47	4	**253**	83
	3		7		25		43		79	

BOND'S DGs

When 45, Alan Bond's **DG's root 6s** above and PDD on the next page depicted striving to achieve something dear to his heart. **DG15** depicted his powerful materialistic urge to acquire a famous trophy. **DG33** was an excellent number to have in order to achieve this aim. It signified his attempts to overcome his adversaries or any obstacles he perceived as blocking his path. **DG51** had the potential in it to be "King" and gain the number **#1** position. **DG87** revealed his strength and cunning to use whatever means to secure his prize.

BOND'S DRs

It is important to note that Bond's DRs changed number families as soon as his WNs were utilised. **SD DR root 6** signified that this was a perfect time to hone his discerning faculties. The **WN DRs root 1s** indicated that this was a perfect opportunity to develop certain aspects of his individuality and leadership capabilities. Between them, their powers of discrimination (**6**) and focus (**1**) fortified each other. Bond used their potential to concentrate, direct and strive for the objective he had set himself. **DR37** signified his potential to develop matters to do with money, wealth, position and the media. **DR91** contains the potential for great achievements and mass appeal. **DR145** split to release **14** indicated furthering his ability to command a large corporation's operation and integrate everything. Its **41** signified the opportunity to harvest riches. However **45** warned to be on the lookout for times of disappointments and **54**; good and bad news. **54** also signalled that the gift of practical wisdom could be cultivated. Two powerful knights, a very savvy queen and an obstinate, never-give-in-**35** are contained in **DR253**; they fuelled his drives.

Bond's personal number families and diamonds exemplify an outstanding array of numbers that perfectly reflected his options and possibilities at that auspicious time. To appreciate fully how his numbers indicated this event, it is suggested that you include those calculations not provided in the basic layout that follows. Bond's birthdate is **22-4-1938**.

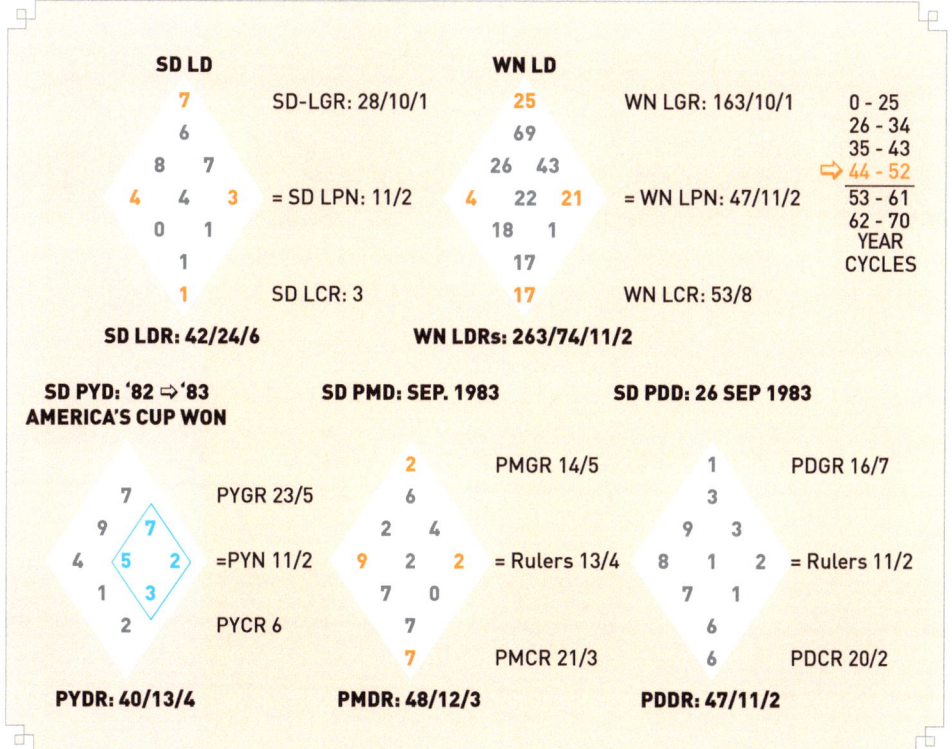

Decade Diamonds & Month, Day, Hour and Minute Diamonds

The single most outstanding feature for this momentous day was that Bond won the prestigious America's Cup when his **LPNF, PYNF, PMNF *and* UDNF essentially matched each other**. We saw this synchronicity occur with "Tiger" Woods but not to this extent. Such exceptional examples validate the importance of transiting numbers triggering major numbers to forecast very special times in one's life.

Bond had a **SD PYG9** and two **SD PYG7s** in that year's PYD. They indicated BIG ideas (**9**), being "hungry for a victory" and having the people on his side (**7**). When paired, they created two **79s** which linked to Bond's highest **DC79** in his decade set, on Page 156. They also linked to the paired **79s** in his **PMD and PDDs**. Being the number of the people's champion and intensified, these **79s** likely indicated his huge success during that time. Note the presence of paired **32** in the challenge sector of the **first DD** and other ◇s on the previous two pages. Its Key is the **6 of Wands** and its name is "success"! This Key when combined with **79**, makes it easy to visualise Bond riding high (**Key32**) and being revered as a hero (**79**) by all and sundry (**PYG7s**).

Years later, Bond tarnished his reputation when he fell into disrepute for embezzling vast sums of corporate monies and for tax evasion. His business enterprise collapsed around 1990 when the rogue within was revealed. He was imprisoned in 1997 and released in 2000. His DDs below show his sudden fall from Grace. (Bond's LD case study is in *Life Diamonds'* Chapter 12.)

	7			16			34			52			88	
5	**17**	2	5	**38**	11	5	**92**	29	5	**146**	47	5	**254**	83
	3			6			24			42			78	

SUSAN BOYLE'S SPECIAL DECADE

Birth Date: 1–4–1961 = LPNF: 85, 76, 67, 22, 13, 4

```
    8            17           26           71           80           89
4  (16)  4   4  (43) 13   4  (70) 22   4 (205) 67   4 (232) 76   4 (259) 85
    0             9           18           63           72           81
```

This happens to be Susan Boyle's "special" decade because the **4 of her forties** matches her **LPNF of 4s**. As already noted this usually denotes an auspicious decade for whatever reason. It was so in her case. It was during her 48th year that she achieved her childhood dream of becoming a famous singer. Note her **17/71** Goals. They picked up the **17s** in her LDs. **G71** signified the judges adjudicating her craft. Their judgement was quickly supported by the public and she gained an immediate (**Ruler34**) reputation (**71**). **G8, G80, G89 and C72** indicated her potential to become wealthy. They excited that potential in her **LPN67⇨Knight of Pentacles**. **C63** aspect of nervousness and little or disturbed sleep was evident when Boyle suffered from their effects due to her whirlwind rise to fame. **Ruler 34 from 43** signified its suddenness. **43** depicted an opportunity for meeting new people, celebrations and making new friends and acquaintances. **Ruler 70** played a significant role. It depicted the unusual way in which she became an instant star and how the unaccustomed stress rendered her "unpredictable", hence, "unreliable" due to sleep deprivation, yet she remained resolute. Being able to remain resolute while in such an intense state of flux is a welcome **70** trait when one is "juggling" many things at once. **G26** is probably the most telling as it indicated Boyle being brave enough (**G8 and 80**) to test her singing ability and become a "star" (**17**).

| SINGING | JUDGES | SUDDEN FAME | THE STAR | SLEEP/ NERVES | FLUX | CELEBRATIONS | RICHES |

This is Susan's story in pictures. It is good to present a cameo that ends on a happy note!

CHAPTER 15: MAKE YOUR DECADES WORK FOR YOU

DD = Decade Diamond	**DG/C** = Decade Goal/Challenge	**YD** = Yearly Diamond
DG = Decade Goal	**CA** = Current Age	**SD** = Single Digit
DC = Decade Challenge	**LD** = Life Diamond	**WN** = Whole Number
DR = Decade Ruler	**P** = Personal	**U** = Universal

GETTING THE MOST FROM DECADES

Past **PYDs** and **DDs** hold the keys to the present and future (UYDs do, too). One way to capitalise on what has occurred in the past is to use it as a guide for present and future directions. This is what this chapter is about. We get down to the nuts and bolts and roll up our sleeves to learn how to get the most from past decade and yearly indications; it may pay to set aside a special journal for this work.

Because Decade Diamonds have long cycles, you may wish to allot ten or twenty pages to the present decade. That would allow space for note-keeping as the decade unfolds via its PYD year by year. Enthusiasts may allow extra space to include UYDs and other diamonds for special times.

To begin this journey into self-direction, calculate three decade sequences of PYDs with their DDs. Arrange them in neat rows with one dual row representing the past, one the present and one the future. Place the sequence of DDs above their PYDs so that each is easy to distinguish and work with.

The rows of PYDs and their accompanying DDs that precede your current decade epitomise your past. What is grasped from the numbers idiosyncrasies, repetitions, patterns and the ways they were used back then, establish the platform from which present and future projections are arrived at. No doubt, a good memory and a good grasp of numbers and Keys' meanings are great assets for this work.

When your work is ready, did you find:

- which PYDs or DDs link to major personal numbers or to their LDs or the Numeroscope (Book 6)?
- which PYDs or DDs have outstanding features?
- your special decade (when the tens number and the LPN are the same)?
- the PYDs or DDs that contain zeros? Anticipate greater benefits or demands for those times.
- emphases/repetition in unit 0/unit 9 years? Their aspects will be intensified and they signify decade beginnings (0) and decade endings (9).
- two PYDs in a decade sequence distinguish your Personal 9 and Personal 1 years? Find them. Personal 9 years signify *ending* a 9-year cycle in your LD. Personal 1 years signify *beginning* a 9-year cycle in your LD. For these reasons these two years are always significant.
- the PYD or DD that indicates the best time for starting, consolidating or finalising matters?
- that a particular PYD or DD seems to contain a warning and requires other calculations to clarify it?
- continuing themes from one year to the next among PYDs or DDs?

When interpreting the trends from your sets of decades, do your best to match your interpretations to your aspirations, aims, circumstances and any possibilities that you perceive you have a good chance of manifesting during the current decade. Create several possible scenarios and jot them down. Use the Key's images to increase your levels of understanding of your options and scope. Aim to reach the highest potential they imply that you recognise you have the ability within to cultivate and nurture. Knowing each number and Tarot Key's positive and negative attributes provides abundant diagnostic material. Knowledge of astrology and the Qabalah enriches what you are able to get from them. Part 4 uses them to decode *lifetime* TAROT SPREADS. They teach how to extract in-depth insights from your numbers and Keys.

Review your decades and other long-term cycles periodically to revise your prospects. Know that you have ample time to make adjustments, modifications, revisions and additions to your projections.

When a PYDs and DDs' numbers link to major personal numbers such as your LPN, Destiny Number (DN = addition of all names at birth) or HPN (your Higher Purpose Number is the total of your LPN and Destiny Number), they usually predict your best or most challenging decades or an admixture of both. For most, the first and possibly the second decade is the exception when you may have been too young to utilise their potential, yet these decades have been known to produce child prodigies: a point to bear in mind.

Develop your own style of recognising your numbers and Keys' signs. Do not be daunted by such intimidating numbers as **16, 22, 40, 57, 63 and 64 and 80, 87, 88 or 89** when they arise. Rather, view them as warnings or proving grounds. Then set out to overcome pessimistic indications by creating and then implementing "possimistic" ones; find, bring out, cultivate and nurture their best aspects in you.

A DECADE'S PATTERN and ORDER

After completing your decade sequences observe how each successive **DD's DG, DC and DR** progress up or down according to their regulated pattern and order. This sequential, orderly forward/backward-moving pattern demonstrates how we are given many opportunities to experience every number in the 0 to 9 range whose starting-points are *governed by the LPN at birth*.

Using a **LPN6** as an example, the first **DG** is **6** providing the child with the opportunity to become acquainted with its attributes. For the second decade, **DG7** replaces **DG6** and then **DG8** replaces **DG7** for the third decade and so on. Each DG's tendencies are given ample time to be fully imprinted and then cultivated and nurtured before ascending to a higher **DG** for the next decade. Hence, the ladder of life is climbed rung-by-rung, step-by-step. If whole numbers are retained upon and beyond reaching a **DG10**, this progression to higher numbers will continue, otherwise the **DG's** revert to single digits again.

Retaining **WN DGs** reveals greater insights. However, if utilised, always remember to include their root digits.

SD and WN DRs follow the same pattern and order as **DGs**; they also increase by one each decade.

It is fascinating to see how **DCs** follow the **DG** pattern in reverse. They sequentially decrease by one each year from birth until the zero challenge is reached. Then the **DCs** begin to increase by one from that decade onwards. Maybe the **DGs and DRs** cover new ground while the **DCs** simultaneously cover old ground in their backwards/forwards motion (a bit like a retrograde planet revisiting and revising old territory)?

DD's compositions may explain the reason behind early and late bloomers. They might also explain why some people become famous or talented much later in life; not during decades that are considered more productive at younger ages.

When you become familiar with your **DD's** pattern and order, you can grasp the spirit of progressing from what you were born in to, to gradually being introduced to new fields of experience that facilitate your evolution. This is somewhat similar to how the Progressed Sun in a horoscope allows new experiences to come into the life when it moves forward from birth through successive astrological signs. As each DD's numbers increase from decade to decade, this phenomenon parallels the horoscope's Progressed Sun. Even though a decade's length is much shorter in duration (ten years as opposed to thirty), the essential underlying principle remains the same.

This progressive advance or regress from number to number is how cyclic life-changes are ingeniously programmed into our matrix's agendas in a regulated way. Hence, this constant provision for progress, change and revision ensures multiple exposures to each number's ways of operating via frequent repetition. It is this repetitive, cyclic premise that teaches us how to recognise, know and utilise their specialised qualities and attributes. This familiarity generates our "flowering".

FIRST DECADE: DG6 with DC6

The following examples use **LPN6** progressions for their DD's basis.

Typical **LPN6** traits naturally underpin the "Work" of the first decade due to its **"multiple imprint"** on it. From this initial imprinting, we are able to grasp how all LPNs with their specialised qualities and attributes indelibly impregnate the first ten years of life. As it is in force for the first ten years, a wide range of **"6"** experiences are lived through (not mastered at this early age). By age ten, each child's LPN traits are well ingrained albeit on subconscious levels at that early stage. This LPN imprinting that occurs from birth to age ten, shows us how to appreciate not only the importance of the LPN but also how it "grounds" itself into and through the Personality during those formative years.

Major lessons that a child might learn from a **DG6** or a **DC6** run along the lines of being introduced to early aspects of: responsibilities, duties and obligations, work and service (household duties and school), love, harmony, relationships and playmates (work associates for those who experience **6** when older). Aspects of compassion, caretaking, conscientiousness, commitment and loyalty, attention to detail and daily routines, family and health regimes are others. The faculty being developed is *discrimination*.

SECOND DECADE: DG7 with DC5

Age 10 ushers in pre-teen and teen years. We see **DG6** replaced by **DG7**. This is due to **1** taking up the 10s' digit position for ten consecutive years; it replaces **0** on the DD's baseline. So, years 10 to 19 have **1** securing the baseline's first position with **LPN6** *remaining* in second position.

1+6 and **1–6** create this decade's **DG/C** pair. Hence, **DG7** and **DC5** are the numbers to see in use during this period. These **"7/5–type"** teenagers may appear to be mature beyond their years because of the more serious, perfectionist and sceptical outlook on life that a **7** is known for. It could be the platform for beginning to specialise early in a range of academic pursuits: education, science or scientific research, mathematics, music, law; or photography, creative or athletic fields.

These teenager's career paths may be clearer due to having a more mature outlook. For some, **DG7** might explain an early interest in religion, science or metaphysics. For others it might explain why they get involved in disreputable and anti-social behaviours, especially if **DC5** is unrestrained. If **DG7** or **DC5** also happen to be major personal numbers, either could signify a major decade.

THIRD DECADE: DG8 with DC4

When the **twenties** are reached, **DG8** and **DC4** rule until **age 29**, as **2** and **6** take first and second place on this DD's baseline. Predictably, **8** and **4** types of experiences are sure to be unfolded and developed via what is encountered.

DG8 might indicate an extremely enterprising decade when the person is busily engaged in building their personal empire and reputation. Finding avenues for mastering a specific skill, or specialising in a particular field would suit a **DG8**. Becoming rich and powerful might be prime motivating drives for some. This becomes more plausible when it is seen that **DC4** supports this by providing **DG8** with a firm foundation upon which to build future wealth and security. Entrepreneurial avenues could appeal. Executive positions may be aspired to. A strong work ethic could develop when **DG8 and DC4's LPN6** is maintaining its influence on them. Health, medical, death and taxes—cathartic experiences—inheritances—banks—loans—debts—insurance or retirement schemes—loss of, or new employment—building up of assets, and an early rise to leadership or executive positions—are some of this combination's possibilities. Overcoming fears and health issues are others.

Experiencing a DG8 early in life might explain why early bloomers, such as athletes and entertainers, reach their peak during their twenties. They often earn big money by mastering and capitalising on **7's** dedication and specialising traits cultivated during the previous decade. If **8** mirrors other major personal numbers, this decade will have its peaks and troughs. It can be notable for favourable and unfavourable reasons. For some it may be a particularly onerous decade fraught with difficulties, financial loss or personal loss, heartbreak, illness, brutality or fears. For others it may be used to secure their future hopes and dreams.

Auspicious or onerous decades, for whatever reason, appear to be those that link to major personal numbers or contain outstanding features. When searching for special decades, they can be bunched together eg, if a person has a **LPN 1**, **Destiny Number 2** and **Higher Purpose Number 3** (1+2; Book 3), then the second, third and fourth decades are tied by those powerful, personal numbers. Hence, this thirty-year span might be an extremely productive time. Decades that do not link directly to major personal numbers might not be as productive; consolidation or change is more likely to be their keynote.

When major personal numbers intensify DDs, one might rise and/or fall during that period. On the other hand, if DDs are strengthened by the presence of personal numbers, this could be the time to make one's mark and consolidate from there onwards. Jamie Oliver did this. What he began in his twenties, he continued building during his thirties. Utilising his **10s' digit 3's** attributes for his thirties' decade, he expanded his business empire at home and abroad. Alternatively, if a set of DD's compositions were being emphasised, this would be the time to pay attention to their signs.

The **first four years** of a decade seem to be its initiating/establishing period. When **year 5** comes along decisions seem to be the dominant theme. This is mainly due to the need for continual adjustment to keep abreast of unfolding trends that have developed from the aims set in place during **year 1**. Hence, this is the year to capitalise on what is proceeding to plan and alter whatever is not or simply change plans. In some respects, **Year 6** seems to be more pivotal than **year 5**. **Year 6** is when the modifications implemented in **year 5** are put into effect; it is a year spent adapting to **5's** adjustments. Rewards in the latter half of the decade reflect how well things were sown in the first half. The pressure appears to build from **year 6** onwards, climaxing in **year 9** when it is important to empty the decade of whatever has become toxic, outworn and obsolete.

INTERPRETATION TIPS: DECADE GOALS and RULERS

Certain features about a decade's Goals and Rulers can do with further explanation.

As they govern long periods, DDs' indications show us ways that we can best facilitate our evolution. Their purpose is to expose us continuously to new experiences, knowledge and learning that stretch us beyond our comfort zones. This stretching process can crack or shatter entrenched beliefs, habits and behaviours that hinder our evolution. These could be such things as maintaining immature behaviours, detrimental beliefs and attitudes, obstinacy and self-created conditions that are out of sync with our Soul's requirements. How slight or severe this cracking or shattering may be, depends upon the state of "readiness and openness" one has for allowing new and better ways and means to become established. Integral to this is to let go of and move beyond the old so that more refined qualities and higher standards are embodied that facilitate evolutionary progress.

Since DD Goals and Rulers increase by one each decade, they provide us with an example that our evolution is sequentially mapped out. When their simple, yet profound ◇s are read correctly, they show how to set about fulfilling that part of our destiny by using their clues to our best advantage. Hence, knowledge of the ways in which the DDs' cyclic rotations operate can be utilised to anticipate well in advance what to cultivate and nurture, *and when*. (LD cycles work in a similar manner.)

However, there are subtle differences between DD Rulers and Goals. The DG is the sum of two numbers, therefore, subordinate to the DR, which is the sum of four. Hence, Rulers are more complex. As they represent the aggregate of the entire DD, they are best described as representing the *over-all* aim or, the *ultimate goal* to be reached by the end of its period. This is the reason why Rulers receive greater emphasis over Goals.

Being complex in nature makes Rulers more difficult to interpret. When interpreting a Ruler, endeavour to understand how each of its parts (include SD, paired and hidden numbers) are channelled through its number and Key's specialised field of expression. Then, attempt to weave a tapestry of appropriate projections together that unifies them. **Depending on whether a Ruler's constituent parts are favourable or unfavourable** *defines its inclinations, emphases and in what vein it is to be interpreted.* DRs, ✳ and ☽ Rulers provide excellent practice for developing this sophisticated skill. Eg, **40** ruling a vertical cross (✚) made up from **26** and **14** tends to make **40** harsher. A woman who had this cross in her LD vented unbecoming extremist behaviours upon others instead of practising self-control, tolerance (**14**) and guarding what she said (**26**). Life reacted in kind; she frequently suffered from activating **40's** harsh aspects.

INTERPRETATION TIPS: DECADE CHALLENGES

In the main, DCs contain positive and neutral qualities as well as negative ones; all numbers do. However, the specific purpose of all Challenges is to direct our attention to our inherent faults, flaws and negative tendencies. Another is to test our mettle and forewarn us of our trials. Their negative indications contain many revelatory insights into our "Shadow side" and "burning grounds" as well as what to fix, prove or prepare for during their long reign.

To conclude Part 3, I think you will agree that DDs add a useful tool to numerology. To have several numerology tools at your disposal serves to confirm long and short term directions as well as your personal array of possibilities.

PART 4

TREASURE HUNT

CHAPTER 16:
UNCOVERING PERSONAL GEMS

YOUR *LIFETIME* TAROT CARD AND ITS SPREAD

Astrology and Qabalah are the Divine tools that we use in this chapter to uncover other aspects to ourselves that cannot be revealed by other means. To achieve this, we merge specific branches of these two sacred sciences with numerology and Tarot to find the special Tarot Key each one of us is born into. Did you know you have such a Tarot Key? Well you do; we all do. I think it is as powerful as our Sun Signs, Life Path and Destiny Numbers because it represents major directions for this lifetime as they do.

Now don't panic. This is really easy to do.

Neither maths nor a sound knowledge of Tarot or the Tree of Life are required. Nevertheless, a basic knowledge of astrology, Tarot and the Qabalah does help. Relevant instructions, diagrams, tables, keywords, pictures of Tarot Keys and several cameos of famous people take you through the steps. They not only show how to locate your special Tarot Key but how to apply its significance and meanings to yourself and your life.

No maths are required because all you need is the day and month of birth. It is that simple. They are used to access the Sun Sign and the Qabalah to find the special birth, Tarot Key.

The most important things to note about this Key are its Sun Sign, sacred element, suit, ruling planet and matching number eg, **42** for the **2 of Cups**. Other things to note are what else we can extrapolate from the Qabalah to enrich and extend its meanings. How to do this is explained as we go along; especially since this discovery may be new to many.

When you familiarise yourself with your birth Tarot Key's ins and outs, you learn to create a *lifetime* Tarot spread from it. This spread completes the set of year, month and day Tarot spreads introduced in Part 2. The value of the birth Tarot Key and its Tarot spread cannot be fully appreciated until their significance and meanings are recognised for their contribution.

Advanced skills learned so far are used for this exercise. New skills are also introduced such as reading charts and tables as well as learning to utilise astrological decans and their Qabalistic associations. The occult streams used for this are listed below.

- **Numerology:** birth *day* and *month*; reversed and reduced compound numbers.
- **Sacred Elements:** Fire, Water, Air, Earth, (Table 1, page 181)
- **Tarot Suits:** Wands, Cups, Swords, Pentacles (Table 1)
- **Astrology:** Sun Sign, Decans and a Decan's Ruling Planet (Table 2, pages 182/3)
- **Key's esoteric name:** Eg, *Love and Union* for Key42 (Table 2)
- **Hebrew Letter names:** Eg, *ZAIN* assigned to LOVERS Key (Table 5, page 190)
- **Hebrew Letter name's objects:** Eg, *sword* or *dagger* for *ZAIN* (Table 5)
- **Tree of Life associations:** for those with this knowledge (Diagrams, page 192)

ASTROLOGICAL DECANS

DECANS are a branch of astrology. They are the **10 degree** divisions of each zodiac sign; hence their name, *decan*.

Each of the **12 signs of the zodiac** are allotted **30 degrees** which equates to **3 decans** to a sign. **Each decan has its own Minor Arcana Key and planetary ruler.** It is this Key and its ruler that we wish to know.

However, the Qabalah uses **CHALDEAN planetary rulers**, not our modern rulers. And only ***Minor Arcana* Tarot Keys** are allocated to each decan. This means *Major Arcana, Royal and Ace Keys are never used*. The natal Key contains *vital*, personal details and themes about a major portion of our Soul and Personality Work for this lifetime, which is why we attach great importance to it.

It is also important to note that the Minor Arcana Keys' placements in each decan are *not sequential*. They begin at **0 degrees, *LEO*** with the **5 of Wands Key**. (See Table 2 on pages 182/183.) This is the **"Struggle and Strife" Key**. How apt that the Key chosen by the "Ancient Ones" to begin their decans is one that equates to our struggle to spiritualise ourselves!

To find your birth Key, the astrological wheel on the next page is divided into each zodiac signs' time allotments and decans along with their corresponding Tarot Keys and planetary rulers. Table 2 on pages 182 and 183 contains the same information except that it includes each Key's esoteric names and modern Planetary Rulers; it may prove easier to follow for those not used to working with astrological wheels. It begins at 0 degrees Leo.

Decade Diamonds & Month, Day, Hour and Minute Diamonds

Steps to Locate the Tarot Key at Birth

1. Find your Sun Sign on the astrological wheel below or from Table 2, pages 182/3.
2. Find the pair of calendar dates your birthday slots into; *this is your decan*.
3. Find the decan's Minor Arcana Tarot Key; *this is your birth Key*.
4. Find the decan's planetary ruler; *this is your birth Key's planetary ruler*.

MINOR ARCANA'S DECANS, PLANETARY RULERS AND DECAN DATES

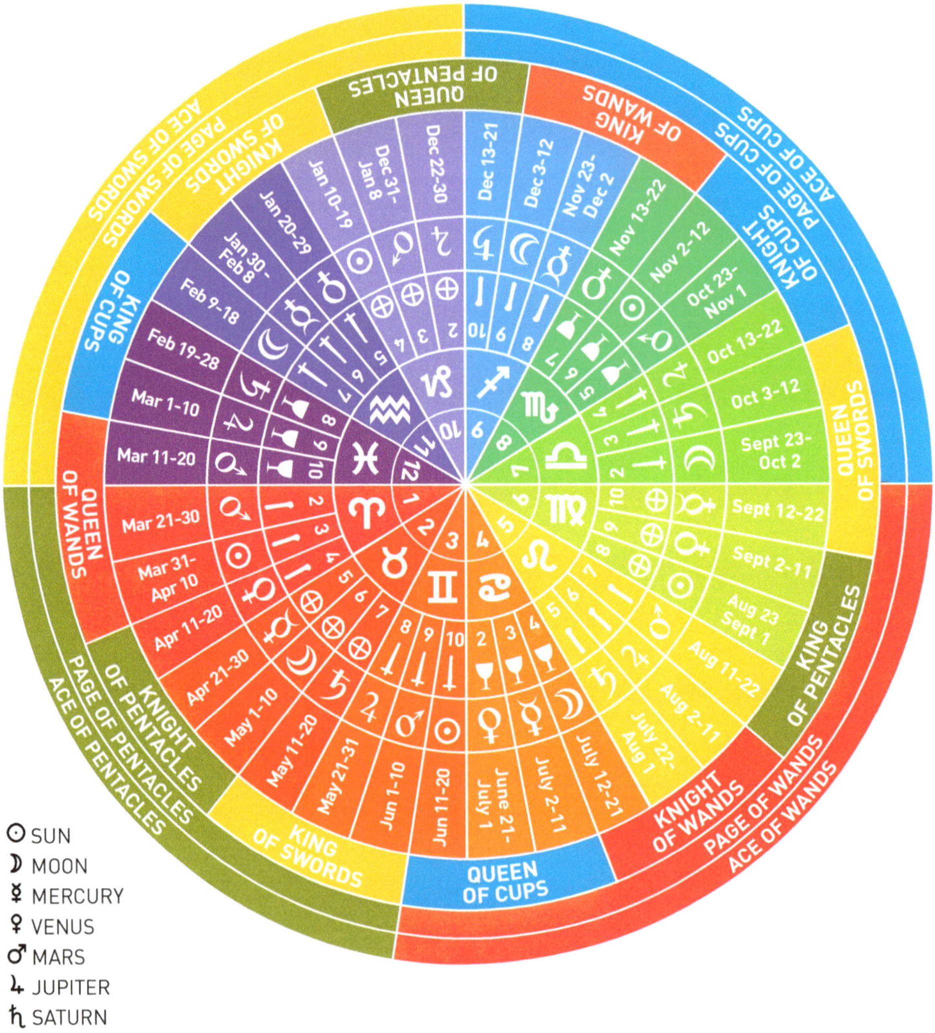

☉ SUN
☽ MOON
☿ MERCURY
♀ VENUS
♂ MARS
♃ JUPITER
♄ SATURN

From wheel centre out: 1: House Numbers **2:** Signs of the Zodiac **3:** Minor Arcana in Decans **4:** Decan planetary rulers (Chaldean) **5:** Decan dates **6:** King, Queen and Knight Keys **7:** Page Keys **8:** Ace Keys. The Zodiac Signs are in their esoteric colours. The Royal and Ace Keys are in their elements' colours.

Now that you have found your birth Key, take it out and study its picture. What does its image portray? What is the number on the face of the Key? What are its symbols? Which suit does it belong to? Which sacred element does it belong to? What is its zodiac's ruling sign? Are any colours dominant? What is its corresponding number? Find it from the **Conversion Table** on page 197.

Everything you can find out about this Key is relevant to you and this lifetime. Everything about it teaches you something about yourself. Hence, it is vital to know it and its *reverse Keys indications* extremely well.

Some birthdays fall on or near the cusp of a decan. This means that they have *two* birth Keys that provide clues to this lifetime. Sometimes, the Keys can be conflicting. Prince William's present us with an excellent example. His birthday falls on **21June1982**. It reveals the **10 of Swords** and the **2 of Cups**; two starkly different Keys. They indicate that there are two sides to him, one very astute, intense and deep and the other very soft, romantic and naive. Such stark contrasts might indicate an inner conflict until balanced.

HOW TO DETERMINE THE CUSP OF A DECAN

A cusp is the borderline between decade divisions. When a birthday falls on or very close to a cusp, it means that we integrate the influences coming from either side. How to determine a cusp is to use **two days before**, the **day of** and **two days after** the birthday to allow for an *approaching* and a *separating* orb either side of the cusp.

An orb is an expanded range of time or the "grey area" that includes predetermined **"before"**, **"of"** and **"after"** periods that surround a cusp. The two *days before* the cusp are seen as *approaching* the cusp. The *actual date* of the cusp is its zenith. The two *days after* the cusp are seen as *separating* from the cusp.

If the birthdate occurs within two days before the cusp, use that decan's Key and the Key for the *next* decan. If the birthdate occurs *on the actual day* of the cusp, the decan for that Key and the *one after* it are used. If the birthdate falls within two days after the cusp the decan *before* and *that particular decan* are used. Both Keys and their planets depict the nature and circumstances of "cusp people". Some cameos that follow, exemplify such birthdays.

Once the birth Key (or Keys) is found, links are traced to its auxiliary numbers i.e., reversed and hidden numbers and their Keys. We use them to develop a "Tarot Key family", as with a number family. This "family" of Keys is laid out to create a most revealing lifetime Tarot spread that provides profound bearings for life.

For those more advanced, the Qabalah opens up self-revelatory links that release more personal "gems". See page 192 for Tree of Life diagrams.

HOW TO CREATE A *LIFETIME* TAROT SPREAD

The steps on this page show how to find Lady Diana's natal Tarot Keys; those opposite, how to create a lifetime Tarot spread from them. (Either spread opposite serves as a single Tarot spread for those who have one key only.)

Main Example:

Name: Lady Diana Spencer
Birthdate: 1 July 1961
Zodiac Sign: Cancer
Cancer Decans: First and second
Decan Rulers: Venus and Mercury
Corresponding Keys: 2 of Cups and 3 of Cups
Key's Esoteric Names: Love and Union (**Key42**) and Abundance (**Key43**)

A LIFETIME TAROT SPREAD'S INSTRUCTIONS

How to create a **Lifetime Tarot Spread** that falls on or near a cusp.

1. FIRST DECAN STEPS
a) Find the corresponding number to the **2 of Cups**; it is **42**.
b) Reverse **42** to uncover **24** and **Key24**⇨**Queen of Wands**.
c) Reduce **42/24** to root **6**⇨**The Lovers**. Reverse **6** to get **60**⇨**6 of Swords**.
d) Use **2** from the face of **Key42** to find the **High Priestess Key**.
e) Reverse **2** to uncover **20** and find **Key20**⇨**Judgement**.
f) Lay out **Keys 42, 24**; root **6, 60**; **2, 20**.

2. SECOND DECAN STEPS
a) Find the corresponding number to the **3 of Cups**; it is **43**.
b) Reverse **43** to uncover **34** and **Key34**⇨**8 of Wands**.
c) Reduce **43/34** to **7** and **70**. Take out **The Chariot** and **2 of Pentacles**.
d) *Use **2** from **Key70's** face to get the **High Priestess** and **Judgement**.
e) Use **3** from **Key43's** face to get **The Empress** and then **30**⇨**4 of Wands**.
f) Use **8** from **Key34's** face to get **Strength**.
g) Use **4** from **Key30's** face to get **The Emperor** and **Page of Cups**.
h) Lay out **Keys 43, 34; 7, 70; 2, 20; 3, 30; 8; 4, 40**.

*****Note:** Only due to lack of space, **Step "d's" Keys** do not appear in their lifetime spread on the opposite page. As luck would have it, they appear in the spread above.
This makes it possible to 'borrow' them mentally just for Lady Diana's case study. However, they *must be included* for a single spread and it is wrong to think otherwise.

Points to Remember:
  ⋄ Interpret all numbers for more insights.
  ⋄ Interpret all planets and signs that rule each Key. (Refer to Tables 3 and 4.)
  ⋄ Never lose sight of the main Key's Zodiac Sign, Suit and Sacred Element
    eg, **Cancer/Cups/Water**
  ⋄ Finally, for those with Qabalistic knowledge, trace the Keys and their numbers to the Tree of Life's Paths to obtain more information. You will be surprised at how much can be obtained from such "humble" beginnings. See page 192.

CASE STUDY: Lady Diana's Lifetime Tarot Spread

1st CANCER DECAN: KEYS, NUMBERS, PLANETS AND SIGNS

	42	24	6	60	2	20
Ruling Planets:	VENUS	NONE	MERCURY	JUPITER	MOON	PLUTO
Ruling Signs	LIBRA	FIRE	GEMINI	SAGITTARIUS	CANCER	SCORPIO

2nd CANCER DECAN: KEYS, NUMBERS, PLANETS AND SIGNS

	43	34	7	70	3	30	8	4	40
	MERCURY	MERCURY	MOON	MARS	VENUS	VENUS	SUN	MARS	NONE
	CANCER	SAGITTARIUS	CANCER	CAPRICORN	NONE	ARIES	LEO	ARIES	WATER

GENERAL INTERPRETATIONS

The lifetime Tarot spread above displays Lady Diana's birth Keys with their number, planet and zodiac sign extensions. As you can see, many clues to her lifetime's orientation can be extrapolated from her principle Keys, the **2 and 3 of Cups**. When the spread is scanned, it is like seeing her life in pictures. Certain aspects within them stand out from the rest and you hear yourself saying, "So that's why" … and, "Now I understand" … and, "Yes, she was like that" … and, "Yes, she did do that"… and, "That definitely happened" … and so on. We get so many "aha moments" from her lifetime Tarot spreads. The same occurs for everyone. Our spreads help us to understand why we are the way we are and do the things we do.

For example, when we see the **2 of Cups** wayshowing major, lifelong trends, we acknowledge straightaway that relationships, unions, love, romance, marriage and sexual expression, attitudes and preferences will present major fields of experiential learning. Even though the Key paints a rosy picture, it has its dark side. We know this because Lady Diana's marriage was far from rosy. Clues to its dark side stem from the Key's Qabalistic attributions: *Peace and War. Wisdom and Folly* are others. Moreover, Lady Diana expressed **2's** hypersensitive attributes besides nurturing unrealistic, **Cancerian** ideals and ideas about love, marriage, home and family, which brought her undone.

Decade Diamonds & Month, Day, Hour and Minute Diamonds

Because Lady Diana's birthday fell on a cusp, the **3 of Cups** emerged as another wayshower for her. I thought the **2 of Cups** was surprisingly accurate but to get the **3 of Cups** *with it* was astounding. The **3 of Cups** is about living the high life, pomp and splendour, entertainment, friendships and enjoying the company of others. It, like its companion Key, paints a rosy picture. Nonetheless, it has a dark side, too. In her own words, Lady Diana said, *"There are three people in my marriage"*. This is what one of its negative aspects represented for her; a third person interfering with her marriage.

We have only pricked the two principle Keys' surface and already we see how accurately they depicted Lady Diana's main, life experiences and circumstances. Imagine the depth and detail to be uncovered when each Key is fully analysed. This is demonstrated further on.

An example of an interpretation technique follows that integrates the numbers and keys from the second decan's Tarot spread. Although **Keys2 and 20** were omitted on page 173, their interpretations are included below.

INTEGRATED INTERPRETATIONS

Abundance is evident in **Keys43, 3 and 30**; it is actually **Key43's** esoteric name. We know that Lady Diana reflected this attribute as she lived an opulent life free of material concerns. Yet, her emotional life (water element) was changeable and chaotic. **Keys34, 7 and 70** reflected that. **Keys7, 70 and 8's** highest requirements were to learn to gain control of her basic instincts to weather those "stormy seas and sudden squalls" (**70**) that unexpectedly descended upon her from out of nowhere (**Key34**).

From all reports, it would be safe to say that Lady Diana was *unfavourably judged* (**Key20**) by her then husband, Prince Charles and the royal family. One of **Key70's** clues is to remain *balanced, stable and calm* midst adversity. Those attributes tested her relentlessly. We saw her become *unbalanced* when things became too much to bear or when she was out for revenge (**Key2's** war aspect). **Key20's** gift for making sound judgements and doing the right thing was affected by this. **Key4's** gift for *rational thinking* was also; especially when Lady Diana acted too impetuously (**Key34**).

The following uses Lady Diana's first decan to demonstrate a more in-depth analysis.

INTERPRETATION GUIDELINES

The best way to develop all that you can from lifetime Tarot Keys is to set up a format to follow until automatic skills develop. A good idea is to start with the divine tool you know best. If numerology is the one, begin with it. Then move on to the next tool you know next best, and so on. What follows is a suggested framework to use starting with numerology.

NUMEROLOGY: Set out the numbers for each Key remembering to reverse and reduce numbers to bring forth hidden information and insights. Then consult the *Life Diamonds* numbers from its 0 to 99 appendix. Consult other resources as well. List positive and negative interpretations beside each number that suit the person's nature, circumstances and aspirations.

TAROT: Convert Tarot Keys to their corresponding numbers (Page 197). Look up their interpretations in the *Life Diamonds* appendix and other resources. Make notes as above.

ASTROLOGY: Interpret astrological components using the Tables provided and personal resources. Make notes from their keywords.

- **ZODIAC SIGN:** Consult Table 4 (Pp 186 and 189). **Cancer** is the *Sun Sign* for the decan which means it underpins *all* of Lady Diana's lifetime Keys. However, we are more interested in which signs rule her major Keys. They are **LIBRA** for **Key42** and **CANCER** for **Key43** (note the double Cancer influence). So you would consult the Zodiac Table choosing relevant keywords and phrases for each sign. The esoteric keynote for all **Librans** is: *"I choose the way which leads between the two great lines of force."* It essentially means to find *balance* in one's life. **Cancerians** esoteric keynote is: *"I build a lighted house and therein dwell"*. It essentially means to *protect and build one's inner Light*. (Keynotes from A.A.Bailey's *Esoteric Astrology.*) These keynotes provide further, significant guidance.

- **SACRED ELEMENT:** Consult Table 1 (P 181). **Water** dominates as **Cancer rules this decan**. Therefore, all Keys in the spread have an *emotional component* to them regardless of their element.

- **SUIT:** Consult Table 1. As **Cups rule this decan** and Cups are ruled by **Water**, *emotions and feelings* lie at the root of all Keys regardless of their suit.

- **RULING PLANET:** Consult Table 3 (Pp 184 and 185). *Caution*: This planet/s is the one that rules the main Key/s and *may not be the same one that rules the Sun Sign*. As the **2 of Cups** and the **3 of Cups** are the two *major* Keys, their ruling planets, **Venus and Mercury**, are the main ones to consider. All other planets in the spread are considered, too, but Venus and Mercury receive more emphasis.

For example, **Venus** is the planet of love, and **Libra** rules relationships and marriage, so they reinforce that Lady Diana will receive major lessons in those areas (**Key 42**). As **Mercury** rules the mind, and **Cancer**, home and family (**Key 43**), it is easy to suppose that a large portion of Lady Diana's preoccupations would focus on nurturing them as well as her love relationships. (Both birth Keys' and their Ruling Planets and Signs are combined here.)

HEBREW LETTERS: Consult Table 5 (Pp 190 and 191). Hebrew Letters apply to *Major Arcana Keys only*. For example, ***ZAIN, the 7th Hebrew letter***, is allotted to **The Lovers Key**. When a letter's meaning is known and which Key it is assigned to, it provides further insights concerning Life Path trends.

HEBREW LETTER OBJECTS: Consult Table 5 (Pp 190 and 191). As ***ZAIN*** stands for cutting tools such as a ***dagger, sword or knife***, it reveals hidden **Lovers Key** aspects. Its objects enlighten us as to why **Key6** can mean severance besides union and why Lady Diana needed to protect herself from possible attack due to their warring nature.

TREE of LIFE: Although the Qabalah is a vast, very advanced, comprehensive subject, I have included four Tree of Life diagrams on page 192 for those with this knowledge. They are rudimentary in construct yet show essential associations on each that are good to know and memorise. Numbers from 1 to 32 link to the Tree's Pathways. Knowing each Path's meanings broadens findings. For example, to know that **Key24** (Lady Diana's *major reversed* Key) is allocated to **Death's Pathway**, indicates that her life would go through *transitioning, transformational periods* that test her ability to cultivate and nurture the type of consciousness that achieves evolution.

What follows is an example of noting specific, numerology interpretations for a spreads' present, reversed and reduced numbers. This type of interpretation focuses on choosing details that are applicable to the subject.

SPECIFIC INTERPRETATIONS:

2: Possibilities—lessons in wisdom, opposites, relationships, unions, values, diplomacy, politics, memory, the past, letting go, moving on, self-esteem, self-worth, nurture, emotions, manipulation, fixation, psychism.

20: Possibilities—lessons in impermanence, ability to contact higher realms, ability to expand consciousness, ability to recreate oneself from good and bad experiences, transitions, depths of feeling, hypercritical, betrayals, harsh or unfair judgements, inability to extricate from untenable positions, avoids making hard decisions, keeps secrets, possible "Skeletons in the closet".

24: Possibilities—lessons in leadership, power, protocol, patriotism, loyalty, equanimity, self-control, poise, sacrifice. Dysfunctional family tendencies.

42: Possibilities—lessons in idealism, pride, placing unrealistic expectations onto others—especially the partner and/or the marriage, placing people on pedestals, gullibility, peace at any cost, self-respect, dependence on others.

6 Possibilities—lessons in intrinsic beauty, peace, harmony, equality, dedication, conscientiousness, obligations and duty, work ethics, realistic goal-setting, organisation, attention to detail, practicality, unconditional love and service, telling the differences between reality, illusion and delusion.

60: Possibilities—lessons in matters to do with love, home, family, marriage and children, miscarriage or abortion, adoption, separation from children by choice, force or divorce or a child chooses to "divorce" the parents, protection of a gifted, intellectually or physically handicapped, ill, abused or sexually abused, problem or illegitimate child, travel, a "rescue" mentality eg, plays the role of saviour/victim or can just as easily revert to victim/saviour.

The next example is of the Dalai Lama. Incredibly, His Holiness' spread is the same as Lady Diana's second decan spread but *includes* **Keys2 and 20**. It is fascinating to see where their similarities and differences lie when their spreads are compared with how each has lived their life.

Practice Examples:

Name: 14th Dalai Lama
Birthdate: 6 July 1935
Zodiac Sign: Cancer
Cancer Decan: Second Decan or 11⇨20 degrees Cancer
Decan Ruler: Mercury
Corresponding Key: 3 of Cups
Key's Esoteric Name: Abundance

The Dalai Lama's natal Key is the **3 of Cups**. It is the same as Lady Diana's Key for her *second* decan. However, when we extrapolate His lifetime Tarot spread from it, **Keys 2 and 20** *must* be included in it (unlike the one on page 173) to avoid missing vital data.

When we compare these two lives against their spreads, we find many similarities appear in their natures and circumstances such as being involved in warfare or the outcomes of war (**Key 34**). Metaphysics ranked high (**20**) as well as being actively compassionate (**Cancer**) when they worked to cheer and protect victims of war, the sick and the needy (**7**). Frequent travel (**Keys 34, 7 and 70**) is another shared trait. Others lie in their opulent life styles, wealth, charitability and heavy duties, as well as ceremonies, celebrations, festivals, dance and entertainment (**Key43's** "*Abundance*" aspect).

Key34's name is *"Shortened Force"*. It means that surprising, spontaneous happenings of an unpredictable nature are catalysts for upsets, hardship and change. Unlike Lady Diana, the Dalai Lama remains steadfastly in control of His feelings and instincts when such times strike. This exhibits elevated **7, 70 and 8** traits (extrapolated from **Key34**). He also exercised *right timing* when He escaped from Tibet. This is a positive **Key34** trait. To learn this skill is critical to ensure success as premature action or applying too much force too soon tends to bring on unwelcome, even disastrous, results. This may have been the case for Lady Diana on the night she died. **Key34** also hints that travel, often by air, spontaneity, impatience, insights, clairvoyance and a wealth of ideas are likely lifetime traits.

Name: Jessica Watson
Birthdate: 18 May 1993
Zodiac Sign: Taurus
Taurus Decan: Third or 21⇨30 degrees Taurus
Decan Ruler: Saturn
Corresponding Key: 7 of Pentacles
Key's Esoteric Name: Success Unfulfilled

Just the opposite to what its esoteric name implies, the **7 of Pentacles** depicts Jessica's potential to achieve something monumental and make money from it, if she so chooses. However, and often typical of this Key, she was satisfied with intrinsic rewards she won from her self-test when she single-handedly mastered the seas at 16. She was tempted by neither fame nor fortune when she arrived home again.

Name: Steve Irwin
Birthdate: 22 February 1962
Zodiac Sign: Pisces
Pisces Decan: First or 0⇨10 degrees Pisces
Decan Ruler: Saturn
Corresponding Key: 8 of Cups
Key's Esoteric Name: Abandoned Success

Steve Irwin provides us with another example of a person whose life runs counter to what their natal Key's name implies. He was the epitome of success; he demonstrated what one could achieve when they turn their back on non-essentials and one-pointedly make many sacrifices to achieve their hopes and dreams.

Part 4 Treasure Hunt Chapter 16 Uncovering Personal Gems

Birthdays that fall on the Cusp of a Decan:

These last four examples are for birthdays that fall on or near the CUSP of a decan. Oprah and "Tiger's" birthdays fall the day *before*, Azaria, the day *of* and Elvis, *two days prior* a cusp.

Name: Oprah Winfrey (Day before cusp)
Birthdate: 29 January 1954
Zodiac Sign: Aquarius
Aquarius Decans: CUSP of 1st and 2nd decan
Decans' Rulers: Venus and Mercury
Corresponding Keys: 5 and 6 of Swords
Keys' Esoteric Names: Defeat; Earned success

Seeing Oprah's two Sword Keys enables us to understand her "warrior" nature at a glance. Being Swords, they depict a life of *struggle and strife* in the form of constant threats to or demands placed on her personal sense of authority and ability to lead. Although first impressions appear gloomy, a **6 Key** endows her with *analysis* and a **5 Key**, *translation*. These qualities, if used correctly, enable Oprah to know and then deal with her flaws and obstacles. The **5 of Swords Key** portrays growing in courage and strength as she surmounts them. The **6 of Swords Key** depicts her innate capacity to love, forgive and leave her troubles behind. Oprah's compassion and patronage for those who have less has earned her the love and respect of millions (♀ in ♒). She is a shining example of someone who extracts the best from daunting Keys.

Name: Azaria Chamberlain (Day of cusp)
Birthdate: 11 June 1980
Zodiac Sign: Gemini
Gemini Decans: CUSP of 2nd and 3rd decan
Decans' Rulers: Mars and Sun
Corresponding Keys: 9 and 10 of Swords
Keys' Esoteric Names: Despair and Cruelty; Ruin

These daunting Keys help to explain Azaria's most unfortunate death. However, for those who may have them, they do contain positive aspects when their keywords and symbols are studied. Their corresponding numbers also contain positive keywords. See Appendices in *Life Diamonds* for interpretations.

The next two examples show the subtle differences between Keys for the day of and before the cusp.

Name: Tiger Woods (Day before cusp)
Birthdate: 30 December 1975
Zodiac Sign: Capricorn
Capricorn Decans: CUSP of 1st and 2nd decan
Decans' Rulers: Jupiter and Mars
Corresponding Keys: 2 and 3 of Pentacles
Keys' Esoteric Names: Harmonious Change; Material Success

Like the **Juggler**, Tiger has great ability and dexterity. He is also unreliable, fails to provide stability in relationships, is devious and plays the trickster. These "**2**" keywords explain some of the **2 of Pentacles'** negative potential he has displayed. However, the ability to make money from building a career and a name for himself is obvious in the **3 of Pentacles Key**.

Name: Elvis Presley (2 Days before cusp)
Birthdate: 8 January 1935
Zodiac Sign: Capricorn
Capricorn Decan: CUSP of 2nd and 3rd decan
Decans' Rulers: Mars and Sun
Corresponding Keys: 3 and 4 of Pentacles
Keys' Esoteric Names: Material Success and Earthy Power

These Keys show Presley's potential to become successful in his chosen career and very wealthy from it. **Key72** depicts his attachment to wealth, material possessions and pleasure. The Hermit's *integrity* quality was inactive (**root9** from **Keys72/27**) because his behaviours deteriorated as his fame and fortune rose. Hence, the gift of raising his spirituality was blocked; he failed to grow his inner Light (**root 9**).

ADDITIONAL POINTS

- **CORE FEATURES:** Obviously, a natal Key's Zodiac Sign, Ruling Planet, Suit and Sacred Element are *the* most important pieces of information to consider when interpreting a spread. This is because they provide vital clues regarding what some of the Soul's main requirements are for its Personality to experience during its earthly sojourn. Therefore, it is in your best interests to know inside out what each signifies.

◆ **KEYS' NAMES:** Did you note in each cameo how much the Key's esoteric name reflected the ways in which each person lived or lives his or her life? Did you notice that they lived as the name implied or its complete opposite?

TABLE 1: SUITS, SYMBOLS and REALMS of CONSCIOUSNESS

Table 1 below reveals keywords for the four Suits, Elements, Symbols and their Realms of Consciousness where specialised aspects of human consciousness unfold and develop. They provide information about each that facilitates their interpretation. The colours represent those assigned to the four Sacred Elements, their symbols and Realms of Consciousness.

SUIT	SYMBOL	MEANINGS
WANDS FIRE	🪄	**Spiritual cultivation** via the Higher Mind's activity, principles, foresight, desires, enterprise, intellect, ideas, inspiration, realisation, optimism, enthusiasm, initiation, creativity, generation, capability, expertise. Divine will.
CUPS WATER	🏆	**Emotional cultivation** via unification, interrelations, feelings, ardour, desires, tastes, reactions, intuition, psychism, reflection, inner responses. Imagination, visualisation, dreams, vision, creativity.
SWORDS AIR	🗡	**Intellectual cultivation** via beliefs, opposites, distinction, analysis, evaluation, translation, acuity, discourse. Intellect fused with desires and emotions. Ethics. Struggle, conflict, animosity, cunning, criticism. Pessimism, cynicism, negativity. Attitudes. Hypocrisy. Bigotry.
PENTACLES EARTH	⛤	**Physical/material cultivation** via synthesis of mind, body and spirit that begets competence, realisation, culmination, results, rewards for effort. Manufacture, craftsmanship, multi-tasking. Values. Materialism. Material security. Revelation. Manifestation.

Table 2 on the next page lists the Keys' esoteric names as well as their corresponding numbers and Keys, their Decan Dates, Decan Rulers and Decan Signs in the zodiac. It also contains the corresponding number to each Minor Key as well as their esoteric names. Modern Planetary Rulers complete the Table. They may be used to obtain more clues.

TABLE 2:
DECANS' DATES, MINOR KEYS, NAMES, PLANETS & SIGNS

DATES	KEY		NO.	ESOTERIC NAME
Jul 22-Aug 1	5 of		31	Strife
Aug 2-11	6 of	Wands	32	Victory
Aug 12-22	7 of		33	Valour
Aug 23-Sep 1	8 of		76	Prudence
Sep 2-11	9 of	Pentacles	77	Material Gain
Sep 12-22	10 of		78	Wealth
Sep 23-Oct 2	2 of		56	Peace Restored
Oct 3-Oct 12	3 of	Swords	57	Sorrow
Oct 13-22	4 of		58	Rest from Strife
Oct 23-Nov 1	5 of		45	Loss in Pleasure
Nov 2-12	6 of	Cups	46	Pleasure
Nov 13-22	7 of		47	Illusionary Success
Nov 23-Dec 2	8 of		34	Swiftness
Dec 3-12	9 of	Wands	35	Great Strength
Dec 13-21	10 of		36	Oppression
Dec 22-30	2 of		70	Harmonious Change
Dec 31-Jan 9	3 of	Pentacles	71	Material Works
Jan 10- Jan 19	4 of		72	Earthy Power
Jan 20- 29	5 of		59	Defeat
Jan 30-Feb 8	6 of	Swords	60	Earned Success
Feb 9-18	7 of		61	Unstable Effort
Feb 19 -28	8 of		48	Abandoned Success
Mar 1-10	9 of	Cups	49	Material Happiness
Mar 11-20	10 of		50	Perpetual Success
Mar 21-30	2 of		28	Dominion
Mar 31-Apr 10	3 of	Wands	29	Established Strength
Apr 11-Apr 20	4 of		30	Perfected Work
Apr 21-30	5 of		73	Material Trouble
May 1-10	6 of	Pentacles	74	Material Success
May 11-20	7 of		75	Success Unfulfilled
May 21-31	8 of		62	Shortened Force
Jun 1-10	9 of	Swords	63	Despair and Cruelty
Jun 11-20	10 of		64	Ruin
Jun 21-Jul 1	2 of		42	Love and Union
Jul 2-11	3 of	Cups	43	Abundance
Jul 12-21	4 of		44	Blended Pleasure

Part 4 Treasure Hunt Chapter 16 Uncovering Personal Gems

CHALDEAN DECAN RULER	DECAN ZODIAC SIGNS	MODERN DECAN RULER
♄ SATURN		☉ SUN
♃ JUPITER	♌ Leo	♃ JUPITER
♂ MARS		♂ MARS
☉ SUN		☿ MERCURY
♀ VENUS	♍ virgo	♄ SATURN
☿ MERCURY		♀ VENUS
☾ MOON		♀ VENUS
♄ SATURN	♎ Libra	♅ URANUS
♃ JUPITER		☿ MERCURY
♂ MARS		♇ PLUTO
☉ SUN	♏ Scorpio	♆ NEPTUNE
♀ VENUS		☾ MOON
☿ MERCURY		♃ JUPITER
☾ MOON	♐ Sagittarius	♂ MARS
♄ SATURN		☉ SUN
♃ JUPITER		♄ SATURN
♂ MARS	♑ Capricorn	♀ VENUS
☉ SUN		☿ MERCURY
♀ VENUS		♅ URANUS
☿ MERCURY	♒ Aquarius	☿ MERCURY
☾ MOON		♀ VENUS
♄ SATURN		♆ NEPTUNE
♃ JUPITER	♓ Pisces	☾ MOON
♂ MARS		♇ PLUTO
♂ MARS		♂ MARS
☉ SUN	♈ Aries	☉ SUN
♀ VENUS		♃ JUPITER
☿ MERCURY		♀ VENUS
☾ MOON	♉ Taurus	☿ MERCURY
♄ SATURN		♄ SATURN
♃ JUPITER		☿ MERCURY
♂ MARS	♊ Gemini	♀ VENUS
☉ SUN		♅ URANUS
♀ VENUS		☾ MOON
☿ MERCURY	♋ Cancer	♇ PLUTO
☾ MOON		♆ NEPTUNE

Use this Table to extract suitable meanings for the planet that rules the decan or Keys in the lifetime Tarot spread. Add their meanings to the person's profile.

TABLE 3: PLANETS AND THEIR MEANINGS

PLANETS	MEANINGS
SUN	**The Sun rules Leo.** It indicates where you are learning to express your own true nature and show off what you can do and achieve. It is where you most wish to be YOU and 'shine'. The Sun guides you to the uncovery of your authentic self. It represents your inner and outer self, basic temperament, will and ego and self-determination, identity and independence. It is the seat of your creative powers, character development and creative self-expression. It centralises or focuses on your administrative, coping abilities.
MOON	**The Moon rules Cancer.** It represents your past life, the Sun, this life. The Moon also represents good memory; fertile imagination; warmth, homeliness, dedication, intense feelings, stubbornness, mood swings, broods; sulks, depression prone; unreliability; irrational thinking; habits; mannerisms; females or feminine side; nurturer
MERCURY	**Mercury rules two signs and their houses;** Gemini (Air) and Virgo (Earth), its signs; 3rd and 6th, its houses. Meanings for Mercury are: Rational, mental capacities that solve our problems; ability to translate internal and external stimuli; ability to communicate what we know, think and feel; plays pranks; can be superficial, flighty and flirtatious or serious, responsible, hard-working and critical
VENUS	**Venus rules two signs and their houses;** Taurus (Earth) and Libra (Air), her signs; 2nd and 7th, her houses. Meanings for Venus are: creative discrimination faculties; artistic expression; beauty; personal attractiveness; popularity; love; harmony; peacemaker; sensual pleasures; envy; jealousy; finances; spending/saving; greed; comfort; laziness; a young female; competitive rivalry; compromise; negotiation; legal issues
MARS	**Mars rules Aries:** Meanings for Mars are: brave or cowardly; fights, defends or runs away; combative issues; accident prone; fearful; creates new experiences; initiates new ideas, interests, plans, projects and relationships; deals with challenges head-on; males or masculine side; procreative; sexual
JUPITER	**Jupiter rules Sagittarius:** Meanings for Jupiter are: an extremist; an optimist; enthusiastic, progressive approach to life; courage to extend personal horizons; desires freedom, urge to progress and grow; exhibits worldliness and wisdom; puts moral codes, beliefs and personal philosophies into practice or is a hypocrite; grandiose ideas and schemes; self-aggrandisement
SATURN	**Saturn rules Capricorn:** It represents our limitations, leadership potential, independence; ambitions; vocational aims, productivity; goal-seeking; successful; responsible; mature, capable, resourceful, strength of character; endurance; awareness of strengths, weaknesses and personal limitations as fears, setbacks and restrictions are dealt with; forms of isolation, alienation and separation; austere; aloof; cold; insensitive, depression prone

The Chaldeans only knew, hence, used the seven, ancient planets listed on the opposite page. The three planets on this page are regarded as "modern". This explains why I have "separated" them from the seven "ancient" planets. The ancient planets were also used by the Golden Dawn Mystery School and these are the planets that rule the decans on the astrological wheel on page 170.

Our "modern" planets were discovered long after the Chaldean "era". William Herschel discovered **Uranus** on 13MAR1781; Johann Gotfried Galle discovered **Neptune** on 23SEP1846; Clyde W. Tombaugh discovered **Pluto** on 18FEB1930.

Their meanings, if applied to lifetime, Tarot Keys, reveal more insights. Eg, the **5 of Cups** is ruled by **Mars and Pluto**. Their dual rulership confirms its melancholy nature. Then, **Mercury and Pluto** rule the **3 of Cups** which explains its unexpected, sinister aspects.

PLANETS	MEANINGS
 URANUS	**URANUS** is the planet of surprises; things suddenly and unexpectedly change for better or worse; reversals are the norm. Uranus rules friends and connections, group activity, striving to achieve common goals, unconventionality and unpredictability, instability, variety, restlessness and change. Independent thought and action rule. Impositions on freedom of expression are unwelcome. Freedom of expression and action are necessary to demonstrate uniqueness. Social, anti-social and rebellious behaviour may be expressed. Uranus teaches equality, non-attachment to material resources and the realisation of group consciousness, shared attitudes, beliefs, tolerance and responsibility. Uranus also rules branches of science, economics, education and politics, humanitarian concerns, research projects and metaphysics. The future is more important than the present hence a need for future financial security in the form of investments, personal insurance and annuities.
 NEPTUNE	**NEPTUNE** reveals where you are most likely to - face your greatest tests – go through phases of stagnation or a form of paralysis - feel nervy, confused, forgetful, vague and uncertain - suffer disappointment and disillusionment – engage in self-destructive behaviours - be your own worst enemy – cause your own undoing - make mistakes and unwise choices - suffer thwarted attempts when striving to reach goals - deal with the unknown and the unforeseen - be prone to deception and lies and unfulfilled promises/contracts - be let down by others - feel depressed and guilt laden - become ill - have contact with hospitals, institutions and welfare services - make sacrifices - be the martyr or doormat - cope with confining conditions - care for another or others - feel weak, frail and vulnerable - reveal your flaws - refine and improve yourself - suffer from 'divine discontent' – engage in self-pity or self-torment - develop spiritual inclinations via religious or metaphysical practices - become virtuous - render selfless service - develop psychic and intuitive faculties - develop soul awareness - tap into super consciousness – self-spiritualisation is the Neptunian goal.
 PLUTO	**PLUTO** indicates radical change and transformation often due to deep, personal insights, catalysts or forces greater than you. It triggers the conscious elimination of outworn behaviour patterns and attitudes, psychological blockages, people and things from your life so that personal transformation, renewal and growth continue. Deep, emotional stress, compulsive, obsessive behaviour, difficulty, struggle and betrayals are Plutonian traits. Issues to do with the past, funerals, death, taxes, alimony, debts, loans, insurances, probate, future material and emotional security, financial institutions, accountants and police are others. Complications, betrayals or separations arise in relationships, partnerships and joint matters. Issues to do with abandonment or isolation may arise. Extremes such as love/hate, trust/betrayal, respect/dishonour, self-mastery/loss of control, faithfulness/infidelity, acceptance/rejection, openness/secrets, believer/sceptic and gain/loss are possibilities. Pluto teaches the pain of attachment, spiteful words and deeds. If allowed, fate, force and destiny have a way of working things out on their own.

TABLE 4: ZODIAC SIGNS AND THEIR MEANINGS

SIGNS	MEANINGS
ARIES  Head & face	**Keyword: "I am"** Development of self-expression. Selfish: head-strong; energetic; enthusiastic; active; egotistical; courageous; needs a cause to support; original; spontaneous; initiator; leadership; impulsive; aggressive; domineering; reckless; quick tempered; conflict; chivalrous; pioneer
TAURUS  Throat	**Keyword: "I have"** Development of desire nature, self-worth, personal values, appreciation, discriminative powers and creative talents. Under Taurus, they manifest gradually within spiritual, emotional, financial and material parameters that are driven by powerful emotive urges to create financial and material security. Productive. Urges to enjoy, exploit and satisfy physical pleasures and sensual appetites. Immovable; stubborn; laid-back; slow on the up-take but sound once grasped; plodding and cautious.
GEMINI  Lungs, collar-bones, arms & hands	**Keyword: "I think"** Development of versatility via an enquiring mind. Curiosity; new or continued studies; siblings; relatives; neighbours; local community; local community affairs; local government; local trade; commerce; early education and teachers and schools; continuous adjustment to one's close environment; commuting; short distance travel; can live on nerves.

Use this Table to extract suitable meanings for the zodiac sign that rules the decan or Keys in the lifetime Tarot spread. Add their meanings to the person's profile.

SIGNS	MEANINGS
LIBRA  Kidneys, Loins & lower back	**Keyword: "I balance"** Developing social skills via powers of persuasion and deliberation to maintain balance, unity and harmony in all relationships. Creative interactive thinking. Aesthetic refinement. Personal grace and charm, integrity and consideration for others Close relationships, associates, friendships, marriage and divorce, business partners. Corporate affairs, contracts, legal matters, economic exchange and competitive edge. Learning how and when to share, compete or negotiate, embrace both sides of an issue and formulate fair judgements. Hesitation and procrastination are embarrassing traits when clear-cut or important decisions elude when anxious or wishing to make favourable impressions. Pride in appearance. Popularity, entertainment, celebrations, reunions and wakes. Libra also provides new social conditions in which reasoning and judgement find solutions to conflict via mediation, arbitration and counselling or from utilising legal channels in an effort to create or restore calm from crisis.
SCORPIO  Sex organs	**Keyword: "I desire"** Development of insight, valour, loyalty, struggle, intensity, commitment and intimacy. This is one's battleground where the rites to maturity are fought and won via catalysts that promote growth, change and transformation. One experiences isolation, alienation and rejection as the battle for greater self-sufficiency and independence is taken to higher levels. Loss and gain, joy, pain and suffering, endings, death and rebirth symbolise this quest for maturity and urge to identify with one's Source. Tenacity, determination, inner strength and fortitude, trust, acceptance and tolerance are nurtured. Power struggles and complications in relationships and joint concerns relating to spiritual, emotional and sexual inclinations, material assets and resources. This is where one fights for causes, faces fears, resists change and clings to unhealthy situations, outworn or toxic relationships and obsolete possessions far longer than necessary. Future security is striven for in the form of assets, investments, insurance and annuity schemes, inheritances. Dealings with institutions and the laws governing them. Suspicion, scepticism, secrets, crime and police, bureaucrats and metaphysics. Death and taxes. Annuities.
SAGITTARIUS  Hips, thighs, liver	**Keyword: "I see"** Development of aspiration and direction resulting from continuous growth opportunities, progress and expansion via activities and experiences that broaden one's sphere of worldly knowledge and depth of understanding. Wisdom and loving understanding are cultivated in this way as one's personal 'worldview' is continuously refined and redefined via contact and experience with ever widening social and global issues such ecology, politics, religion, philosophy and natural and superphysical laws. Sagittarius governs the areas of courage, faith, dreams, higher law, academic learning, sports, global concerns, foreign cultures and religious beliefs. Obligations concerning morals and ethics, honesty and benefaction are tested. When positive: wisdom, intuition, vision and enterprise, prosperity, success, freedom of choice and action are cultivated. Hypocrisy, elitism, falsity, double standards and self-aggrandisement are negative indications. Religious leaders, judges, lawyers, entrepreneurs, corporation heads, wealthy or influential people, publishers, awards and broad networking practices belong here. Sagittarius also represents expansion; growth in consciousness or weight gain; confers wealth and/or poverty as well as good or bad luck or fortune; is magnanimous.

SIGNS	MEANINGS
CANCER 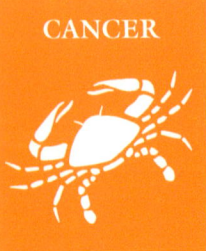 Breast & stomach	**Keyword: "I feel"** Development of one's ability to adapt to constant pressure and change and express one's feelings. Changes occur mainly within the areas of emotional expression, family and domestic issues, property and things related to the past. Women; mothering; parents; family unit; family resources; births; deaths and endings. A safe, secure home to withdraw to is essential when upset or threatened. Family business. Defensive; shy; nervous; easily frightened; a chameleon.
LEO  Heart, sides & back	**Keyword: "I will"** Development of one's character and new facets of creative self-expression via experimentation and new experiences mainly in the areas of self-discovery activities, creative pursuits and leisure activities. Character development, self-awareness, pride in accomplishments, love and romance, sexual exploration, speculation, parenting, children and middle to high education. Charm, charisma, an exhibitionist, has an aura of "royalty" or impressiveness; has the potential to "shine"; status-seeker. Inflexibility, arrogance, lords it over others, proud, vain.
VIRGO  Intestines	**Keyword: "I analyse"** Development of refining and improving all day-to-day activities related to service, work, work associates, social skills at work, employees, trade, domestic and health regimes and pets. Financial independence from work. Seeks satisfaction from efforts. Perfectionist. High morals and ethics. Capable of self-analysis. Works on character flaws and imperfections in habits then devises practical ways to improve on them. Keenly aware of duties and obligations. Versatile. Clinical. Adaptable, resourceful, efficient and self-disciplined; Conscientious, dedicated, prudent, chaste, responsible, discriminate and productive.

SIGNS	MEANINGS
CAPRICORN  Knees	**Keyword: "I use"** Developing new opportunities and experiences with the focus on being successful at attaining career and/or personal goals. Opportunities arise that foster the intelligent use of will, sagacity, strategy and independent action to achieve these ends. One's mettle, maturity and leadership ability are tested by setbacks and difficulties, greater demands, higher degrees of responsibility, extra duties, failure and sometimes publicity. Respect, status, and traditional views prosper here. Fate and destiny play their role but free will prevails. Depression develops from being too serious or pessimistic in outlook or suffering severe setbacks. Career issues, professionalism, etiquette, personal goals and corporate affairs dominate. Authority figures, the elderly, those who command respect, are mature or well established.
AQUARIUS  Ankles, blood	**Keyword: "I know"** Develops ability to handle sudden upsets, reversals and surprises and events or incidents that are beyond one's control which makes this sign full of excitement, thrills and crises via its unpredictable nature. By being confronted with the unusual and the unexpected, you learn to exercise the unique stuff of which you are made. Individual talents and personal genius help you to develop and accept all points of view that awaken an appreciation of the infinite complexities, differences, uniqueness and universal wisdom inherent in everything. Reciprocal love, friends, colleagues, unions, groups, associations and others' children are represented here besides the politics involving them. Stocks, share portfolios and other types of investments that secure future financial security are interests. Learning tolerance and to accept all points of view awakens you to a Higher Purpose within everything. One's hopes and dreams seek expression here. Working with others towards a common goal to achieve better working, social or humanitarian conditions is the aim. Social sense of community, A reformist.
PISCES  Feet	**Keyword: "I believe"** Develops the essence of spirit via opportunities that encourage growth in a higher purpose, personal refinement, greater spiritual fortitude and self-discipline. These inmost qualities are hard won via struggle, forms of confinement and pain and suffering. Loving-kindness is the goal achieved from working alongside others and administering help and support to those less fortunate. However, often one's higher sensitivities and ideals are not always in tune with the harsh realities of life with the danger being that proneness to fatalism or indifference to personal or universal affairs brings about self-undoing. If not mindful of this, the tendency is to give up on plans and dreams rather than set practical goals and persist with them despite setbacks. Depression, disappointment and disillusionment are often experienced. Pisces generates insights into the supernatural aspects of life that provides a bridge to higher consciousness via meditation or other means.

TABLE 5:
HEBREW LETTER PLACEMENTS & MEANINGS ⇔ MAJOR ARCANA KEYS

HEBREW LETTER	LETTER NO.	LETTER OBJECT	KEY NO.	KEY'S NAME	HEBREW LETTER MEANINGS
Aleph	1	Bull	0	Fool (young)	**Bull**, patience, plodding, naive, strength, fortitude, endurance, dependability, worker, vitality, virile, fierce when roused, cultivator, agricultural power, civilisation **Involution**
Beth	2	House	1	Magician	**House**, temple, abode, refuge, environment, location, area, architectural principles, construction/destruction, concentration, specialisation, order
Gimel	3	Camel	2	High Priestess	**Camel**, travel, transport, commerce, trade, networking, interaction, contact, communication, association
Daleth	4	Door	3	Empress	**Door**, womb, passage, transition, inner subjective world to outer objective plane, creation, conception, origin, beginning, formation, development, open/close
Heh	5	Window	4	Emperor	**Window**, admits light and air, to see, outlook, attitude, point of view, to frame, to classify, to compose, to constitute, to manifest, looking within and without
Vau or Vav	6	Nail	5	Hierophant	**Join**, pin, sew, nail, staple, glue, fasten, build, unite, merge, fuse, combine, blend, gel, 'and' as a conjunction to join
Zain	7	Sword	6	Lovers	**Sword**, **dagger**, **knife**. Cutting tools used in warfare, surgery or butchery. Need for protection. Opposition, division, separation, resistance, antagonism, disposing
Cheth	8	Fence	7	Chariot	**Fence or field**, particular as opposed to the general, a specific area set apart for cultivation whether inner for the spirit or outer as work or for cultural purposes, property rights, location, to enclose, to protect
Teth	9	Serpent	8	Strength	**Serpent**, wisdom, secrecy, regenerative power, to renew, restore, revive, redevelop, stimulate, rejuvenate, refine, Kundalini
Yod	10	Open hand	9	Hermit	**Open hand**, instrument for all higher activities of the human mind, dexterity, skill, power, might, supremacy, sign of the Supreme Spirit
Kaph	11	Fist	10	Wheel of Fortune	**Fist**, grip or grasp, to grasp as to grip or hold or grasp as to comprehend

HEBREW LETTER	LETTER NO.	LETTER OBJECT	KEY NO.	KEY'S NAME	HEBREW LETTER MEANINGS
Lamed	12		11	Justice	**Ox-goad**, that which incites to action, urges, motivates, prods, oversees, controls, manages, guides or as a verb means initiate, instruct, encourage, inspire, chastise
Mem	13		12	Hanged Man	**Water**, the first mirror, 'made in God's image', reflected life, reproduce, replicate, imitate, copy, repeat
Nun	14		13	Death	**Fish**. As a noun fish, as a verb to move, sprout, grow, germinate, produce, develop, generate, manufacture
Samekh	15		14	Temperance	**Prop or Support**, help, assistance, walking-stick, to brace, foundations. Improvement, refinement, purification, transmutation, metamorphosis
Ayin	16		15	Devil	**Eye**, vision, orb or circle suggesting limitation, bondage, appearances, Avidya: a symbol of false knowledge or illusion
Peh	17		16	Tower	**Mouth**, to feed, initiating process of assimilation, internalisation, absorption, incorporation and digestion; organ of speech, power of the word
Tzaddi	18		17	Star	**Fish hook**, to hook, to draw out, to entice, to procure by artfulness, to harvest, mental processes in meditation
Qoph	19		18	Moon	**Back of Head**, instinctual mind that governs, heals and regenerates all automatic bodily functions, maintains bodily life during sleep, Medulla Oblongata
Resh	20		19	Sun	**Face or Head**, guiding power, reasoning power, direction, administration, collection, containment, centralising and organising many things together as the brain does, things we face in life, inner and outer appearance
Shin	21		20	Judgement	**Fangs or Teeth**, sharpness, acuity, pierces, tears, grinds, digestion, acidity, breaks down, decay, corrosion, penetration, destructive action, toxic, deadly, poison
Tau or Tav	22		21	World	**Mark or Cross**, making one's mark, signature, finality, termination, closure, culmination, zenith
Aleph			22	Fool (old)	**Mountain Top**, love, shares, cultivator, nurturer. Knowledge, understanding, wisdom. Tolerance. Climax. Completion. **Evolution**, **Unity**, **Superconsciousness**

FOUR TREES OF LIFE SHOWING VARIOUS ATTRIBUTES

Use these Trees to obtain more insights from your numbers and keys.

TREE 1

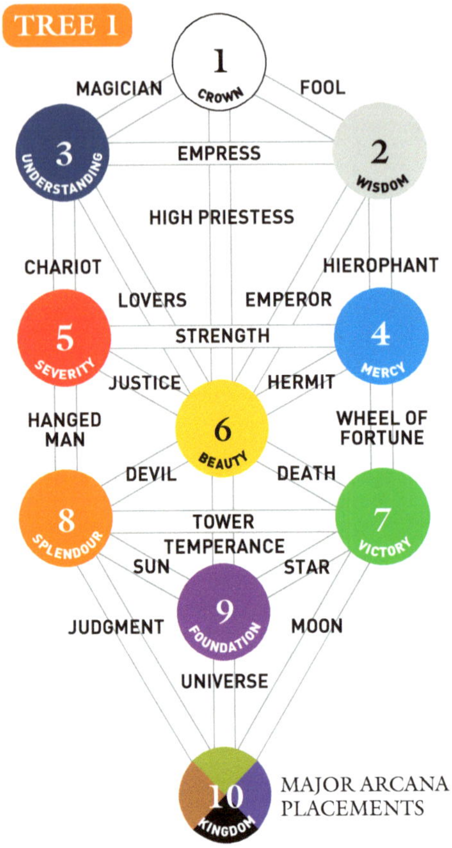

MAJOR ARCANA PLACEMENTS

TREE 2

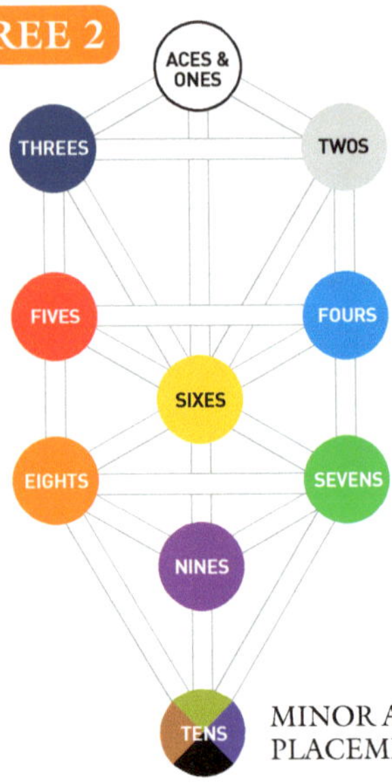

MINOR ARCANA PLACEMENTS

TREE 3

KING, QUEEN, KNIGHT, PAGE PLACEMENTS

TREE 4

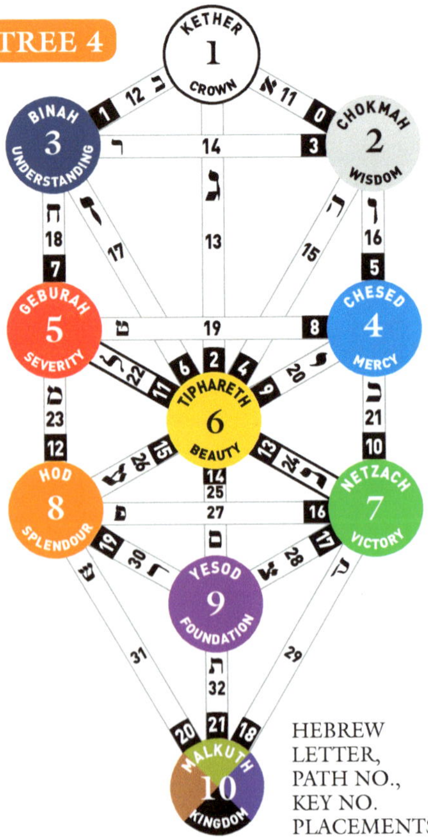

HEBREW LETTER, PATH NO., KEY NO. PLACEMENTS

Part 4 Treasure Hunt **Chapter 16** Uncovering Personal Gems

GENERAL TIPS

1. **Important:** Take Natal Keys and lifetime spreads seriously due to their lifelong imprint. Refresh their meanings from time to time to detect overlooked aspects that may not have caught your eye during prior reviews. Try to obtain clear Soul and Personality guidelines from them and then utilise that information for your Highest Good.

2. **Common Themes:** When researching lifetime spreads for your family, close friends and famous people, search for similarities and differences that are common among them. For example ….

   Woods and Presley were born into the **second decan of Capricorn**. Two aspects that they shared from **Key71** were *self-gratification and self-aggrandisement*. They showed in the ways they strove to build status and material wealth from honed skills.

   Another aspect that they shared is found in **Key71's root8**. It typifies the struggle involved to gain control over their base instincts or animal nature, namely sexual appetite. *To learn to control one's base instincts is one of this key's major lessons* and so it was for Woods and Presley. No doubt they used them well to outdo their opponents.

   Both men were dedicated workers as **Key71** implies, but do not fall into the trap of thinking that everyone born with this Key is automatically industrious and likely to become famous and wealthy from unfolding and developing his or her unique gifts. Bear in mind that countless variables influence the ways that these numbers and Keys are expressed. This explains why marked differences occur between personalities and circumstances.

   For example, I know a young man also born into the **second decan of Capricorn**. He has chosen to be a layabout and live on social security for most of his working life instead of capitalising on **Key71's** special gifts. He also squanders his social benefits.

   Yet, what is so interesting about these three men is that they had/have high libidos. Each one activated the shame aspect of **Key17**, **Key71's** reverse, by allowing their desire nature (**root8**) rule them; all three also engaged in substance abuse.

3. **Hidden Clues:** Important information lies in the decan's ruling zodiac sign, planet, Key and Key's numbers. Eg, **Key71's** sign is **Capricorn**, its ruling planet, **Saturn**, its **Key**, **The Devil**, *the Great Tempter*. Information gained from them reinforces why these men had such a struggle to control their morals and desires. As with **root8**, *the Great Tempter* also tests base instincts, morals, sexual appetites and behaviours. However, as mentioned before, beware of jumping to hasty conclusions re **Keys15 and 71's, 8 trends** because they also ruled **St Joan of Arc's Capricorn decan** (6th Jan) and she could not have been more moral, devout and chaste! In her case, she displayed **Key 15's** *saint* rather than *sinner* aspect; she also epitomised control over her base instincts (**Key8** aspects).

   Moreover, the decan's **root zodiac,** its **Ruling Planet, Key** and its **Key's numbers** *overshadow* all three decans in a sign. If they do not appear in the lifetime spread, it pays to include them as they often reinforce findings as above. **Capricorn and Saturn, The Devil, 15/51 and 6/60** provide excellent additional information to add to Tiger, Elvis and St Joan's lifetime spreads. We understand how relevant **The Devil Key** was for the three men and St Joan regarding exercising self-control, but so was **number 60**, as two of the men are estranged from their children and St Joan left her family when **17**. Separations from family are **60** traits, which is opposite to bondage epitomised by **The Devil Key**. These points demonstrate how the zodiac sign and its offshoots can add essential, missing details to a reading.

4. **Natal Keys sometimes provide elusive information that verifies what are obvious characteristics and happenings in a person's life when nothing else seems to.** I was reading for a friend who was born on the 19th March 1951. Males have been and still occupy a major part of her life. They were mainly her father, two uncles, her husband and her four sons who affected her life in positive and negative ways. Her Life Diamonds' numbers and Keys did not reveal such a powerful, male dominance. However, her natal Tarot Keys did. My friend was born on a decan's cusp, which meant she had the **10 of Cups** and the **2 of Wands** as her natal Keys.

   Now we get to the interesting part.... *both Keys are ruled by* **MARS**!

   Just as an aside, her professions to date were a mother, a teacher, then a real estate agent and now the editor/owner of an alternate newspaper. Her natal Keys, in particular, revealed her talent for selling real estate.

5. **Links to Horoscopes:** For those who have their horoscope, factor in the degree, house placement and aspects to your decan's ruling planet/s to obtain further insights.

6. **Background Information:** *This information is vital to all forecasts.* Always gear the interpretations to suit the person, their circumstances and aspirations.

7. **Keepsake:** Since the nature of this work is so self-revelatory, you may wish to keep your natal Key and its lifetime Tarot spread with other lifetime data such as LDs, birth matrix (YDs and DDs) and astrology charts.

Conclusion

This holistic system of numerology is dedicated to all those who are searching for answers. It unfolds and develops a refining process that uncovers and describes your nature and circumstances at any point in life. The fine details revealed by each successive study describe your major and minor themes. The aim is to uncover information that leads to self-realisation, from that a sense of fulfilment and from that, ways of determining your future. It provides essential tools that facilitate journeying into self-knowing with the ultimate aim being to uncover your authentic self and from that *consciously* learning how to create your own reality, both within and without.

AIDS FOR GREATER PROFICIENCY

- Be open to explore new numerological concepts
- Cultivate a sound knowledge of numerology and Tarot
- Memorise Tables and diagrams
- Memorise many number and Tarot Keys' keywords
- Memorise abbreviated terms
- Persist with dedicated practice on a wide range of subjects
- Trust your capabilities as they grow
- Think outside the square
- Increase your knowledge
- Devise your own methods

APPENDIX 7: MEANINGS FOR ACRONYMS AND SYMBOLS

Life Diamond	Personal Yearly Diamond		Universal Yearly Diamond
LD: Life Diamond	PYD: Personal Yearly Diamond		UYD: Universal Yearly Diamond
LG: Life Goal	PYG: Personal Yearly Goal		UYG: Universal Yearly Goal
LGR: Life Goal Ruler	PYGR: PY Goal Ruler		UYGR: UY Goal Ruler
LC: Life Challenge	PYG: Personal Yearly Challenge		UYC: Universal Yearly Challenge
LCR: Life Challenge Ruler	PYGR: PY Challenge Ruler		UYCR: UY Challenge Ruler
LDR: Life Diamond Ruler	PYDR: PY Diamond Ruler		UYDR: UY Diamond Ruler
Personal Month Diamond	**Personal Day Diamond**		**Universal Day Diamond**
PMD: Personal Month Diamond	PDD: Personal Day Diamond		UDD: Universal Day Diamond
PMG: Personal Month Goal	PDG: Personal Day Goal		UDG: Universal Day Goal
PMGR: PM Goal Ruler	PDGR: PD Goal Ruler		UDGR: UD Goal Ruler
PMC: Personal Month Challenge	PDC: Personal Day Challenge		UDC: Universal Day Challenge
PMCR: PM Challenge Ruler	PDCR: PD Challenge Ruler		UDCR: UD Challenge Ruler
PMDR: PM Diamond Ruler	PDDR: PD Diamond Ruler		UDDR: UD Diamond Ruler
Personal Hour Diamond	**Personal Minute Diamond**		**Decade Diamonds**
PHD: Personal Hour Diamond	PMinD: Personal Minute Diamond		DD = Decade Diamond
PHG: Personal Hour Goal	PMinG: Personal Minute Goal		DG = Decade Goal
PHGR: PH Goal Ruler	PMinGR: PMin Goal Ruler		DC = Decade Challenge
PHC: Personal Hour Challenge	PMinC: Personal Minute Challenge		DR = Decade Ruler
PHCR: PH Challenge Ruler	PMinCR: PMin Challenge Ruler		
PHDR: Personal Hour ◊ Ruler	PMinDR: PMin Diamond Ruler		PMG = Personal Month Grid
Miscellaneous	**Miscellaneous**		**Symbols**
CA: Current Age	L = Life	D = Diamond	◊ Diamond
LPN: Life Path Number	P = Personal	SD = Single Digit	♥ Heart Number
PYN: Personal Year Number	Y = Year	WN = Whole Number	☐ Inner Square
UYN: Universal Year Number	U = Universal	F = Family	⨉ Grail
PMN: Personal Month Number	N = Number	M = Month	✡ Star of David
PDN: Personal Day Number	G = Goal	D = Day	✚ Vertical Cross
PHN: Personal Hour Number	C = Challenge	H = Hour	✖ Diagonal Cross
PMinN: Personal Minute Number	R = Ruler	Min = Minute	✱ Wheel of Life
DN: Decade Number			↻ Top Cycle Ruler

APPENDIX 2: CONVERSION TABLE FROM NUMBERS TO TAROT KEYS

MAJOR ARCANA	WANDS	CUPS	SWORDS	PENTACLES
0 The Fool	23 King: Spirit	37 King: Spirit	51 King: Spirit	65 King: Spirit
1 Magician	24 Queen: Soul	38 = Queen: Soul	52 = Queen: Soul	66 = Queen:: Soul
2 High Priestess	25 Knight: Astral	39 = Knight: Astral	53 = Knight: Astral	67 = Knight: Astral
3 Empress	26 Page: Phys. B.	40 = Page: Phys. B.	54 = Page: Phys. B.	68 = Page: Phys. B.
4 Emperor	27 Ace = 1	41 = Ace = 1	55 = Ace = 1	69 = Ace = 1
5 Hierophant	28 = 2	42 = 2	56 = 2	70 = 2
6 Lovers	29 = 3	43 = 3	57 = 3	71 = 3
7 Chariot	30 = 4	44 = 4	58 = 4	72 = 4
8 Strength	31 = 5	45 = 5	59 = 5	73 = 5
9 Hermit	32 = 6	46 = 6	60 = 6	74 = 6
10 Wheel of Fortune	33 = 7	47 = 7	61 = 7	75 = 7
11 Justice	34 = 8	48 = 8	62 = 8	76 = 8
12 Hanged Man	35 = 9	49 = 9	63 = 9	77 = 9
13 Death	36 = 10	50 = 10	64 = 10	78 = 10
14 Temperance				
15 The Devil	**TIPS:**	**TIPS:**	**TIPS:**	**TIPS:**
16 The Tower	1. REDUCE all numbers from ACE ⇨ 36 then +1: Eg, 30:3+1⇨4 of Wands 33:6+1⇨7 of Wands. 34:7+1⇨8 of Wands 36:9+1⇨10 of Wands	1. MATCH UNITS in 41⇨50 to SAME Keys' Nos.: Eg, 41⇨Ace 44 ⇨ 4 of Cups 48 ⇨ 8 of Cups 50 ⇨ 10 of Cups	1. REDUCE all whole numbers from 55 ⇨ 64 then MATCH to Keys: Eg, 55 = 1 ⇨Ace of Swords 59⇨5 of Swords 64 ⇨ 10 of Swords	1. ADD 2 to all units from 70 ⇨ 78: Eg, 70+2⇨2 of Pentacles 71+2⇨3 of Pentacles 77+2⇨9 of Pentacles 78+2 ⇨10 of Pentacles
17 The Star				
18 The Moon				
19 The Sun				
20 Judgement				
21 The World	2. Memorise ROYAL Keys and ACE	2. Memorise ROYAL Keys and ACE	2. Memorise ROYAL Keys and ACE	2. Memorise ROYAL Keys and ACE
22 The FOOL				

APPENDIX 3:
ALL NUMBER FAMILY CALCULATIONS

LPNF FORMULA: BIRTH DAY + BIRTH MONTH + BIRTH YEAR

There are many ways to calculate a LPNFs.
The PYNF below contains more detailed steps.

Birthdate: 16-1-1971

1. To find the highest LPN split 1971 thus: 19 and 71.
2. Add the numbers without reducing any: 16+1+19+71 = LPN**107**
3. Reduce 1971 to 18. Add: 16+1+18 = LPN**35**
4. Reduce 18 to 9 then add: 16+1+9 = LPN**26**
5. Reduce 16 to 7 then add: 7+1+9 = LPN**17**
6. Reduce 17 to its root digit = LPN**8**
7. **LPNF** ⇨ **107, 35, 26, 17, and 8** (also **80** as 8's reverse)

Note: Each number in the LPNF's group must reduce to the same root digit.

PYNF FORMULA: BIRTH DAY + BIRTH MONTH + CURRENT CALENDAR YEAR

The number of steps is governed by compound numbers appearing anywhere in the equation.

STEP 1: No Reductions
a. To begin, 2010 is split into 20 and 10.
b. Next, retain the whole birthday (27) and month (6) numbers.
c. Add: 20+10+27+6= **PYN**⇨**63**
d. **63** is the highest, *personalised*

STEP 2: Century Number Reduction
a. Reduce 20 to **2** and retain **10**.
b. Do not reduce other numbers.
c. Add: 2+10+27+6= **PYN**⇨**45**
d. **45** is the second highest, *personalised* PYN.

STEP 3: Year Number Reduction
a. Retain **2** and reduce **10** to **1**.
b. Do not reduce other numbers.
c. Add: 2+1+27+6= **PYN**⇨**36**
d. **36** is the third highest, *personalised* PYN.

STEP 4: Birth Day Number Reduction
a. Retain **2** and **1**.
b. Reduce 27 to **9**.
c. Add: 2+1+9+6= **PYN**⇨**18**
d. **18** is the second lowest, *personalised* PYN.

Note: When all SDs appear as totals, no further steps are required except to reduce **18** to **9** to complete the number family. If the birth day number is high like 29, use it first, then 11 and finally, 2. Then go to step 5.

STEP 5: Birth Month Number Reduction
If the month number is 10, 11 or 12, reduce until the final SD step is reached.

STEP 6: Additional Step
Set out the numbers this way:

> 2010 (use full **year** number)
> 27 (use full birth **day** number)
> 6 (use full birth **month** number)
> Then ADD: **2043** ⇨ **Root 9**
> (Use **43** as a "PYN" – see Chapter 3.)

STEP 7: Compile the PYNF
Set out **2010's PYNF** including its root digit: **63, 45, 36, 18 and 9**. (also **90** as 9's reverse)

Note: Each number in the PYNF's group must reduce to the same root digit.

PMNF FORMULA: CURRENT MONTH NUMBER + PYNs from PYNF

STEP 1: Calculate the **PYNF**
STEP 2: ADD **current month's number** to all **PYNs**
STEP 3: Their totals = the **Personal Month Number Family (PMNF)**

PDNF FORMULA: CURRENT CALENDAR DAY + CURRENT PMNs from PMNF

STEP 1: Calculate current **PYNF**
STEP 2: Calculate current **PMNF**
STEP 3: ADD the **current calendar day's number** to all **PMNs**
STEP 4: Their totals = the **Personal Day Number Family (PDNF)**

PHN FORMULA: CURRENT HOUR IN REAL TIME + CURRENT PDN

STEP 1: Calculate current **SD PDN**
STEP 2: Calculate **current hour in 24-hour clock time**; reduce if necessary.
STEP 3: ADD **current hour number** to **PDN**; reduce to a SD or keep as a WN.
STEP 4: Their totals yield the **Personal Hour Number (PHN)**

PMinN FORMULA: CURRENT MINUTE + ACTIVE PHN (REAL CLOCK TIME)

STEP 1: Calculate current **SD PHN**
STEP 2: Calculate current **minute**; reduce if necessary
STEP 3: ADD **current minute number** to **PHN**; reduce to a SD or keep as a WN.
STEP 4: Their totals yield the **Personal Minute Number (PMinN)**

APPENDIX 4:
ALL DIAMOND CALCULATIONS

LD FORMULA: BIRTH MONTH + BIRTH DAY + BIRTH YEAR

SD LD CALCULATIONS

1. **Baseline:**
    - (a) Reduce birthdate's Day, Month and Year numbers to SDs or keep WNs
    - (b) **BASELINE:** Month first, Day second, Year third
    - (c) **LPN:** Month + Day + Year = LPN
2. Calculate all Life Goals and Challenges, Cycle Rulers, Constellations and Magickal Facets.
3. Calculate each cycle's time periods in ages and years
4. Shade or highlight the current cycle
5. CHECK CALCULATIONS
6. Record notable features
7. Calculate Interim and WN LDs to broaden and confirm findings

PYD FORMULA: CURRENT AGE + LPN

SD PYD CALCULATIONS

1. **Baseline:**
    - (a) Calculate the Single Digit Life Path Number (SD LPN)
    - (b) Calculate CA from the **last birthday** for PYD's year or a specific point in time
    - (c) Split CA to take up 1st and 2nd baseline places; put the SD LPN in 3rd place
    - (d) ADD CA + LPN = PYN. Eg CA 26 + LPN3 ⇨ 2+6+3 ⇨ 11, then 1+1 ⇨ SD PYN 2
2. Calculate all yearly Goals and Challenges, Cycle Rulers, Constellations and Magickal Facets.
3. Calculate each cycle's period
4. Shade or highlight current cycle
5. CHECK CALCULATIONS
6. Record notable features
7. Calculate Interim and WN PYDs with UYDs to broaden and confirm findings

A PYD's Three, 4-Monthly Cycles Calculations: Birthday ⇨ 16th, January	
1st 4-month cycle:	16 JAN ⇨ 15 MAY
2nd 4-month cycle:	16 MAY ⇨ 15 SEP
3rd 4-month cycle:	16 SEP ⇨ 15 JAN

Appendices

UYD FORMULA: CURRENT AGE + CURRENT YEAR

SD UYD CALCULATIONS

1. **Baseline:**
   - (a) Calculate Single Digit Universal Year Number (SD UYN)
   - (b) Calculate CA from **last birthday** for UYD's year or a specific point in time
   - (c) Split CA to take up 1st and 2nd baseline places; put SD UYN in 3rd place
   - (d) ADD CA + UYN to get Baseline Ruler Constellations
2. Calculate all yearly Goals and Challenges, Cycle Rulers, Constellations and Magickal Facets.
3. Calculate each cycle's period
4. Shade or highlight current cycle
5. CHECK CALCULATIONS
6. Record notable features
7. Calculate Interim and WN UYDs with PYDs to broaden and confirm findings

| A UYD's Four, 3-Monthly Cycles' Calculations: | 1st of January ⇨ 31st March
1st of April ⇨ 30th June
1st of July ⇨ 30th September
1st of October ⇨ 31st December |

PMD FORMULA: CURRENT CALENDAR MONTH + PMN + PYN

STEPS FOR CALCULATING SD and WN PMDs

1. **SD Baseline:**
   - (a) Select **current month's number**; reduce if a WN for a SD◇
   - (b) Select **current SD PYN** from its PYNF
   - (c) Add a) and b) to get **PMN**. reduce if a WN for a SD◇
   - (d) **Baseline:** Place SD Mth No. first, **SD ♥ PMN second**, SD PYN third
2. Calculate all Goals, Challenges, Cycle Rulers, Constellations and Magickal Facets
3. Calculate Interim and WN PMDs to broaden and confirm findings
4. Apply "Points to Remember" from Chapter 3

A PMD's 4 x 1 Weekly Cycles' Calculations:
- ✦ **1st week** (first mini ◇): Day 1 → Day 7
- ✦ **2nd week** (second mini ◇): Day 8 → Day 14
- ✦ **3rd week** (two opposing ▲▼s): Day 15 → Day 21
- ✦ **4th week** (cosmic ◇): Day 22 → Last Day of the month

ALL DIAMOND CALCULATIONS *continued*

PDD FORMULA: CURRENT CALENDAR DAY + PDN + PMN

STEPS FOR CALCULATING SD and WN PDDs

1. **SD Baseline:**
   (a) Select **current Day Number** or reduce if a WN.
   (b) Select **current SD PMN** from its PMNF.
   (c) Add a) and b) to get **Personal Day Number (PDN)**. Reduce to a SD.
   (d) **Baseline:** Place SD Day No. first, **SD ♥ PDN second** and SD PMN third.
2. Calculate all Goals/Challenges, Cycle Rulers, Constellations and Magickal Facets.
3. Calculate Interim and WN PDDs to broaden and confirm findings.
4. Apply "Points to Remember" and Checklist from Chapter 3.

Note: DAYLIGHT SAVINGS TIMES—Use real clock time.

A PDD's 4 x 6 Hourly Cycles' Calculations:

1st	6 hours begins at	**MIDNIGHT**	1st mini ◇: Midnight—6am (first cycle)
2nd	6 hours begins at	**6 a.m.**	2nd mini ◇: 6am—noon (second cycle)
3rd	6 hours begins at	**NOON**	2—opposing ▲▼: Noon—6pm (third cycle)
4th	6 hours begins at	**6 p.m.**	Cosmic ◇: 6pm—midnight (fourth cycle)

PHD FORMULA: CURRENT HOUR IN REAL TIME + PHN + PDN

STEPS FOR CALCULATING SD PHDs

1. **SD Baseline:**
   (a) Select **active Hour Number** in **24 hour clock time**; reduce if a WN.
   (b) Select **current SD PDN** from its PDNF.
   (c) Add a) and b) for **Personal Hour Number (PHN)**. Reduce to a SD.
   (d) Put SD Hour No. first, **SD PHN second** and SD PDN third on baseline.
2. Calculate all Goals/Challenges, Cycle Rulers, Constellations and Magickal Facets.
3. Record significant features. Apply "Points to Remember".
4. **Interim and WN PHDs** may be calculated broaden and confirm findings.

Midnight to 1 a.m.—Reduce 24 to 6 for this hour's duration.

Note: DAYLIGHT SAVINGS TIMES—Use 24-hour real clock time.

A PHD's 4 x 15 MINUTE Cycles' Calculations:

1st	:	first mini diamond	: 0 mins.—15 mins.
2nd	:	second mini diamond	: 16 mins.—30 mins.
3rd	:	two opposing triangles	: 31 mins.—45 mins.
4th	:	large outer diamond	: 46 mins.—60 mins.

ALL DIAMOND CALCULATIONS *continued*

PMinD FORMULA: CURRENT MINUTE + PMinN + ACTIVE PHN

STEPS FOR CALCULATING SD PMinDs

1. **SD Baseline:**
   - (a) Select **active SD Minute Number** or reduce if a WN.
   - (b) Select **current SD PHN** using 24 hour clock time.
   - (c) Add a) and b) for **Personal Minute Number** (**PMinN**). Reduce to a SD.
   - (d) Put SD Minute No. first, **SD PMinN second** and SD PDN third on baseline.
2. Calculate all Goals/Challenges, Cycle Rulers, Constellations and Magickal Facets.
3. Record significant features. Apply "Points to Remember".
4. Interim and WN PDDs may be calculated to broaden and confirm findings.

Note: DAYLIGHT SAVINGS TIMES—Use 24-hour real clock time.

A PMinD's 4 x 15 SECOND Cycles' Calculations:

1st	: first mini diamond	:	0 secs.—15 secs.
1nd	: second mini diamond	:	16 secs.—30 secs.
3rd	: two opposing triangles	:	31 secs.—45 secs.
4th	: large outer diamond	:	46 secs.—60 secs.

DD FORMULA: CURRENT 10'S DIGIT + LPN

STEPS for CALCULATING SD and WN DDs

1. **LPNF**: Calculate in advance
2. **CURRENT AGE**: Calculate in advance
3. **SD DD's BASELINE**: CA 10's digit—space—**SD LPN**.
4. **WN DD's BASELINE**: CA 10's digit—space—**WN LPN**.
   Work from second lowest to highest LPN until all WN LPNs are used.
5. Calculate WN DD **GOALS** (WN DGs) and **CHALLENGES** (WN DCs). *Do not reduce*
6. **RULERS**: ADD all SD or WN numbers—write unreduced Rulers in centre of each DD.
7. **HIDDEN NUMBERS**: Obtained from WN reductions.

A DD's COMPOSITION
- ◇ A 10's digit, a SD or WN LPN, Goals, Challenges and Ruling number/s.
- ◇ Four long-term SDs (unless WNs are used).
- ◇ Up to twelve compound numbers from pairing of SDs.
- ◇ Hidden numbers from reducing paired or whole numbers.

Appendix 5:
ALL TAROT SPREAD CALCULATIONS

HOW TO CALCULATE A PERSONAL YEAR TAROT SPREAD

YEAR **2010**; Birth DAY **27**; MONTH **6**.

Preparation
◇ Calculate 2010's **PYNF**: **63, 45, 36, 18** and **9** (using 27th June)

ASSEMBLE TAROT SPREAD
STEP 1: **Top Row**: Present Numbers—**63, 45, 36, 18** and **9**—**convert to Keys**
STEP 2: **Bottom Row**: Missing Numbers—**54** and **27**—**convert to Keys**

HOW TO CALCULATE A PERSONAL MONTH TAROT SPREAD

Preparation
◇ Calculate 2010's **PYNF**: **63, 45, 36, 18 and 9**. (using 27th June)
◇ Month for analysis: **JULY** *(Do not reduce if a compound number)*
◇ Add **7 of JULY** to all Personal Year Numbers.

ASSEMBLE TAROT SPREAD
STEP 1: **Top Row**: Present Numbers—**70, 52, 43, 25, 16** and **7**—**convert to Keys**
STEP 2: **Bottom Row**: Missing Numbers—**61** and **34**—**convert to Keys**

HOW TO CALCULATE A PERSONAL DAY TAROT SPREAD

Event Date: 21-4-2010 = UDNs 28, 10, 1

Preparation
◇ Calculate 2010's **PYNF**: **63, 45, 36, 18 and 9**. (using 27th June)
◇ PMNF for April ⇨ **67, 49, 40, 22, 13 and 4** (add **4** to each PYN)
◇ Add **21** to all numbers in May's PMNF

ASSEMBLE TAROT SPREAD
STEP 1: **Top Row**: Present Numbers—**88, 70, 61, 43, 34, 25** and **7**—**convert to Keys**
STEP 2: **Bottom Row**: Missing Numbers—**79, 52** and **16**—**convert to Keys**

HOW TO FIND YOUR *LIFETIME* TAROT KEY AT BIRTH

EXAMPLE: Birthday is 27th JUNE

1. Find the Sun Sign on the decans' astrological wheel or Table 2.
2. Find which pair of calendar dates the birthday slots into. This is the decan.
3. Note the decan's Tarot Key.
4. Note the decan's planetary ruler.

HOW TO CREATE A *LIFETIME* TAROT SPREAD FROM YOUR NATAL KEY

1. Find the corresponding number to the **2 of Cups**; it is **42**.
2. Reverse **42** to uncover **24** and **Key24**⇨**Queen of Wands**.
3. Reduce **42/24** to **root 6**. Reverse **6**⇨**The Lovers** to get **60**⇨**6 of Swords**.
4. Now use the number on the face of **Key42**, which is **2**. Use it and the **High Priestess Key**.
5. Reverse **2** to uncover **20** and **Key20**⇨**Judgement**.
6. Lay out the mini **Tarot spread** for **Keys 42, 24, 6, 60, 2 and 20**. Do not forget **root 6** and **60**.
7. Now interpret **all Numbers and Keys** in a *lifetime* vein.

EXAMPLE: LIFETIME TAROT KEY for 27th JUNE

Zodiac Sign: Cancer
Cancer Decan: First
Decan Ruler: Venus
Corresponding Key: 2 of Cups
Key's Esoteric Name: Love and Union (**Key42**)

EXAMPLE: LIFETIME TAROT SPREAD for 1st CANCER DECAN

42	24	6	60	2	20

Ruling Planets: VENUS | NONE | MERCURY | JUPITER | MOON | PLUTO
Ruling Signs: LIBRA | FIRE | GEMINI | SAGITTARIUS | CANCER | SCORPIO

RECOMMENDED RESOURCES

The Tarot—Paul Foster Case, B.O.T.A. Publications revised addition, 1990 (The Master's Hand - brilliant)

Tarot Prediction, An Advanced Handbook of Images for Tomorrow —Emily Peach; The Aquarian Press, 1988 (Excellent for beginners)

An Introduction to the Golden Dawn Tarot —Robert Wang; The Aquarian Press (Brilliant - detailed)

Numerology and the Divine Triangle —Faith Javane and Dusty Bunker; Para Research, 1985 (Excellent interpretations for numbers to 78; also astrology correspondences for each number)

Numerology, The Romance in Your Name—Juno Jordan; De Vorss and Company, 1989 (Excellent beginners' numerology book)

Easy Tarot Guide —Marcia Marcino; ACS Publications, 1990

Tarot Constellations—Patterns of Personal Destiny—Mary K. Greer; Newcastle Publishing, 1987

Seventy-Eight Degrees of Wisdom—A Book of Tarot. Parts 1 and 2—Rachel Pollack; The Aquarian Press, 1983

The New Age Tarot—Guide to the Thoth Deck—James Wanless; Merill-West Publishing, 1987

The Pictorial Key to the Tarot —Arthur Edward Waite; Samuel Weiser, 1984

IN PRINT

LIFE DIAMONDS—Your Mini Maps to Life

LIFE DIAMONDS—Your Mini Maps to Life totally revises and updates Pythagoras' Pinnacles and Challenges to meet today's vastly changed times.

The **LIFE DIAMOND** is a simple map to life that depicts **individual lifetime pathways that lead to unravelling your Soul's Agenda for this lifetime.** Except for the first life cycle, its life-long directions are set in nine-year cycles. Each cycle's numbers and Tarot Keys conceal specific clues that show you how to reach your unique goals and triumph over your unique tests by:

- ⟡ Increasing the limited number range from 0 to 9 to 99 and beyond!
- ⟡ Introducing number-pairing techniques
- ⟡ Matching numbers with their corresponding Tarot cards
- ⟡ Developing a holistic approach to Numerology
- ⟡ Synthesising Numerology, Tarot, Astrology, Sacred Geometry and Qabalah
- ⟡ Using graded steps from beginner to advanced levels
- ⟡ Using a large number of case studies and interpretation tips
- ⟡ Providing practical ways to apply its methods to suit daily and spiritual aims
- ⟡ Providing new interpretations for all numbers to 99 and all 78 Tarot Cards.

Learn to *personalise* your numbers to reveal detailed clues about this lifetime's, requirements, signs and changing destinations. Discover the **esoteric side** to your numbers. It conceals your spiritual potential.

Imagine … your birthdate and simple sums hold the secrets to your Life!

Make LIFE DIAMONDS one of your true *Wayshowers*.

IN PRINT

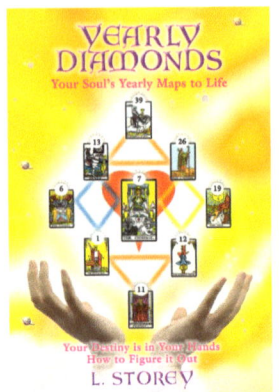

YEARLY DIAMONDS—Your Soul's Yearly Maps to Life

YEARLY DIAMONDS the *Life Diamonds'* companion, introduces two types of *esoteric*, **yearly forecasts**; one **Personal**, one **Universal**. They supplement each other so are best worked together. Their comprehensive, yearly forecasts are derived from the same holistic numerology system introduced in **LIFE DIAMONDS**—*Your Mini Maps to Life*.

PERSONAL and UNIVERSAL YEARLY DIAMONDS break down their Life Diamond's long cycles into more manageable yearly cycles. Hence, Soul Paths and everyday Life Directions become easier to define and follow.

PERSONAL and UNIVERSAL YEARLY DIAMOND forecasts, although profound, *are extremely* quick and easy to calculate. They contain unprecedented depth, detail, accuracy and timing by replacing the Life Diamond's generalities with specifics. Hence, those searching for enlightening, yearly trends will find this in their Yearly Diamonds' personalised numbers and Tarot Keys.

This study is made both interesting and inspiring by the frequent use of fascinating case studies and cameos that depict snapshots of years in babies and famous and ordinary people's lives. The methods unfold from beginner to advanced levels of proficiency.

Advanced numerology methods reveal many tips and interpretation secrets to update numerology so that it remains abreast of modern ways of living and being.

PERSONAL and UNIVERSAL YEARLY DIAMONDS
contain indispensable yearly guidance for all Seekers on the Path.

FORTHCOMING TITLES

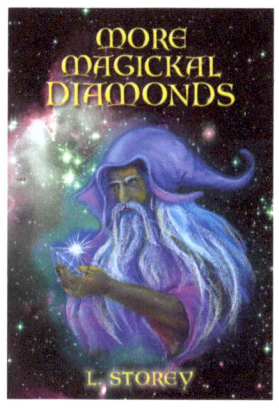

MORE MAGICKAL DIAMONDS

Brimming with new material, **MORE MAGICKAL DIAMONDS** introduces very simple diamonds that uncover individual vocational and personality traits using birthdates and names. Previous diamond books provided maps geared to time and life cycles. However, **Magickal Diamonds** deals with specific, personal aspects. They help to explain who and what we are, and what we are attracted to, and why.

This workbook magickally adapts diamonds to suit the **Achievement Number**, the **Shadow Achievement Number**, the **Life Experience Number** and the **Destiny Number**. The **Higher Purpose Number and its Diamond** are exceptional. They reveal this lifetime's quest by highlighting the pathways that lead to the ultimate goals set by your Soul.

A **list of possible vocations** for every number from 1 to 99 appears as one of this book's gems.

Personality Diamonds extract esoteric insights and potential from names. They provide a comprehensive, analysis of a person's character not achieved if using "old" numerology methods.

A new, extremely simple, fast, esoteric way of **reading names** is introduced. Its unique method uncovers previously untapped, personal gifts, scope and promise that have lain concealed in our names for aeons. When this method is applied, **a person's character, gifts, impediments and potential is unmasked in moments**!

Other new methods introduce in-depth, holistic, **esoteric interpretations for the 26 LETTERS**. Letters and names' esoteric secrets are now revealed!

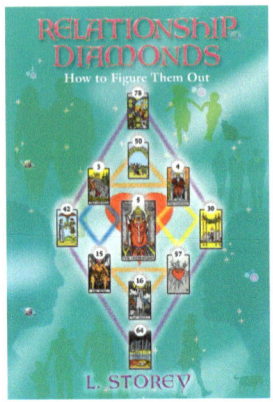

RELATIONSHIPS—*How to Figure Them Out*

RELATIONSHIPS—*How to Figure Them Out* synthesises all methods introduced in previous books. It extends numerology practice to create an advanced, yet simple system that is adapted to suit the study of **all types of relationships**. It makes a most significant contribution to numerology.

RELATIONSHIP DIAMONDS reveal *any* **relationship's compatibility status** as well as its strengths, weaknesses and directions. These diamonds cover:

♥ Lovers ♥ Families ♥ Same Sex Couples ♥ Teams

♥ Marriages ♥ Siblings ♥ Associates ♥ Groups

♥ Friends ♥ Relatives ♥ Pets

Many case studies, cameos, diagrams, interpretations and helpful tips systematically explain how to interpret a relationship's dynamics. Questions everyone wants the answer to such as: **Are we compatible? Will we be happy? Will it work? Will it last? Will it fail? What do we have in common? What do we need to work on? What are our weaknesses? What can we achieve as a couple?** are treated.

Imagine being able to find a family unit or any type of group's purpose, compatibilities and challenges from their diamond …. this is unprecedented!

RELATIONSHIP DIAMONDS introduces an unparalleled technique that *progresses* Relationship Diamonds year by year. It enables yearly forecasts to be made for all types of relationships. They introduce simple means to track their unfolding trends.

This journeybook takes the art of interpretation to new heights when it integrates all methods in prior books. It prepares the way for ***NUMEROSCOPES***; the most profound, Pythagorean, numerological configuration of all, and possibly, the last journeybook.

www.ingramcontent.com/pod-product-compliance
Lightning Source LLC
Chambersburg PA
CBHW041831300426
44111CB00002B/47